INTERCULTURAL COMMUNICATION

Routledge Applied Linguistics is a series of comprehensive resource books, providing students and researchers with the support they need for advanced study in the core areas of English language and Applied Linguistics.

Each book in the series guides readers through three main sections, enabling them to explore and develop major themes within the discipline:

- Section A, Introduction, establishes the key terms and concepts, and extends readers' techniques of analysis through practical application.
- Section B, Extension, brings together influential articles, sets them in context, and discusses their contribution to the field.
- Section C, Exploration, builds on knowledge gained in the first two sections, setting thoughtful tasks around further illustrative material. This enables readers to engage more actively with the subject matter and encourages them to develop their own research responses.

Throughout the book, topics are revisited, extended, interwoven and deconstructed, with the reader's understanding strengthened by tasks and follow-up questions. *Intercultural Communication*:

- introduces the key theories of intercultural communication
- explores ways in which people communicate within and across social groups
- is built around three themes – identity, otherization and representation – which are followed and developed over the book's three sections
- gathers together influential readings from key names in the discipline, including: James Paul Gee, James P. Lantolf, Les Black, Richard Dyer, Jacques Derrida and Alastair Pennycook.

Written by experienced teachers and researchers in the field, *Intercultural Communication* is an essential resource for students and researchers of English language and Applied Linguistics.

Adrian Holliday, **Martin Hyde** and **John Kullman** are based in the Department of Language Studies at Canterbury Christ Church University College, UK. Adrian Holliday is a Reader in Applied Linguistics and Head of the Graduate School, Martin Hyde is a Principal Lecturer and Deputy Director of the International Office and John Kullman is a Senior Lecturer.

ROUTLEDGE APPLIED LINGUISTICS

SERIES EDITORS

Christopher N. Candlin is Senior Research Professor in the Department of Linguistics at Macquarie University, Australia and Professor of Applied Linguistics at the Open University, UK. At Macquarie, he has been Chair of the Department of Linguistics; established and was Executive Director of the National Centre for English Language Teaching and Research (NCELTR); and was foundation Director of the Centre for Language in Social Life (CLSL). He has written or edited over 150 publications and from 2004 will co-edit the new *Journal of Applied Linguistics*. From 1996 to 2002 he was President of the International Association of Applied Linguistics (AILA). He has acted as a consultant in more than 35 countries and as external faculty assessor in 36 universities worldwide.

Ronald Carter is Professor of Modern English Language in the School of English Studies at the University of Nottingham. He has published extensively in applied linguistics, literary studies and language in education, and has written or edited over 40 books and 100 articles in these fields. He has given consultancies in the field of English language education, mainly in conjunction with the British Council, in over 30 countries worldwide, and is editor of the Routledge Interface series and advisory editor to the Routledge English Language Introduction series. He was recently elected a Fellow of the British Academy for Social Sciences and is currently UK Government Advisor for ESOL and Chair of the British Association for Applied Linguistics (BAAL).

FORTHCOMING TITLES IN THE SERIES

Translation: An advanced resource book
Basil Hatim, Heriot-Watt University, UK and The American University of Sharjah, UAE and Jeremy Munday, University of Surrey, Guildford, UK

Grammar and Context: An advanced resource book
Ann Hewings, Open University and Martin Hewings, University of Birmingham

Intercultural Communication

An Advanced Resource Book

Adrian Holliday, Martin Hyde
and John Kullman

Routledge
Taylor & Francis Group

LONDON AND NEW YORK

First published 2004
by Routledge
2 Park Square, Milton Park, Abingdon, Oxon OX14 4RN

Simultaneously published in the USA and Canada
by Routledge
270 Madison Ave, New York, NY 10016

Reprinted 2006 (three times)

Routledge is an imprint of the Taylor & Francis Group, an informa business

© 2004 Adrian Holliday, Martin Hyde and John Kullman

Designed and typeset in Akzidenz, Minion and Novarese by
Keystroke, Jacaranda Lodge, Wolverhampton
Printed and bound in Great Britain by
TJ International Ltd, Padstow, Cornwall

British Library Cataloguing in Publication Data
A catalogue record for this book is available from the British Library

Library of Congress Cataloging in Publication Data
A catalogue record for this book has been requested

ISBN10: 0–415–27060–X (hbk)
ISBN10: 0–415–27061–8 (pbk)

ISBN13: 978–0–415–27060–1 (hbk)
ISBN13: 978–0–415–27061–8 (pbk)

Contents

Contents

Contents cross-referenced

Series Editors' Preface

The Routledge Applied Linguistics Series provides a comprehensive guide to the key areas in the field of applied linguistics. Applied Linguistics is a rich, vibrant, diverse and essentially interdisciplinary field. It is now more important than ever that books in the field provide up-to-date maps of what is an ever-changing territory.

The books in this series are designed to give key insights into core areas of Applied Linguistics. The design of the books ensures, through key readings, that the history and development of a subject is recognized while, through key questions and tasks, integrating understandings of the topics, concepts and practices that make up its essentially interdisciplinary fabric. The pedagogic structure of each book ensures that readers are given opportunities to think, discuss, engage in tasks, draw on their own experience, reflect, research and to read and critically re-read key documents.

Each book has three main sections, each made up of approximately ten units.

A: An **Introduction** section, in which the key terms and concepts that map the field of the subject are introduced, including introductory activities and reflective tasks designed to establish key understandings, terminology, techniques of analysis and the skills appropriate to the theme and the discipline.

B: An **Extension** section, in which selected core readings are introduced (usually edited from the original) from key books and articles, together with annotations and commentary where appropriate. Each reading is introduced, annotated and commented on in the context of the whole book, and research/follow-up questions and tasks are added to enable fuller understanding of both theory and practice. In some cases, readings are short and synoptic and incorporated within a more general exposition.

C: An **Exploration** section, in which further samples and illustrative materials are provided with an emphasis, where appropriate, on more open-ended, student-centred activities and tasks designed to support readers and users in undertaking their own locally relevant research projects. Tasks are designed for work in groups or for individuals working on their own. They can be readily included in award courses in Applied Linguistics or as topics for personal study and research.

The books also contain a glossarial index, which provides a guide to the main terms used in the book, and a detailed, thematically organised further reading section which lays the ground for further work in the discipline. There are also extensive suggestions for further reading.

The target audience for the series is upper undergraduates and postgraduates on language, applied linguistics and communication studies programmes as well as teachers and researchers in professional development and distance learning programmes. High-quality applied research resources are also much needed for teachers of EFL/ESL and foreign language students at higher education colleges and universities worldwide. The books in the Routledge Applied Linguistics Series are aimed at the individual reader, the student in a group, and at teachers building courses and seminar programmes.

We hope that the books in this series meet these needs and continue to provide support over many years.

The Editors

Professor Christopher N. Candlin and Professor Ronald Carter are the series editors. Both have extensive experience of publishing titles in the fields relevant to this series. Between them they have written and edited more than 100 books and 200 academic papers in the broad field of applied linguistics. Chris Candlin was president of AILA (International Association for Applied Linguistics) from 1997–2002 and Ron Carter is Chair of BAAL (British Association for Applied Linguistics) from 2003–2006.

Professor Christopher N. Candlin,
Senior Research Professor
Department of Linguistics,
Division of Linguistics and Psychology
Macquarie University
Sydney NSW 2109
Australia

and

Professor of Applied Linguistics
Faculty of Education and Language Studies
The Open University
Walton Hall
Milton Keynes MK7 6AA
UK

Professor Ronald Carter
School of English Studies
University of Nottingham
Nottingham NG7 2RD
UK

Acknowledgements

The editor and publishers wish to thank the following for permission to use copyright material.

Atlantic Syndication for cartoon by Blower, 'Country by country guide to women and the world', *Evening Standard*, 10.6.98

Benetton for images from its advertising material

Blackwell Publishers for material from B. Fay (1996) *Contemporary Philosophy of Social Science: A Multicultural Approach*, pp. 55, 57, 59, 60

Cambridge University Press for material from Gerhard Baumann (1996) *Contesting Culture: discourses of identity in multi-ethnic London*, pp. 1–2, 4–6; and Yoshio Sugimoto (1997) *An Introduction to Japanese Society*, pp. 1–4, 11–13

Guardian Newspapers Ltd for Stephen Moss, 'Mind your language: the semantics of asylum', *Guardian*, 22.5.01. Copyright © 2001 The Guardian

Hong Kong City Polytechnic for material from C. Roberts and S. Sarangi (1993) '"Culture" Revisited in Intercultural Communication' in T. Boswood, R. Hoffman and P. Tung (eds) *Perspectives on English for Professional Communication*, pp. 97–102

Martin Jacques for material from his interview with Professor Stuart Hall included in *New Statesman*

Boye Lafayette De Mente for material from 'Beware of Using Logic in Japan' by Boye Lafayette De Mente, 7 October 2000, Executive Planet.com website

Open University Press for material from Teun A. van Dijk (2000) 'New(s) Racism: A discourse analytical approach' in Simon Cottle (ed.) (2000) *Ethnic Minorities and the Media*, Chapter 2

Oxford University Press for material from A. Pavlenko and J. P. Lantolf (2000) 'Second language learning as participation and the (re)construction of selves' in J. P. Lantolf (ed.) (2000) *Sociocultural Theory and Second Language Learning*, pp. 162–169, 172–174

Palgrave Macmillan for material from J. Solomos and L. Back (1996) *Racism and Society*, Macmillan, pp. 186–190

Rogers, Coleridge and White Ltd on behalf of the author for material from Christopher Hope, *Darkest England*. Copyright © Christopher Hope 1996

Sage Publications for material from Hugh O'Donnell (1994) 'Mapping the Mythical: A geopolitics of national sporting stereotypes', *Discourse and Society*, 5:3, pp. 345–380; Ulf Hannerz (1999) 'Reflections on varieties of culturespeak', *European Journal of Cultural Studies*, 2:3, pp. 393–407

Taylor & Francis Books Ltd for material from G. Matthews (2000) *Global Culture/ Individual Identity: Searching for home in the cultural supermarket*, Routledge, pp.

19–23; J. P. Gee (1999) *An Introduction to Discourse Analysis*, Routledge, pp. 12–13, 17–18, 49, 68–9, 78; B. Burkhalter, 'Reading Race Online: Discovering racial identity in usenet discussions' in M. A. Smith and P. Kollock (eds) (1999) *Communities in Cyberspace*, Routledge pp. 63–69, 72–73; V. Burr (1996) *An Introduction to Social Constructionism*, Routledge, pp. 2–5, 21–28; S. E. Hampson, 'The Social Psychology of Personality' in C. Cooper and V. Varma (eds) (1997) *Processes in Individual Differences*, Routledge pp. 77–81; R. Dyer (1997) *White*, Routledge, pp. 1–4; A. Pennycook (1998) *English and the Discourse of Colonialism*, Routledge, pp. 171–2, 174–5, 180; and Miriam Cooke (1997) 'Listen to the Image Speak', *Cultural Values*, 1:1, pp. 101–102, 104, 105, 106; R. Rosaldo (1993) *Culture and Truth: The Remaking of Social Analysis*, pp. 202–204

The University of Birmingham for material from Jess Olsen (1998) 'Through White Eyes: The packaging of people and places in the world of the travel brochure', *Cultural Studies from Birmingham*, 2:1

Westview Press, a member of Perseus Books, LLC, for material from Harry C. Triandis (1995) *Individualism and Collectivism*, pp. 1–2, 4–5. Copyright © 1995 by Westview Press, a member of Perseus Books Group

Every effort has been made to trace the copyright holders but if any have been inadvertently overlooked the publishers will be pleased to make the necessary arrangement at the first opportunity.

How to use this book

The book is divided into three sections:

Section A Introduction: Defining concepts, which aims to present concepts that will
   be the basis for study throughout the book
Section B Extension, which will develop and continue to explore these concepts in
   dialogue with a series of readings
Section C Exploration, which will realize the discussions of the first two parts within
   a series of research tasks, and which will establish a methodology for addressing
   intercultural communication.

Each section will also be divided into three themes.

Theme 1 Identity deals with the way in which we all bring with us our own discourses
   and feelings of culture and negotiate these in communication.
Theme 2 Otherization deals with a major hindrance to communication in the way
   in which we over-generalize, stereotype and reduce the people we communicate
   with to something different or less than they are.
Theme 3 Representation looks at the way in which culture is communicated in
   society, through the media, professional discourses and everyday language.
   It focuses on how we need critically to recognize and address the ways in which
   these representations influence our own perceptions if we are to communicate
   effectively

It is a tenet of the book that the disciplines presented in Section A and applied to research
tasks in Section C are usable in all intercultural communication contexts, and as it is
argued that all communication is intercultural, that this book is ultimately about
developing skilled communication strategies and principles in a globalizing world.

   Examples that are drawn on and which are from the writers' own cultural milieux
and experiences are thus simply catalysts for illustrating larger principles that readers
are expected to apply and use in their own cultural milieux and contexts. Because the
book is not based upon the principle that cultural differences exist as real and tangible
entities, but are intersubjective and negotiated processes (admittedly affected by power
structures) the book cannot attempt to be a manual of cultural differences and therefore
does not aim to collect exotic examples of cultural behaviours. To do this would indeed
be to enter into the process of otherization decried as a major problem in intercultural
communication in the world today. The examples used are simply those that the authors

have felt sufficiently familiar with and confident enough to be able to describe and use
to promote the readers' thoughts and sensibilities about their own communicative
behaviour in the interactions, wherever these may be.

The use of examples in the book from, for example, the Middle East in Section A
and from Britain and the Spanish-speaking world in Section C, is thus a consequence
of the locatedness of the authors. It is expected that readers will be able to generalize
out from these examples; and in Section C there is an invitation for readers to bring
their own cultural milieux into research activities.

SECTION A
Introduction: Defining concepts

Each unit in Section A will comprise the presentation of an *experience* or situation in the form of an example, and a *deconstruction* of this example through which basic concepts will be introduced. By deconstruction we mean 'taking apart' to enable greater insight and analysis. This is an essential skill which will prepare readers to be able to look at their own interaction with others analytically and with fresh eyes in order to solve the puzzle of what is going on. It is particularly important, where we feel that much intercultural communication is marred by prejudice, to be able to take apart and undo this prejudice. The concepts introduced in Section A can then be responded to in the rest of the book. The emphasis is not only on people with different nationalities, but also with other senses of belonging, whether community, class, occupational, gender and so on. There will then be a final section in each unit which focuses on what is needed for successful communication. This will take the form of *disciplines* about what to be aware of in the process of intercultural communication, which will then be collected together at the end of each theme.

These disciplines will not be based on what a person from culture X is like and therefore how we should communicate with them. There is enough published along these lines, which we consider to be largely essentialist and reductive. By essentialist we mean presuming that there is a universal essence, homogeneity and unity in a particular culture. By reductive we mean reducing cultural behaviour down to a simple causal factor. The disciplines will thus be basic principles about understandings which need to be achieved in order to interact with different individuals in different contexts. This order of example, deconstruction, disciplines, binds the book together and our belief is that intercultural communication should grow from an understanding of people, culture and society generally. The deconstruction of the examples will attempt an understanding, and observations about communication will grow from them. Each unit will also finish with a task which will help you to link the examples and concepts it provides with your own experience.

The examples in each unit are reconstructed from actual experience. They have been edited, sometimes mixed together, the characters, genders, nationalities changed, with fictitious names and situations, so that no one can be recognized, and also to bring out the issues we have found important. The approach in this part of the book is therefore novelistic. The deconstruction of what happens in each example is subjective. We do not however feel that the subjectivity is problematic. As in more formal qualitative research, each instance speaks for itself, its value being in the resonance or dissonance each example creates – in the degree to which the reader can say 'This makes sense to me; I can recognize this type of thing from my own experience', or 'This makes no sense; I need to think about this more'.

The examples are all about particular people in particular situations. They have been taken from a range of nationalities and social groupings. However, really, it does not matter which nationality or group they come from, as the aim is not to describe what someone from a particular culture is like and then suggest how to communicate with them. Each example shows one or two people struggling with their differences, perceived or real, sometimes succeeding, sometimes failing, sometimes understanding, sometimes falling into an essentialist trap. If the balance is more on the side of people failing, followed with discussion on how they went wrong, this is because in the majority of cases we do indeed get things seriously wrong, and this is something which needs to be dealt with. It needs to be realized that the reason for failure is essentialism.

Section A introduces a non-essentialist view of culture which is then followed up in the rest of the book. It focuses on the complexity of culture as a fluid, creative social force which binds different groupings and aspects of behaviour in different ways, both constructing and constructed by people in a piecemeal fashion to produce myriad combinations and configurations.

The difference between 'non-essentialism' and 'essentialism', which are terms used by social scientists in their discussion about the nature of culture (e.g. Keesing 1994), is described in Table 1. We realize that this, like all other dichotomies, is harsh and ignorant of the fact that in reality views range between the two extremes. Nevertheless, essentialism in the way we see people and culture is the same essentialism which drives sexism and racism. The equivalent condition, culturism, similarly reduces and otherizes the individual and underlies many of the problems in the world today. By otherization we mean imagining someone as alien and different to 'us' in such a way that 'they' are excluded from 'our' 'normal', 'superior' and 'civilized' group. Indeed, it is by imagining a foreign Other in this way that 'our' group can become more confident and exclusive. Essentialism therefore needs to be defined strongly, recognized and fought against wherever it is found. This particular definition of essentialism might be different to that of others. As with racism and sexism, the concept needs to be discussed and continuously revisited.

It is perhaps noticeable that the entries on the right-hand side of the table (for non-essentialism) represent more complex and perhaps obscure ideas than those on the left-hand side. In this sense, essentialism is the 'easy' answer for culture, which has become popular, usable and marketable in, for example, management studies and foreign language education where people are looking for simple formulae for communicating with clients, students and colleagues from 'other places and backgrounds'. For this reason, the tone of this book is to go against these 'easy' answers, to struggle with dominant discourses and to problematize what is normally thought.

The final row in the table addresses the final question posed by this book, developing strategies for intercultural communication. Again, whereas the essentialist side provides an answer, the non-essentialist side poses more of a problem which is complex and requires an understanding of things which are not at all clear and different to what we imagine. Thus, the angle on communication within the theme of *identity* will be how identity is constructed and how individuals define their own identities. Within the theme of *otherization*, the focus will be how to avoid the trap of over-generalization and reduction when describing and interacting with others. Within the theme of *representation* the emphasis will be on deconstructing the imposed images of people from the media and popular discourse.

The purpose of this book is to engage in a dialogue with the reader. We do not believe there is only one route to achieving successful intercultural communication. You will therefore encounter different perspectives, possibly contradictory, within the book.

Table 1 Essentialism vs. non-essentialism

	Essentialist view of culture	How people talk about it	Non-essentialist view of culture	How people talk about it
Nature	i 'A culture' has a physical entity, as though it is a place, which people can visit. It is homogeneous in that perceived traits are spread evenly, giving the sense of a simple society.	'I visited three cultures while on holiday. They were Spain, Morocco and Tunisia.'	ii Culture is a social force which is evident where it is significant. Society is complex, with characteristics which are difficult to pin down.	'There was something culturally different about each of the countries I visited.'
Place	iii It is associated with a country and a language, which has an onion-skin relationship with larger continental, religious, ethnic or racial cultures, and smaller subcultures.	'Japanese culture', 'European culture', 'Hindu culture', 'Black culture', 'Japanese secondary school culture.'	iv It is associated with a value, and can relate equally to any type or size of group for any period of time, and can be characterized by a discourse as much as by a language.	'There is a more homogeneous culture of food in Japan than in Britain.' 'Schools in Britain have a more evident culture of sport than schools in Japan.'
Relation	v The world is divided into mutually exclusive national cultures. People in one culture are essentially different from people in another.	'When crossing from Japanese culture to Chinese culture . . .'; 'People from Egypt cannot . . . when they arrive in French culture.'	vi Cultures can flow, change, intermingle, cut across and through one another, regardless of national frontiers, and have blurred boundaries.	'There is more of a culture of . . . in China than in India', 'Schools throughout the world have a lot of cultural similarities.'
Membership	vii People belong exclusively to one national culture and one language.	'No matter how long she lives in Italy, she belongs to Austrian culture', 'Which culture do you originally come from?' 'One can never totally learn a second culture.'	viii People can belong to and move through a complex multiplicity of cultures both within and across societies.	'I feel most British when I travel abroad to places where that is meaningful. A sense of Iranian culture from my family and upbringing comes into play when I listen to Iranian music, speak the

Behaviour	ix 'A culture' behaves like a single-minded person with a specific, exclusive personality. People's behaviour is defined and constrained by the culture *in* which they live.	German culture believes that . . .', 'In Middle Eastern culture there is no concept of . . .'; In Chinese culture, people . . .'; 'She belongs to Norwegian culture, therefore she . . .'	x People are influenced by or make use of a multiplicity of cultural forms.	language and think of global politics. At the moment the strongest cultural force in my life comes from the international women's group to which I belong, through conferences, journals and email contact. These are the people to whom I feel culturally closest. The people I find most culturally strange are my children's friends and the village where I was a child. My Iranian-ness enriches my perceptions of and participation in British society, and vice versa.'
Communication	xi To communicate with someone who is foreign or different we must first understand the details or stereotype of their culture.	'When you want to greet a Swedish business man, you need to know that in Swedish culture . . .'	xii To communicate with anyone who belongs to a group with whom we are unfamiliar, we have to understand the complexity of who she is.	'What you have to understand about her is that she does not conform to the stereotype of Middle Eastern women that we see in the media, which she considers false and ignorant. In reality she is different to what we expected.'

Theme 1
Identity

This theme will explore how people construct their own identities.

PEOPLE LIKE ME
'This is whom I want to be represented by'

Experience

This unit explores the complexity of people's cultural identity in terms of how they want to represent themselves. Consider Example A1.1.1.

Example A1.1.1 Being represented

Parisa had been coming to international conventions on food processing for several years. She had made several good friends, especially from among the Europeans; but there was a gnawing problem which always came back unresolved. She was the only person at the convention who came from Iran; and no matter how friendly and sincere, she knew that her European colleagues saw her in a particular way which just wasn't her at all. It was from their passing comments, their casual, unguarded turns of phrase, in which they seemed to show surprise when she was creative, assertive or articulate, as though she *ought* to be somehow unable to be good at all the things she did. One of her colleagues did not actually say 'Well done!' but certainly implied it in her tone of voice. She also felt isolated as the only person from her particular background at these conventions. There was nobody else to represent who she was. It also hurt her when someone said that she was 'Westernized' and 'not a real Iranian'. This seemed like a no-win situation. If her behaviour was 'recognized', she was not real; and if she was considered 'real', she wasn't supposed to behave like that.

Then something happened which both confirmed her fears and gave her support. She invited three of her colleagues to see one of the films which was showing as part of a festival of Iranian films at the local university. They came willingly – very interested – and then to another one. When she asked one of her colleagues what she found so fascinating, her colleague replied that she was particularly impressed by the female characters who portrayed such strong women. Indeed, one of them played a major executive role in a film crew. She hired and fired people and drove around in a jeep.

Her colleague said that she had no idea such women existed in Iran, and that she always thought Muslim women were supposed to be subservient. Parisa was also pleased because the women on the film were certainly 'real' Iranians in that they wore the hejab, and the woman who drove the jeep wore the black hejab and long coat that she imagined fitted the 'stereotype'.

Shortly after this, another Iranian arrived at the convention. Parisa was very pleased that he was educated, worldly, urbane, well-dressed and also extremely articulate. This was no more or less than *she* would expect of an Iranian man; but she was pleased because here was further evidence for her other colleagues of the sort of people she belonged to. Moreover, it was very clear that he had tremendous respect for her as an equal, an academic and a professional. Parisa wondered though if they considered *him* a 'real Iranian'. After all, he wore a tie and didn't have a beard.

Deconstruction

Apart from the problem of being stereotyped and otherized, perhaps on the basis of the popular media images, which may depict Muslim women as lacking in power, Parisa's predicament in Example A.1.1.1 is that she lacks other images on the basis of which the people around her can judge who she is. Although her colleagues have got to know her and see her as their friend, they lack real knowledge of what sort of group she belongs to in order to place her. In this sense, they are also in a predicament, and indeed vulnerable to the stereotypes with which they are presented from other sources. Two concepts which need to be focused on are:

■ the multi-facetedness of Other people and societies
■ the way people talk.

Multi-facetedness

At one level one might say that Parisa wants to be associated with a certain type of Iranian person – educated, worldly, a working woman in the same way as her new male colleague is a working man – which she does not perceive as conforming to the popular stereotype. However, at another level it is more complex than this. Her society, like all others, is complex and multi-faceted, and in order for anyone to show who they really are, this complexity has to be visible. The Iranian films that her friends saw show this complexity, as often art forms are able to do more than any other media form. The woman, covered in black Muslim clothes, driving a jeep, being her own person, educated and a working woman, yet looking like all other women, hiring and firing extras for the film she is involved in making, begins successfully to show the layers and depths of a complex society in which identity is multi-faceted and shifting.

Another element in Parisa's quest to be recognized is her desire to be associated with other people. Again, at one level she wants to be associated with people like her in that they are middle class and so on, but at a deeper level, they should represent the same many-faceted complexity that she sees in herself. Thus, the new male colleague is also different to what she imagines her other colleagues would expect – not conforming to the stereotype, while at the same time being what 'she would expect of an Iranian man' in his civility, good manners, worldliness, and, moreover, respect towards her and the qualities she wishes to be noticed for by others.

The way in which these elements contribute to a person's recognition of where she comes from is depicted in Figure 1. As well as evidence of complexity, layers and facets, there is the unexpected juxtaposed with what is expected. The unexpected is inevitable where any society must always be far more than any outsider can imagine.

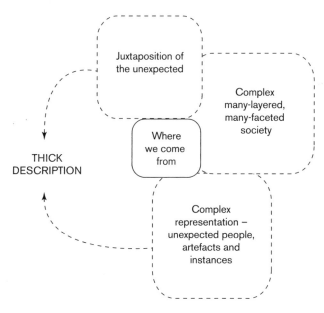

Figure 1 Elements of where we come from

The principle of discovery is also implicit in *thick description* – seeing the complexity of a social event by looking at it from different aspects. The figure shows that the knowledge derived from understanding the juxtaposition of unexpectedness (e.g. the woman in the film), complexity (e.g. the layers in the film), and encounters with people, artefacts and instances (e.g. Parisa's new colleague, the film, how the new colleague treats Parisa) results in thick description. Thick description as a term comes from anthropology and qualitative research and involves two elements:

■ deriving meaning from a broad view of social phenomena which pieces together different, interconnected perspectives
■ exploration, in which sense is made from an ongoing emergence of social phenomena, which may not immediately seem to connect, and which may indeed be unexpected.

One possible explanation of Example A1.1.1 is that something which troubles Parisa is the knowledge that her colleagues feel she is not a 'real' Iranian because she appears 'Westernized'. She also suspects that her new compatriot colleague will also be seen as not being 'real'. The fact that her colleagues consider her Westernized is more to do with their essentialist view of culture and the way in which they construct her particular 'national culture'. Because they see it as essentially different (Table 1 cell v) from their own 'Western' culture they cannot imagine that it would share features which they consider essentially Western. There is also a marked 'us'–'them' attitude. Hence, if Parisa in any way behaves like 'us', she must have become like 'us' and left the essentialist attributes of 'them' behind. The non-essentialist view has no difficulty with the notion that cultural attributes can flow between societies (Table 1 cell vi). Parisa desperately needs her colleagues to understand that her society is sufficiently complex and big to include the cultural attributes which they *consider* Western, but which are in fact normal for many people who come from Iran.

The way people talk

At a deeper level than these issues is what Parisa gleans from 'passing comments, their casual, unguarded turns of phrase, in which they seemed to show surprise when she was creative, assertive or articulate' – 'no matter how friendly and sincere' her European colleagues seemed. There are several possibilities here.

1. The thinking implicit in these comments is essentialist. Once again, there is the belief that the behavioural traits belonging to 'that' culture must be all packaged in the same stereotypical personality (Table 1 cell ix). Hence, if Muslim women are 'subservient', they cannot be 'creative, assertive or articulate'.
2. This thinking is deep in everyday discourse; and people are probably unaware of it.
3. They do not see it as derogatory.

In all three cases the passing comments are in conflict, in Parisa's view, with apparent friendliness. The possibility of 1 is especially worrying because it implies a deep-seated essentialism in people's attitudes and socialization – an issue which will be taken up in Theme 2 Otherization. If 3 is the case, her colleagues are in effect being profoundly patronizing in that they assume they think it appropriate to comment on, perhaps praising, unexpected 'achievement' for someone from 'her culture' – rather as they would a child who achieves above their years – 'well done!'

Communication

Especially considering the above points about the way people talk, there are important considerations in this unit with regard to communication. We have seen how Parisa herself feels, not only about direct communication but also about asides and tones of voice. Parisa *may* be more sensitive than many, but this one instance – as in the case of any qualitative analysis – illuminates a particular predicament which makes one see intercultural communication in a certain way. It becomes clear that for Parisa's colleagues to communicate with her effectively they do not need information about her presumed national culture. This would be prescriptive and indeed essentialist in that it would tend to define the person before understanding the person. Rather than being a matter of prescribed information, the non-essentialist strategy is a moral one to do with how we approach and learn about a person as a human being (Table 1 cell xii). There are several disciplines that might be observed here.

1. Respond to people according to how you find them rather than according to what you have heard about them.
2. Avoid easy answers about how people are. Bracket – put aside simplistic notions about what is 'real' or 'unreal' in your perception of 'another culture'.
3. Appreciate that every society is as complex and culturally varied as your own.
4. Learn to build up thick descriptions of what happens between you and others – to work out how to communicate as you go along.

 Task A1.1.1   Thinking about Parisa

➤ Think of a situation you have been in that is like the Parisa example and describe it in similar detail.
➤ Explain how you can better understand one or more people in the situation with the help of Figure 1 and the disciplines listed above.
➤ What can you learn from this about intercultural communication?

 UNIT A1.2   **ARTEFACTS OF CULTURE**
Telling cultural stories, closing ranks

Experience

This unit continues to unravel the complexities of cultural identity by looking at what might lie behind what people say about their culture.

Example A1.2.1   Chinese teachers

Janet is American and got to know Zhang and Ming, who are Chinese, when they were doing their master's course together. She found that Zhang talked a lot both in class and at other times about Confucianism and how it was the basis of Chinese culture. They soon got into an ongoing discussion about what teachers and students could be expected to do in his university English classes. He said that because of Confucianism, just as it was impolite for children to question their parents, it was impolite for students to question their teachers. This meant that all sorts of things which happened in classrooms in the West, like discovery learning and classroom discussions, were culturally inappropriate in China.

As the master's course progressed, Janet noticed that Zhang was getting increasingly unhappy. She asked Ming what Zhang's problem was. He explained that some people found it more difficult than others to cope with being in a foreign environment. She had noticed that Zhang was very silent when there was a class discussion, and she asked Ming if this was to do with Confucianism. Ming said that this was certainly a factor; but when Janet told him what Zhang had told her about students having to obey their teachers in China, Ming said that this was not strictly true – that he knew lots of teachers who were prepared to be engaged in discussion by their students, that students were certainly not always prepared to submit to teachers who would not listen to them, and that in modern China many parents no longer held the sort of authority that Zhang was talking about. Janet told him that this shocked her because it was not just from Zhang that she had heard about this. There were so many books she had read about Chinese culture which reported how it was bound by Confucianism. There were also two other people on the course who said that all the Chinese people they had met said the same thing. Ming said that there were different ways of looking at this. On the one hand, it could not be denied that Confucianism had been a very powerful influence on Chinese society for thousands of years. On the other hand, not everyone had to be bound by this influence; and different people could be influenced in different ways.

Janet then read an article which said that people in the developing world had tended to exaggerate their own cultural identity in order to counter the powerful influence of the West. She read Kubota (2002). When she put this idea to Ming he said that there was no need to read too much into Zhang's statements about Confucianism. He thought it was really far more simple than that. He had seen so many American people in China who had seemed far more 'American' than anyone he had seen here. Surely was it not the case that *all* people drew more heavily on certain cultural resources when they felt culturally threatened by strange behaviour. So does that mean that Confucianism is a 'cultural resource' she wondered.

Deconstruction

In this example we see an American teacher trying to make sense of conflicting messages about Chinese culture. The first impression that Zhang presents her with tends towards the essentialist view – that 'Chinese culture' is characterized by Confucianism, which in turn determines the behaviour of parents, children, teachers and students (Table 1 cell ix). The conflicting impression that Ming presents is more non-essentialist – that what Zhang says is not necessarily true, that the influence of Confucianism is far from straightforward. If we assume that Janet has read Unit A1.1 and learnt that the essentialist view denies the complexity of one's identity and society, Zhang's point of view becomes even more puzzling for her. What, therefore, are the reasons for Zhang's essentialist point of view? Ming and Janet herself have already gone some way in answering this question.

■ When people are in a difficult, strange environment, they can close ranks and exaggerate specific aspects of their cultural identity.

■ Different cultural resources can be drawn upon and invoked at different times depending on the circumstances.

In both cases, because of the strength of statement, there can be an *appearance* of essentialist national culture. We shall now look in more detail at these phenomena, and at a related third.

■ What people *say* about their cultural identity should be read as the image they wish to project at a particular time rather than as evidence of an essentialist national culture.

Closing ranks

The factor which Janet read about, reaction to a powerful cultural threat from the West, could certainly be a reason for closing ranks – though there could also be threats from other national, international or global quarters. In this case they could be invading a person's, or indeed a whole society's, home territory. There may indeed be a connection here with religious and ethnic fundamentalism. Difficult, strange environments are also encountered, as Ming states, when travelling to foreign places. Adrian Holliday remembers an example of this where otherwise left-wing, long-haired young Englishmen displayed a deep interest in British military music from the Coldstream Guards while living in Iran in the 1970s. An interesting inverse of this may be where people in strange environments also construct essentialist descriptions of 'local people'. British people in very diverse foreign locations commonly see the 'locals' as 'subservient, hierarchical, corrupt, inhibited by extended families and arranged marriages, lacking in individualism, unable to make decisions' and so on. Such descriptions are more likely to be British constructions of the opposite of what they consider themselves to be than grounded in the behaviour they observe around them.

The case of the Chinese people reported by both Zhang and Janet's British colleagues to be Confucian in all their actions, and that of the interest in military music for the young Englishmen abroad, may be a reaction to perceived Western pedagogies or at least 'modern' pedagogies which they find too difficult to deal with. This reminds one also of the observed behaviour of Japanese students in British classrooms. Their silence and apparent 'passivity' may be more a reaction to the, to them, strange classroom rules which confront them than an effect of cultural behaviour in Japan.

Cultural resources

Confucianism for the Chinese teachers thus becomes a convenient cultural resource around which to marshal their threatened identity (Table 1 cell x). As can be seen by the way in which the British abroad define the foreign Other as opposite to themselves, the particular resources which are chosen may well be the ones which are most opposite to the cultural features of the threat. There are also arguments that the very strong description of Japaneseness which has recently pervaded international commerce is actually a ploy to promote a marketable exoticness (e.g. Moeran 1996).

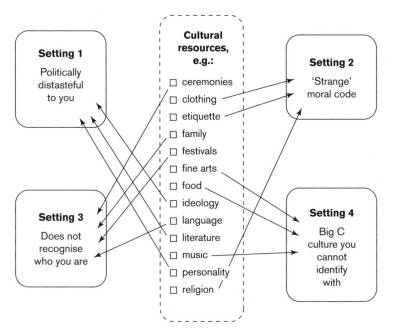

Figure 2 Making use of culture

Figure 2 is a rough attempt to show how different cultural resources can be used by a particular person in particular settings. By cultural resources we mean aspects of culture that exist in our society which we can draw on at different times and for different reasons. The central bubble lists quite randomly the sorts of things which *might* be resources. There could be many other things on the list. The surrounding bubbles are examples of cultural settings which are 'foreign' and present a particular threat in different ways. The arrows match resources to settings, showing that only some resources would be relevant to dealing with each setting. 'Particular' is the key word here because this is *by no means* a set of universals. Every person who reads this would use different resources to deal with each setting, and you might indeed find it fascinating to imagine how the arrows might link different resources to the settings if it were you. It is also important to note that you would appear quite culturally differently in each setting. If you used the resources in the same way as in the figure, in each setting your 'culture' may appear to be characterized by the following.

■ You find the politics of the society or social group in Setting 1 'distasteful'. You counter this by drawing on a particular aspect of personality, literature and ideology from your own society or group and present *your culture* as being left-wing activist.

■ You find the moral code in Setting 2 'strange'. You reassure yourself by drawing on religious beliefs, clothing and etiquette in your own society or social group and present *your culture* as a religious one with particular dress codes.

■ The people in Setting 3 do not understand who you are because they have no knowledge of where you come from. You strengthen your identity by drawing on ceremonies, festivals and family values in your society or social group and present these as the basis of *your culture.*

■ You cannot identify with the 'high culture' (arts etc) of Setting 4. You draw on the fine arts, 'cuisine' and music of your society or social group and present these as the defining ingredients of *your culture.*

One may think that the 'you' in each of these cases is being deceitful or duplicitous, playing with or selecting what they like from their culture in this way. This would be an essentialist view. The non-essentialist view would be that culture is a shifting reality anyway, and people make of it what they need to as live their identities in different circumstances. This view of culture as a shifting reality can be compared with Text B0.1.1 by Hannerz in **Unit B0.1**, where there is a reference to people being 'more or less Confucian', and to the multiplicity of cultural identity reported by Baumann in Text B0.1.2, also in **Unit B0.1**.

Artefacts of culture

There are dangers with the non-essentialist view just as there are with the essentialist view. It would be a grave mistake for the essentialist to think Ming was not a 'real' Chinese because he did not conform to the Confucian essence. In the same way it would also be a grave mistake to think that Zhang was not to be taken seriously because he was being 'naïve' about the role of Confucianism. Even though it might be the case that Zhang's statements about how Confucianism determines the behaviour of teachers and students might be considered essentialist, these statements are still extremely meaningful to him, just as the behaviour of all the people mentioned in this unit would be extremely real to them. In each case, these are constituents of how individuals need to work their own personal identities. If we as communicators are to take people from other backgrounds seriously, we should take every fact of what they do and say seriously. In this sense, every instance of behaviour becomes an artefact of who people are. Thus, what *can* be said about Zhang is that his discourse about Confucianism is part and parcel of his cultural identity. The *way* he talks about Confucianism is an artefact of what *he* believes about Confucianism; and this in itself may indeed be cultural. Indeed, if more and more Chinese were heard to talk about Confucianism in this way, one may conclude that there is a tendency for some Chinese to say that Confucianism influences every part of their lives. Table 2 demonstrates this. On the left, essentialist descriptions are based on prescription, while on the right, non-essentialist descriptions are very cautious and

Table 2 What people say

Essentialist description based on stereotypes	*Non-essentialist description based on observation*
In Chinese culture people's behaviour is determined by Confucianism.	Some Chinese feel it important to say that their behaviour is determined by Confucianism. Others say that this is an overgeneralization.
In Japanese culture students are silent and passive in the classroom.	Some Japanese prefer to remain silent when in British language classrooms.
In 1970s British culture young people liked military music.	Some young British people found military music comforting while living abroad.

qualified, based on no more than what can be observed. Indeed, the non-essentialist descriptions should also be *ephemeral* – that is, perhaps true at a particular time, but changing. For those British readers, the bottom left statement will show the ridiculousness of some essentialist comments; yet it would have been easy for Iranians to generalize thus when they saw the way two particular British people behaved while in their country.

Communication

The lessons to be learnt about communication from Example A1.2.1 build on those in the previous unit. Janet has indeed learnt some of the lessons from Unit A1.1 and listens carefully to Zhang and Ming and places what she learns against what she has heard from her own compatriots about things related to Confucianism – thus creating her own thick description. Taking a non-essentialist line, she sees Ming, despite his doubts about Confucianism, as just as 'real' a Chinese as Zhang. If she believes Ming's doubts about Confucianism, how should she therefore respond to Zhang? The answer may be that she should follow these disciplines, which follow on from the four disciplines listed on page 10.

5. While respecting whatever people say about their own culture, take what they say as evidence of what they wish to project rather than as information about where they come from.
6. Take what people say about their own culture as a personal observation which should not be generalized to other people who come from the same background.

Task A1.2.1 Thinking about Zhang and Ming

➤   Think of a situation you have been in that is like the Zhang and Ming example and describe it in similar detail.
➤   Explain how you can better understand one or more people in the situation with the help of the explanations in the Deconstruction section, Table 2 and the disciplines listed.
➤   Use Figure 2 and describe what sorts of cultural resources were being used by one of the participants and why.
➤   What can you learn from this about intercultural communication?

IDENTITY CARD
'I am who I can make myself and make others accept me to be'

Experience

This unit explores the principle that while one person may be exchanging information with another person, they are both, be it intentionally or unintentionally, also sending messages about their cultural identity – about how they want the other person to see them. The example is different to those in previous units in that it does not concern people from different societies. It is about people in the same society, but from very different cultural groups. This is to illustrate the non-essentialist point that cultural difference by no means has to be connected with national difference (Table 1 cells vi and viii). Also, by looking at a small, rather than a large culture, it is easier to see the details of cultural formation. See the discussion of small cultures in Holliday in Text B0.2.3, Unit B0.2, Section B. Consider the event given in Example A1.3.1.

Example A1.3.1   Girls on the bus

A public bus in south-east England was mainly occupied by school children returning home to the villages after attending school in the city. Several of the other passengers were annoyed by what they considered noisy bad language from some of the children. The most vociferous and extreme swearing was from a group of girls. The bus stopped and a further schoolgirl got on. She joined the group, one of whom shouted, 'Hello, you big fat tart', to which the new girl loudly retorted, 'Fuck off bitch'. This exchange seemed to serve as a greeting as the two did not appear in any way genuinely angry with each other. The volume of their utterances was also noticeably loud enough for all the bus occupants to hear – in other words, it was unnecessarily loud for communication to occur just between themselves. The first interactant then admired a new item of jewellery her friend had around her neck: 'Where did you get that, you dirty slag?' The friend answered: 'None of your business, you fucking nosy cow!'

    After this, the first interactant's attention became fixed upon a school boy, who was smaller than the girls, sitting several seats away. 'Darren! Oi, Darren! Fucking listen to me Darren! Are you a poof, Darren?' The girls laughed and the boy looked embarrassed and at a loss as to how to reply. 'No I'm not,' he finally protested, and looked out of the window, no doubt hoping the girls' attention would wander to someone else. Then another girl's voice: 'Darren, Michaela says you're a poof.' Darren's bus journey was going to be a longer one than he might have hoped!

There are a lot of terms you might not be familiar with in this example. See Task C1.4.2, in Unit C1.4.

Deconstruction

In this example we see a group of schoolgirls asserting their cultural identity to the outside world who are represented by the culturally different Other people on the bus, who are in turn shocked and perhaps disgusted by their explicit display. In many ways, the girls are doing the same as Parisa in Unit A1.1 and Zhang in Unit A1.2, but whereas they were pulling elements from their distant homes to reinforce identity in the face of strangers, these girls are on their home ground and we see the details of actual cultural formation – still, though, in the face of strangers. There are several related concepts at work:

■ the multiplicity of identities
■ the creation of an identity card
■ the marking out of territory.

Cultural identity and multiplicity

The two girls derive and achieve an identity by signalling belongingness to the particular culture of swearing girls on the bus. Belongingness among the members of any group partly involves the learning and use of particular discourses. It is a person's familiarity and ease of use of these discourses that demonstrates their membership of a particular group – that is, the cultural territory to which they stake a claim. In the case of Example A1.3.1, the discourse is one of swearing – the mastery of a complex code which only insiders can fully understand and which can be used to exclude outsiders. Thus, apparent insult is read as greeting or endearment between the initiated girls, but as real insult and exclusion when directed at the boy.

However, the two girls are not only members of the culture of swearing girls on the bus. As with Parisa, Zhang and Ming in Units A1.1 and A1.2, they belong to a complex society which allows a multiplicity of choices. They could also define themselves as members of an age group, a nationality, an ethnic group, a social class, a religion, a scout group, an aerobics class, a hockey team, a school class group. We are all, as individuals, members of a vast number of different cultural groups (Table 1 cell viii), and hence have a multiplicity of identities. Adrian Holliday notes that he has an identity as a member of his family, part of which (through his wife) is Iranian, the university where he did his graduate studies, a professional group, part of which (through Applied Linguistics) is international, a university department, a local community of artists, and so on, besides being a member of a particular nation, which at the moment is moving between 'British' and 'English'. With each identity he has a certain communal bond with a group of other people: we are linked through a common experience, we have our icons, our ideologies and our communal history to draw on, and we encapsulate all of this in our discourses. Because all of us inhabit different cultural groups, we are in fact all unique in our cultural identities.

Identity card

There is also a very strong sense of cultural assertion in Example A1.3.1: '*This* is how we *are!* We use bad language; we shock; we make boys feel uncomfortable; we don't care about annoying people around us.' And in the paragraph above we use the term 'define themselves' rather than simply 'are'. The two girls are not simply *being* members of a culture; they are *doing* the culture in order to *communicate* something to the people around them. In this sense, they are *playing* a particular identity card.

In a way they are playing with the cultural stereotypes expected by other members of their society. Swearing is often considered a territory occupied only by males displaying their toughness. Indeed it would seem that girls have invaded this traditional male territory and taken it over. They have also invaded the misogynistic male lexicon of derogatory terms for women: 'slag', 'bitch', 'tart', 'cow'. They thus subvert the potentially wounding power of these terms, neutralize them by their frequency of use, and convert them into the normal phatic functions of greeting and 'small talk'. And in so doing, they increase the shock effect by voicing yet twisting what the audience of bus passengers may consider taboo. On the other hand, these terms have become very much the domain of women generally in their in-talk, whereas outsider men will use them at their risk.

The girls are very vocal and thus also occupy the acoustic space of the bus: the old notions of men not swearing in the presence of the 'weaker' and 'daintier' sex are completely challenged – indeed inverted – here. This incident would seem to have a lot to do with the notion of 'girl power'. Further attack is made upon maleness by the bullying of the boy and the questioning of his sexuality. Again the weapons of reductionist and derogatory sexual labelling are used by the girls on the boy rather than vice versa.

Although we are not fully in control of the resources that make up our identity, and we cannot choose our ethnicity, sex and so on, we can decide how to play the hand of cards that we have been dealt. We can work with the discourses available to us according to how we wish others to see us and how we wish to influence others' perceptions of the hand of cards we have been dealt. Indeed, through such discourse action over time these very cards can become viewed in different ways. This is true, for example, of how women have changed the way femininity is constructed and perceived over the last century, or of how anti-slavery discourses in the early 19th century changed the way that Black Africans were perceived in British society. Identity is therefore not in essence a stable concept, but one that is achieved through the skilled manipulation of discourses in society.

Territory

By being creative with the act of swearing, the girls are in effect marking a powerful new territory – an identity terrain which they occupy in their struggle for presentation of self against the identities that are imposed upon them by others. This territory is fought over and at times conceded during interactions. In the case of Example A1.3.1, the act of swearing becomes a critical marker of this territory.

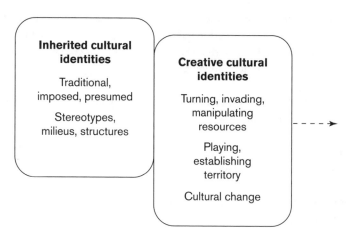

Figure 3 Two sides to identity

Figure 3 shows two sides to cultural identity. The left-hand bubble represents a state of affairs which, though imposed by the way in which society defines us – and indeed other societies define us, in the case of national cultural perceptions – can be seen as the resources of the material that we have to work with. In the case of the girls on the bus, these might comprise 'traditional' notions that girls do not swear, but are sworn at. The right-hand bubble signifies a dynamic movement away from this establishment, in which, through playing with the resources, individuals or groups can create new identities and, indeed, create culture change. Although a similar process, this is subtly different to what can be seen in Unit A1.2, as represented in Figure 2. There, cultural resources are used ephemerally to defend identity; here they are used to create the fabric of identity.

Communication

Being sensitive to and understanding others' cultural productions and the way in which they play with the various identities available to them (discourses on their identities currently available in the context of their interactions) is a crucial part of good intercultural communication. A good interpersonal communicator, therefore, needs to be aware of issues surrounding the concept of identity. Before we can communicate with people who are different to ourselves, we need to understand something about how they present themselves as being or belonging to certain groups. This goes deeper than the observations about Zhang in Unit A1.2, where we note that one should respect what people say about themselves and see this as an artefact of who they are without over-generalizing. The creative element in Example A1.3.1 takes this further. Hence the first discipline for this unit must be that we should do the following (disciplines 1–4 appear on page 10, and 5–6 on page 15).

7. Understand how people are creating and indeed negotiating their cultural identity in the very process of communicating with us.

We need therefore to see communication with anyone as a dynamically creative process. Also, this surely teaches us something about ourselves, which should be evident from all the examples in this theme – that the whole thing is, of course, a two-way process, in that we should also do the following.

8. Appreciate that you are creating and negotiating your own cultural identity in the process of communicating with others.

Furthermore, as the process of communication is also personal – as all the examples in these units are to do with interaction between individuals – we should do the following.

9. Appreciate that the creation and negotiation of cultural and personal identity are the same thing.

 Task A1.3.1   Thinking about the girls on the bus

➤   Think of a situation you have been in that is like the girls on the bus example and describe it in similar detail.
➤   Explain how you can better understand one or more people in the situation with the help of Figure 3 and the disciplines outlined.
➤   What can you learn from this about intercultural communication?

Theme 2
Otherization

This theme will explore a major inhibition to communication by looking at how, so easily, we can construct and reduce people to be less than what they are. Continuing from Units A1.1, A1.2 and A1.3 within the Identity theme, the angle on communication will be how we must discipline our own perceptions if we are to communicate successfully. However, Units A2.1, A2.2 and A2.3 will look more deeply at the forces that prevent us all from seeing people as they really are. The weight of responsibility is on 'us' to understand ourselves, rather than on essentialist categories of 'them'.

COMMUNICATION IS ABOUT NOT PRESUMING
Falling into culturist traps

Experience

Continuing to follow the principle that we should try to understand people before we can communicate with them, in this unit we explore how easy it is to be misled by our own preconceptions and to fall into the trap of otherization. As with Unit A1.3, we use an example from within our own society to demonstrate how the tendency to reduce the foreign Other is deep within the roots of society generally. We hope therefore to show how even easier it is to misconstruct people from other societies. Consider the experience given in Example A2.1.1.

Example A2.1.1 The Smith family

A while ago John had neighbours, the Smiths, who belonged to a Christian sect related to the Amish. John and his family took this as a matter of fact because Mr Smith told them so several weeks after moving in during a residents' meeting. However, from the very first John's family saw of them they had suspected something of the sort. There were six children. The girls and Mrs Smith were dressed in long dresses with aprons, which came down to their mid-calf, and wore headscarves over long hair. The boys had long shorts with braces [US, suspenders], which also came down to mid-calf. Mr Smith was clean-shaven, except for a beard around his chin. As they were moving in John and his family could see that their furniture was like old-fashioned wooden school furniture; and they didn't seem to have a television, stereo or video. There was, however, a piano and John could hear them making their own music for entertainment in the evenings. They were also American.

Several events took place after the family moved in which began to reveal the way in which John was thinking about them.

One afternoon, John was in his garage pottering about when Mr Smith came out and got into his large people carrier. He guessed he was waiting for the rest of his family before going out with them. He really was amazed when Mr Smith turned on the car's CD player and listened to music. He had thought that because the Smiths didn't have a television or stereo in the house their religion forbade them from listening to such things.

It was the time when the whole country seemed involved in the events surrounding Princess Diana's death. Mr Smith's American parents were staying with them and his wife had encountered his mother in the driveway. Mrs Smith senior told her that because there was no television or radio in her son's home, and no one was allowed to read newspapers, it was difficult for her and her husband to find out what was going on, and they felt they were missing a critical aspect of being in England. Despite the incident with the car stereo, this confirmed to John that the Smith family were indeed fundamentalists, and that he had been right all along about how they abstained from modernity. He was therefore shocked and indeed concerned that it would be an inconsiderate invasion of their religious *culture* when his wife suggested inviting Mr and Mrs Smith senior, and indeed the whole Smith family, in to watch Diana's funeral on the television. John really felt that this invitation would put the whole family in a very difficult position. It would be like inviting Muslims to eat pork. His wife said that it would be impolite to invite Mr and Mrs Smith senior alone, and that anyway they all had the choice to refuse.

John was amazed again when the whole Smith family accepted the invitation and all ten of them came into their living room, the children sitting on the floor, to watch the whole funeral. He was even more amazed when Mrs Smith later wrote his wife a note to say that they had all really appreciated the opportunity.

Deconstruction

This example shows John reducing his neighbour according to a prescribed stereotype – very much as Parisa's colleagues reduced her to a stereotype in Unit A1.1. What makes this particularly significant is that it is so easy to fall into traps like this. It is therefore extremely important to deconstruct exactly how this can happen.

It seems clear from Example A2.1.1 that John had made a mistake both about the nature of the Smith family and about how to communicate with them, whereas his wife had been successful at least to the extent of achieving significant interaction that seemed to be appreciated by both sides. In an attempt to explain why this happened we are going to explore the four interconnected concepts, some of which will be familiar, some less so, and link them with the concept of essentialism introduced in Units A1.1, A1.2 and A1.3:

■ stereotype
■ prejudice

- otherization
- culturism.

From stereotype to otherization

John had formed a *stereotype* based on his observation of wooden furniture, abstention from exposure to the media, austere clothing, a large family, Mr Smith's chin beard, Mrs Smith's and the daughters' long hair, put together with the popular image of the Amish presented in the Hollywood movie, *Witness*. Many argue that it is natural to form stereotypes and that they indeed help us to understand 'foreign cultures' – that they act as a template, or as an ideal type, against which we can measure the unknown. We disagree with this view. One reason is that we do not behave sufficiently rationally in intercultural dealings to be able to work objectively with such templates. A major reason for this is that stereotypes are often infected by *prejudice*, which in turn leads to *otherization*. This process is summarized in the top half of Figure 4. We have chosen the words for the bubbles in the figure carefully because this is a complex, dangerous area.

The 'foreign Other' (bubbles A and C) refers not only to different nationalities, but also to any group of people *perceived* as different – perhaps in terms of so-called ethnicity, religion, political alignment, class or caste, or gender. This is 'so-called' ethnicity because the term is particularly relative and disputed (e.g. Baumann 1996 in Unit B0.1). We also do not list culture because all the other things listed can be said to have cultures or to be cultural. Interest (bubble B) could similarly be ethnic, religious, political, class or caste, or gender. This would colour, bias or infect the way in which the foreign Other is seen. Emergent evidence (bubble B) would be based on what can be learned on the basis of deeper understanding. This is clearly very difficult to achieve, as interest of one sort or another is always with us. Attempts are made in various types of social science. Reduction (bubble C) is where the different facets, the variety of possible characteristics and the full complexity of a group of people are ignored in favour of a preferred definition. In our view, as the figure implies, stereotyping, prejudice and otherization interact with each other; however, it is the negative impact of the latter which makes the other two undesirable.

A basic feature of this process is the way in which information is brought from outside the situation, a priori. The reference to the movie, *Witness* (above), shows that it was images that John already had about Amish people that gave rise to his stereotype of his neighbours. (We shall explore the influence of such social representation in more detail in Theme 3.) If he had simply observed what he saw and heard of them in situ, without these prior images, he would have had a far more complex picture of them. To compound this, were his a priori negative feelings about so-called 'fundamentalist' Christians – his prejudices – so that his final otherization of his neighbours reduced them to people who would *never* watch television, would *always* think it evil and, by extension, would not *appreciate* the complexities of such *modern* phenomena as Diana's funeral. One may think, so what? Amish people *are* strange and odd, and restrict their behaviour and opt out of 'normal' life. The point is that John judged his neighbours, and categorized them, and decided what they would and would not be *before* really investigating who they were as individuals.

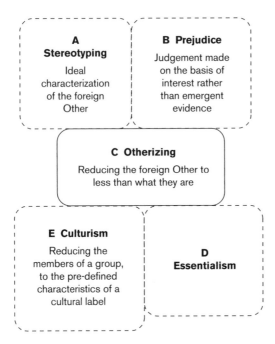

Figure 4 Constituents of otherization

Culturism

The lower half of Figure 4 reveals another aspect of otherization, which addresses the issue of culture. Following our comment regarding bubbles A and C (23), the groups of people who we characterize as the 'foreign Other' can be said to share between them something cultural. The problem is that 'we' can very easily take this too far and allow the notion of 'culture' to become greater than the people themselves. Just as we too easily form stereotypes which can pre-define what people are like, we can *imagine* or *reify* 'cultures' as objects, places and physical entities within which and by which people live (Table 1 cell i). By reification we mean to imagine something to be real when it is not. Hence, essentialism is born (bubble D). Therefore, in Example A2.1.1:

■ John saw the Amish as a religious culture characterized by the stereotypical traits of austere appearance, disdain for modernity and so on, which would govern the behaviour of the Smith family. He thus saw them through the filter of 'in Amish culture. . . .' (Table 1 cell ix)

From essentialism there is just a small step to *culturism* (bubble E). This is similarly constructed to racism or sexism in that the imagined characteristics of the 'culture' (or 'women' or 'Asians') are used to define the person. Thus:

■ whatever Mrs Smith did, John *explained* it as being Amish. And if she did something which did not fit the explanation, it was that she had somehow lost her culture, was no longer, or 'not really' Amish, or had been 'secularized'.

24

Again, the reader might think this argument inconsequential, because 'everyone knows' that the Amish 'are in fact like that'. Nevertheless, if one applied the same culturist rule to women, we would get:

■ whatever Mrs Smith did, John *explained* it as being due to her being a woman. And if she did something which did not fit the explanation, it was that she had lost her femininity.

Communication

The disciplines for intercultural communication arising from this unit carry the same basic message as those in Unites A1.1, A1.2 and A1.3, except that here they can draw attention to the factors which help *prevent* us from misinterpreting other people's realities. In the light of the experience of this unit, we must therefore do the following (disciplines 1–4 appear on page 10, 5–6 on page 15 and 7–9 on pages 19–20).

10. Avoid falling into the culturist trap of reducing people to less than they are – in the same way as we must avoid racist and sexist traps.

Task A2.1.1   Thinking about the Smiths

➤ Think of a situation you have been in that is like the Smiths example and describe it in similar detail.
➤ Pinpoint where the elements of otherization depicted in Figure 4 show themselves in the situation, and list the perpetrators and victims.
➤ What can you learn from this about intercultural communication? How might you go about conforming to the discipline described?

CULTURAL DEALING
What we project onto each other

Experience

This unit looks at the problem of otherization on a macro scale when two communities of people come together and behave according to their images of each other. Consider this example (first used in Holliday 2002):

Example A2.2.1   Tourists and business

Agnes has joined a tour group which is travelling through North Africa visiting archaeological sites. The group is made up of German, Italian, French, Swedish and

British tourists. They stay in a small hotel near one particular site for three days. It is 30 kilometres from the nearest town, but there is a village nearby. The villagers work in the hotel and have also set up a string of small shops in which they sell local handicrafts and souvenirs.

Agnes forms a brief relationship with François. She is really amazed at herself for succumbing to his charms. She thinks it is, after all, such a cliché. She has of course seen the film *Shirley Valentine*, in which a middle-aged Englishwoman falls in love with a local restaurant owner while on holiday on a Greek island. She has never had such a casual relationship before; but her marriage is struggling and she has come away to escape. She is also sure that François, who seems a real gigolo, does this sort of thing with every European woman who comes along.

François is amazed at himself for getting involved like this. He is unmarried and has never had an affair with a woman before. He is engaged to be married, and has a high sense of personal morality. Indeed, he will not have had sex with his fiancée, and his relationship with her will have been carefully chaperoned. He has actually fallen in love with Agnes, but is at the same time smitten by remorse because he is being unfaithful to his fiancée, whom he also loves deeply. After a very short time he becomes horrified at Agnes's behaviour. She suddenly 'throws herself at him' and is readily prepared to have sex. It must after all be true what everyone says about European women – that they are loose, have no morals and will have sex with anyone.

They part in anger. She goes back to her fellow travellers and indulges more than ever in the stories of how North African men swindle tourists and mistreat their women. He goes back to his village and indulges more than ever in the stories of the corrupt West.

Deconstruction

Here we can see François and Agnes getting into a very difficult relationship made more so by a complexity of personal and cultural complications. Basic concepts here are as follows.

- When people from different backgrounds meet, a middle culture of dealing is set up within which they interact, which in turn is influenced by respective complexes of cultural baggage.
- What people see of each other is influenced by the middle culture of dealing, which may be very different to what they think they see which is a product of otherization.

Middle cultures of dealing

Figure 5 can be interpreted not in the essentialist terms of 'European culture' and 'North African culture' (Table 1 cell iii), but in terms of a far more complicated mélange of interacting and overlapping cultural entities (Table 1 cell vi). This is demonstrated in Figure 5. Bubbles B and D represent the small cultures of the tourists and of the villagers *while* they are trading with the tourists. These are the cultures which initially come into

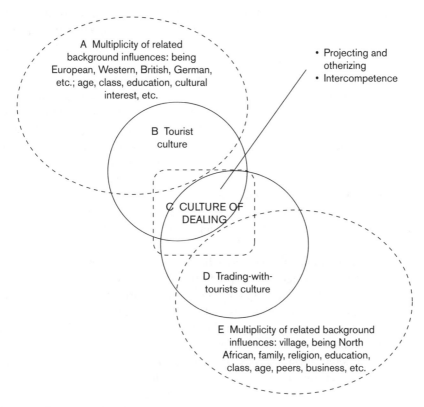

Figure 5 Culture of dealing

contact with each other and which act as the primary source of information for each group. The broader cultural influences of being European or villagers and so on are in the background in bubbles A and E. What exactly these influences, as cultural resources, might be will also depend on the specific circumstances (Unit A1.2 Figure 2). In this case, village and family might have a stronger impact on François because of their proximity, and being European on Agnes because of the group of people she is with as a tourist. The tourist culture and the trading-with-tourists culture (bubbles B and D) are more temporary and yet specific to the activities in hand. Anyone who has seen a group of tourists, among whom are their own compatriots, will recognize that they are behaving very differently (in bubble B) to when they are at home (bubble A), forming a new type cohesiveness among themselves with perhaps new artefacts such as cameras, water bottles, sun hats, backpacks and so on. At the same time, the village trading culture (in bubble D) will have different characteristics to the culture of the village itself (bubble E), with perhaps use of languages, currencies, codes of politeness and so on which are tuned to the foreign customer. This trading-with-tourists culture (in bubble D) may be seen as an extension or outcrop from the village culture (in circle E); and it will not be the only one. Similar cultures (bubble D) will grow when people go to school or university, travel to cities or deal with other people who come to the village – thus exemplifying that the village culture (bubble E) is always far from the confined exclusivity in the essentialist sense.

Bubble C, in the centre of the figure, represents a further extension of all the other cultures where the actual interaction between François and Agnes takes place. This is a culture of dealing because it is set up between the two interactants who enter into a relationship of culture-making.

We do not wish to give the impression in this model of behaviour that the cultures in bubbles B to D are 'subcultures' which are hierarchically subordinate, or deviant, to the respective 'parent' cultures (bubbles A and E). A more open-ended picture seems more appropriate, in which the 'small cultures' of the tourists, the village, the tourist–tourism business and so on have a multiplicity of relationships both within and transcending larger entities (Table 1 cells iii–iv). Furthermore, Figure 5 presents only one way of seeing what happens between the villagers and the tourists. Another way of seeing this might be in terms of discourses, rather than small cultures, as discussed in Unit A3.2 and by Gee in Unit B1.3. Whether these can be called discourses or cultures might depend on the degree to which they are represented by ways of talking or behaviour and artefacts.

This model of multiple cultures means that what François and Agnes actually see of each other is very much defined by the specific situation in which they meet. The cultural influences of Europe, from where Agnes comes, are only part of the picture. The culture of tourism is closer, and its influence is evidenced in Example A2.2.1 by the reference to the *Shirley Valentine* film in which the behaviour of a middle-aged English woman is changed by being away from home in an 'exotic' place. For François, it is the culture of trading with tourists which brings him into contact with Agnes, leaving the social influences of the village and his engagement relatively distant. When François and Agnes actually meet, it is within the very new culture of their dealing with each other that they see each other's behaviour directly. It could be argued that in this new culture their behaviour becomes intercompetent (Holliday 2002:152) – anomalous, sometimes mixed up, still approaching the competence people achieve in longer-standing cultures, as they learn how to behave in this very new culture. Put more simply, they see each other very much out of character in this clumsy new culture.

Nevertheless, the basis upon which they *perceive*, or think they see, each other is very different. Inaccurate otherization and culturism become rampant. Although Agnes, as a tourist, is behaving differently because she is on holiday, François explains her behaviour – as a 'loose immoral' woman – according to the common stereotype of Europeans he brings from his village. Agnes similarly explains his behaviour – as a 'swindler, gigolo and misogynist' – according to the common stereotype of people who work in the bazaars of North Africa she brings from home. They both thus miss totally the fact that each of them is involved in an intense moral struggle precipitated by the strangeness of the situation in which they find themselves.

What needs to be realized here is that in a non-essentialist paradigm, we are not looking at the foreign Other as though it is locked in a separate foreign place. In all the examples so far used there are people who are operating at cultural borders. Moreover, their struggle for identity is very much connected with this border activity – how they are being seen by people who do not know them. We showed in Unit A1.3 and in Unit A2.1 that this is to do with people moving not just between different societies but also between small cultures within a particular society. Figure 6 shows that what we actually see in a person's behaviour and what they say about themselves interacts *both* with the cultural resources they bring with them and the new culture they encounter. Hence, Zhang's talk about Confucianism in Unit A1.2 is his projection onto the circumstances in which he finds himself in the foreign society of the master's programme.

What is particularly unfortunate here is that very often the resources we bring with us from our familiar cultural experience (right-hand bubble of the figure), and which we then project onto the unfamiliar culture which we confront (left-hand bubble) are very often stereotypes that arise from our own discourses about the Other. Then, after subsequently unsuccessful interaction with the Other, we return, like François and Agnes, to the same comfortable discourses – hence the two-way arrows in Figure 6.

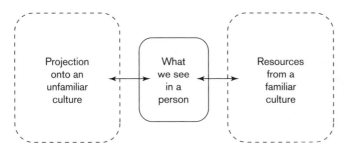

Figure 6 Identity on the cusp

Communication

As a result of this unit it is possible to build on the disciplines from Unit A1.3, which dealt with communication as cultural negotiation. From our understanding of the complex cultures surrounding communication, we need to do the following (see other disciplines listed previously).

11. Be aware that what happens between yourself and others is influenced very much by the environment within which you are communicating and your own preoccupations.

Because of this, we need to do the following.

12. Become aware of our own preoccupations in order to understand what it is that people from other backgrounds are responding to.

This in effect means that we need to research ourselves just as much as we research those who are strange to us. This links with the disciplines in Unit A1.1 about building a thick description of the whole communication scenario.

Task A2.2.1 Thinking about cultural dealing

➤ Think of a situation you have been in where there is an element of cultural dealing and describe it, using Figure 5 to help you.

➤ Evaluate Figure 5 and try to improve on it so that it fits the situation you have described better.

➤ Explain how you can better understand one or more people in the situation with the help of Figure 6 and the disciplines listed.

➤ What can you learn from this about intercultural communication?

UNIT A2.3

POWER AND DISCOURSE
We must be careful what we say

Experience

This unit considers how careful we must all be when talking about and to people who we consider to be Other, because we may be unaware of the power our words may carry. Indirectly, the unit will consider the issue of political correctness, a much-contested concept. Consider Example A2.3.2.

Example A2.3.1 Understanding supervisor

Jeremy is a lecturer in an Australian university. He was very pleased when he heard he was going to supervise a black student from South Africa. Several years ago he had been involved in a three-year science education project in secondary schools in South Africa, and he felt he knew the place more than his colleagues. He felt he would clearly be the best person to help Jabu to get through her research project. He had also read quite a few things on cultural differences, which interested him a great deal.

Jabu first met Jeremy during a class he was teaching on introducing science research. She was the only 'overseas' student there and felt quite angry when, during introductions, he announced to all the other student that he knew her 'context' very well. She was not sure whether it was something about his tone of voice – as though he was speaking about someone who had a handicap of some sort – or his speed of voice – as though she might not understand normal English – or that she was being separated out from all the other students as needing some sort of special attention – which annoyed her. Or perhaps it was that Jeremy was making out that he understood her and was on her side. What could he possibly know about her and her background which would give him this right!? Even her closest friends at home did not presume they knew her so well that they could speak for her like this – except perhaps her mother, and every daughter knows that story!

She could see, at their first tutorial, that he really was trying his best; but he still maintained his slow tone of voice. At least he wasn't shouting as some people did when they thought you might not understand. Then he began to explain to her that he understood something about what he called 'black culture in South Africa' and would therefore be able to help her to meet deadlines and to 'understand concepts' that might be 'alien' to her. He even said that he knew what it was like, with 'the history of black people' that she 'suddenly had to compete in every sphere'. It took her a moment to understand what he was getting at. Then she realized that he was having the ignorant audacity to be thinking that she might have difficulty keeping up with 'white people'.

This sort of thing became the norm for Jeremy and Jabu's meetings. When she showed him work he always made a big thing about saying how well she had done – as though he was surprised that she could do it at all. Then there were lots of informal 'friendly' bits of conversation, in which he always put on a very 'kind' face, about 'food', 'rituals', 'marriage practices' and 'ceremonies' 'in black culture'; and once he even asked her if she was 'still in contact with her tribe'. He was also supervising a German student; and she was sure he never asked *him* about 'food', 'rituals', 'marriage practices', 'ceremonies' and 'tribes'.

One day Jabu really felt like giving up the whole thing and going home. She was walking down the corridor towards Jeremy's office. He was standing in the corridor talking to a colleague. He hadn't seen her, and he was saying, 'Well she does have some difficulty meeting deadlines; but of course that's something deep in black African culture, isn't it?' She knew as a matter of fact that she was having no more difficulty than any of the other students; and anyway, even if she was, why should it have anything to do with being black African? There was a Welsh student who always missed deadlines, and no one would dare suggest this was anything to do with 'Welsh culture'.

Deconstruction

This example clearly shows two very different perceptions of what is going on. Jeremy believes he is being supportive, inclusive and understanding, whereas Jabu feels she is being treated badly and indeed the victim of racism. Jeremy is, we are sure, trying his best to do what he can for Jabu; but in our view he is making a basic mistake which derives from his essentialist notion of her culture, which prevents him from dealing with her as she sees herself. Her predicament is similar to that of Parisa in Unit A1.1, though it remains unresolved in this example. Jeremy falls into the same trap as John does in Unit A2.2; but in his naivety he does not realize it; and this lack of realization goes deep into his language. We shall discuss the details of this problem in terms of the following concepts.

- Thinking you are being understanding when in fact you are patronizing.
- False sharing.
- Culturist language.

Being patronizing

This is detailed in Table 3. Basically, in row i, Jeremy does not base his understanding of Jabu on what he observes of her, but on pictures he himself has constructed from his own experience in South Africa. Here, he makes the usual essentialist mistake of imagining that everyone in South Africa is the same; and the basis of his construction in the first place is likely to have been stereotypical (Table 1 cell ix). His reading into 'cultural difference' also implies an essentialist fascination with comparable, collectible cultures as objects (Table 1 cell i). All of this drives his behaviour – talking not really to her but to an image of who she is. Moreover, his treating her as a cultural category sets her apart from the other students (Table 5 row ii). Making her 'special' inhibits her ability to integrate and makes her feel labelled less capable than the other students (Table 5 row iii). This notion of 'special needs' is also strengthened by the essentialist idea that arriving in a 'new' culture, like learning a new language, puts Jabu in a deficit position. See for example (Table 1 cells vii–viii and x). ('Special needs' is an issue which also affects the inclusion of children from diverse backgrounds and abilities within state education.)

Table 3 Difficult communication

Jeremy thinks he is being understanding and inclusive because:	*Jabu feels patronized, otherized and the victim of racism because:*
i He shows he understands her cultural circumstances and special needs.	She does not want to be made 'special' by someone who could not possibly understand. He has no right to presume she has special needs. He is treating her as inferior to others because of a limited understanding of who she is. She feels invaded.
ii He rationalizes her shortcomings in terms of her culture.	He makes her a special cultural case. He implies the inferiority of her culture. He fails to imagine she could be like others.
iii He speaks slowly and carefully.	Before he even meets her, he assumes she will have difficulty understanding. He treats her as though she is handicapped.
iv He shows interest in her culture.	He over-emphasizes 'exotic' aspects, which imply backwardness.
v He makes reference to cultural concepts she will understand.	He uses language which implies her inferiority.

The final straw for Jabu is when she overhears Jeremy in the corridor making what can be no less than a culturist comment – that her lateness in meeting deadlines is caused by her being a 'black African'. The blatant error in this judgement is revealed by Jabu's observation that she certainly is not being treated equally with other students. Indeed, it is Jeremy's over-generalization that her lateness is a product of her national culture which prevents him from seeing a far more common explanation – that she is really more like other students than different to them.

False sharing

This category of otherization is complex. It corresponds with row iv in Table 5. Again, Jeremy is probably right and sincere in wanting to share; but he is sharing with an image of Jabu which he has constructed, while the real Jabu exists in a very different world. What reveals Jeremy's mistake is Jabu's observation that if she were German, he would not be making references to 'marriage practices', 'ceremonies' and 'tribes'; and as German society must be complex just like hers, he must have selected these topics when he talks to her because they have some sort of exotic value, which in turn implies, for her, some sort of backwardness. This type of otherization is often difficult to pin down. Jeremy could equally have cultural imaginations about German society, which would indeed be reflected in his choice of topics when talking to his German student – perhaps connected with being organized or militaristic. In Jabu's case, coming from a part of the world where there is a colonial history, there is indeed an expectation of another type of cultural imagination, akin to Orientalism in the Middle and Far East, where certain aspects of societies have been sensationalized by the West to feed a deep view that they are indeed 'backward' and 'lascivious'. (See the discussion of Orientalism in Unit B2.1.) The key word in Jeremy's choice of topics is 'tribe'. Although this term might be in common usage to refer to certain types of social grouping, perhaps even by Jabu herself, when used by Jeremy it rings of 'primitive', lacking in state organization and 'pre-literate', and colours his reference to the other things on his list. Therefore, 'marriage *practices*', 'ceremonies' and 'rituals' become 'primitive'. Jabu is thus being 'tribalized' by Jeremy (see, e.g., Nzimiro (1979), Wagner (1981:29), and Baumann (Text B0.1.2) in Unit B0.1). This is therefore similar to the situation seen in Unit A1.3, where we see a group of school girls using terms of abuse to create social cohesion which would be considered misogynistic if used by outsider men.

Culturist language

The significance of Jeremy's use of 'tribe' and 'practices' draws attention to the role of language in otherization (Table 5 row v). A major point here is that he does not seem to be aware of the effect of the language he is using, and investigating this hidden area takes us into critical discourse analysis and the uncovering of the way everyday talk hides our ideologies (e.g. Fairclough 1995 and Holliday 2000). Although we do not have the full text of what Jeremy says to Jabu, from what we do have in Example A2.3.1, it is possible to see the traces of Jeremy's essentialist culturist ideology in some of his phraseology. Talking of helping Jabu to 'understand concepts' that might be 'alien' to her is not in itself particularly significant in a tutorial supervision context. However, when this is put alongside 'the history of black people' and that she would 'suddenly have to compete in every sphere', understanding concepts seems to become dependent on racial factors. This is certainly the connection which Jabu makes – 'keeping up with white people'.

This attention to language raises the issue of political correctness. What has become known as 'PC' in some circles has been attacked quite a lot for (a) preventing people from speaking their minds and stating the obvious, and (b) being over-sensitive to apparently innocent language which carries hidden racist or sexist references – for example, 'clearing the decks' being a non-PC gender-related phrase because it refers to the navy, which is a male-dominated institution. (It refers to removing unnecessary objects from a warship's deck in preparation for battle, and it used to mean tidying up in preparation for a new activity.) While we would tend to agree with (b), where the sanitization of language might indeed be being taken too far, we do not agree with (a). We really do feel that Jeremy needs to be extremely careful with his language. We certainly regard his statement that Jabu's inability to meet deadlines is connected with 'something deep in black African culture' as something that needs to be 'politically corrected'. This is not just Jeremy speaking casually in an unguarded moment when he thinks Jabu is not listening. The question tag, 'isn't it?' is there to involve a colleague in a discourse which is essentially racist and culturist. This type of unguarded language is thus in danger of normalizing a potentially very destructive way of speaking and thinking about others. Responding again to objection (a) above, Jeremy may indeed be stating what seems to *him* to be obvious. The point is that, as Jabu rightly rationalizes, what he says is *not* based on immediate empirical evidence, but on inaccurate stereotyping leading to prejudice (Figure 4 bubbles A and B).

We would therefore state that political correctness is very necessary in the sense that everyone needs to:

- take great care of connections they make between people, their behaviour and generalizations about the categories in which we place people – culture, gender and race being but examples;
- be disciplined in considering evidence which is not connected to these categories.

The discipline in the second point is a form of *bracketing* – a device used in qualitative research for avoiding the easy answers which most readily spring to mind because of their presence in dominant discourse (e.g. Holliday 2002:22, 185). Jeremy thus needs to be aware that he is already conditioned by an essentialist dominant discourse which will always tend to explain the behaviour of people from certain parts of the world in terms of their national or ethnic culture. If he really wants to help Jabu, he should attend to this rather than indulging unguardedly in his prior experience of her exoticness.

We think it is important to spend a moment to comment about the relationship between culturism and racism in this example. Basically Jeremy is otherizing and reducing Jabu to less than what she is by means of a prescribed image of what he thinks she is. Whether this is racist, culturist or even sexist depends on which aspect of her persona, in his eyes, is the driving force behind his image of her. If it is her blackness, which implies for him, and subsequently her, race, then this is racism. If it is her gender, then this is sexism. If it is her culture, then this is culturism. Although Jabu reads Jeremy's attitude as racism, his primary interest is in her culture. Therefore, we see his reducing of her as culturism.

Communication

This unit is very much about restraint. Learning from Jeremy's mistakes, we need to do the following (see other disciplines listed previously).

13. Avoid being seduced by previous experience of the exotic.
14. Monitor our own language and be aware of the destructive, culturist discourses we might be conforming to or perpetuating.

Task A2.3.1   Thinking about Jabu

➤ Think of a situation you have been in that is like the Jabu example and describe it in similar detail.
➤ Explain how you can better understand one or more people in the situation with the help of Table 3 and the disciplines listed.
➤ What can you learn from this about intercultural communication?

Theme 3
Representation

This theme will take a more macro look at how society constructs the foreign Other on our behalf.

CULTURAL REFUGEE
We have been different to what we are now

Experience

This unit will look at the issue of refugees, not just because it is extremely important in today's world, but because the refugee predicament as cultural traveller with problematic status serves to teach us a lot about the nature of culture and cultural representation. Consider Example A3.1.1.

Example A3.1.1   Life before

When Martha first met Reza he seemed to her the typical newly arrived refugee, drably dressed and unsure of himself. She was new to teaching people like him but found a lot of support from conferences, colleagues and textbooks; and it made a lot of sense to her to follow the approach within which her job was not just to teach the English necessary for Canadian citizenship, but to empower her students by encouraging them to express their identity. Reza was a good example of this need. He was from Afghanistan. She was lucky that there was so much information around in the media about the plight of people in Afghanistan. Martha felt that coming to the West would enable Reza 'to express himself and articulate his identity in ways he had never been able to before'. She knew that even in Kabul, people had absolutely nothing.

At first, as everybody said, Martha found Reza clearly unable to deal with the requirements of Western society. He was terribly prejudiced against basic freedoms. Even when she was sure he had the basic English, he refused to talk about his culture, he seemed to resent having a female teacher, which one would expect from a culture 'where women were not even considered second-class citizens', and the only coherent statement she heard him make was that he would never let his daughter marry a Canadian. There was an odd incident she would always remember. He cut his finger rather badly. When he came back from the hospital he was extremely agitated and kept on talking about the nurse who had stitched it. Martha presumed that he just could not cope with being touched by a woman. Eventually she had to give up on him as a hopeless bigot.

Martha then met Reza a year later. He was sitting in the cafeteria while waiting for a friend who was signing up for her programme. Martha thought he looked somehow different – less angry and desolated. She accepted his invitation to sit down and have coffee. He told her he was working as a supervisor in a furniture factory. His English was better; and it seemed more appropriate now to ask him about his life before he was a refugee. Martha was astonished when he told her he was a judge, but that he hadn't been as successful as his sister, who was a university professor in the US, and his eldest daughter, who was specializing to be a gynaecologist in Moscow. He said he remembered her being annoyed with him in class, and that she needed to understand what a difficult predicament he was in at that time, entering a new country at the bottom of the system as a casual labourer, and feeling totally powerless and isolated – a member of the Canadian underclass who found it hard to appreciate the 'freedoms' of the West about which they had heard. He explained that although it might seem silly and unimportant now, the last straw had been the accident with his finger. All he had wanted to do at that point, despite everything that was happening there, was to return home to get it treated. She asked him why, when surely there was no decent medical care in Kabul. Reza said that this is just one of the things that everyone misunderstood about Afghanistan. In fact there were excellent hospitals there, where of course he would not be treated like a refugee who couldn't think. He finished by saying that he felt his greatest achievement in Canada was seeing his teenage daughter doing well at school and taking part in the full range of activities that young people deserved.

Deconstruction

In this example we see Martha working with Reza, a refugee in her language class, according to representations of the foreign Other which are present in society. She then discovers that he is very different to these representations. Reza's plight is not dissimilar to that of several of the people in these units who are culturally misunderstood; and Martha is no more nor less to blame for not seeing his reality than other people who misunderstand them. This unit does not tell a different story, but focuses on a different aspect of how cultural misunderstanding comes about through the following sources of representation in influencing Martha in the way she sees Reza:

■ media images
■ professional images.

To deal with this, we shall discuss the need to:

■ bracket popular representation.

Media images

A major source of Martha's prejudging of Reza, a refugee from Afghanistan, is the information she gets from the national media. In modern society we are constantly fed images of the foreign Other by television, radio and the press, in the explicit form of news, documentaries and current affairs discussion, which report and describe people and events across the world, often with graphic visual material, and more subtly through the images of people and places that we see creatively manipulated in advertising and elsewhere. Afghanistan is a particularly good example here because of the very large amount of material there has been about the 'war against terrorism' which has depicted many, but very similar, images of the country and its people. It is not therefore at all surprising that Martha should see Reza in these terms – derelict, war-ruined streets with little evidence of urban facility, and a society in which women are covered and deprived of the most basic rights. It is not just Afghanistan which suffers from such a limited media image. Many more countries less well known to the West, usually in the developing world, are represented very selectively in world media in terms of their most saleable, sensational, 'exotic' images which are the basis of the reductive Orientalism discussed in Unit A2.3. Hence, it would be easy for many Western people not to know that many Arabs do not wear the kufiyah or the *hejab* (traditional scarf- or shawl-like headwear for men and women respectively), that many Arabs are not Muslim, that many Muslim women do not wear the *hejab* or veil, that many people in the developing world do not live in traditional souks, bazaars, shanty towns, thatched villages or war-torn streets with livestock, and that a very large slice of the population all over the world is middle-class, owns cars and computers, lives in orderly suburbs, and dresses and goes about its daily business very much like 'we' do. Significant for Martha to know is that many refugees, though they have fallen on hard times because of war, political oppression or economic catastrophe, have in the not-too-distant past had what one might consider to be sophisticated, educated lives.

What is perhaps strange is that while people may be naturally cynical about much of what the media shows us, they may well be often less critical of images of the 'exotic'. This is shown in Figure 7, which is our own interpretation of the relationships between the individual and forces of representation in society. The representations created by the media are in bubble B. There is a subtle dialogue between this and the tastes and opinions of the public in bubble E. The nature of this dialogue will vary from society to society, depending on the freedom of the media; but in the West, the representations in the media will very largely respond to public demand – and at the heart of this demand is the desire to essentialize.

Professional images

Apart from the possible Othering of the developing world, in the case of 'the war in Afghanistan', the representations we see cannot be disconnected from a particular political point of view which depicts a derelict country in need of rescue by the West. During colonial times, images of the South and East as deficit cultures were often constructed, consciously or unconsciously, to justify 'civilizing' conquest. This strategy

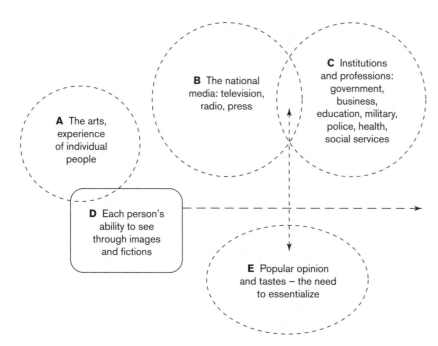

Figure 7 Forces of representation

for reproducing certain types of representation can, we think, be connected with the professional image which Martha gets from 'conferences, colleagues and textbooks'. In our view, the discourse of the professionalism which Martha employs also projects a 'civilizing conquest' over refugee students. Instead of simply teaching Reza the language he needs to live and work in a new country, justified by the image of Afghanistan as derelict, Martha is intent on 'empowering' him to 'express' his identity in ways 'he had never been able to before'. She thus sees 'them' and 'their culture' as lacking basic human capacities. It is also noticeable that she is disappointed because Reza is 'not a woman', thus denying her the opportunity of 'liberating' even more deeply oppressed individuals.

There is a similar relationship here between popular tastes and opinions and professional representations (Figure 7 bubbles E and C) as there is with the media. In bubble C we have also listed other institutions and professions which produce representations of the foreign Other, all of which, in turn, to varying degrees, with their own strong discourse of reality, feed, influence and provide the content for the media in bubble B.

Bracketing popular representations

The relationship between bubbles B, C and E in Figure 7 imply an almost hegemonic set of beliefs and images in which the mainstream opinion, tastes, media and institutions of a society collude to produce established representations of the foreign Other. By hegemonic we mean achieving a domination which pervades all aspects of society to such a subtle degree that it may be invisible. There can, however, be breakthroughs, the source of which we have placed on the left of the figure. This is of course an extremely simplistic representation in itself of very complex social forces; but we wish to make the simple point that the individual actor (bubble D) in whatever society is able to form their own images and break away from – see through – the established essentialism. Some of the resources which can be used here (bubble A) have already been exemplified in these units. The conference colleagues in Unit A1.1 are introduced to a film by Parisa and see an alternative (to the established) picture which reveals a more complex reality of who she is. Janet and John in Units A1.2 and A2.1 arrive at such pictures through encounters with individual people in Zhang and Ming and the Smith family, as do the observers of the school girls in Unit A1.3. Something happens which makes us bracket the easy answer and look at things differently. We have listed the arts generally in the bubble because we think that it is in this domain – broadly from quality television drama through to music and painting and, indeed, more critical television documentary – that more critical, creative images *can* come. We have not listed travel and international contact because, as we see with Jeremy in Unit A2.3, and Agnes and François in Unit A2.2, *contact* with 'other cultures' may confirm rather than question the essentialist point of view.

Returning to Martha's experience, there were several cultural presumptions she formed in her initial encounter with Reza which she will need to reassess in the light of her second encounter. She explained both his unease in class and his dissatisfaction with regard to his hospital visit as a misogynous dislike of contact with female teachers and nurses. Apart from one statement about how he did not want his daughter to marry a Canadian, these presumptions stem directly from the overall cultural stereotype of Afghanistan and all its male population being entirely in support of limiting women's rights. Such a view is enforced by news footage, documentaries and political speeches. The fact that few, if any, of these report any men in Afghanistan itself supporting women's rights, serves to package together the Taliban, the ruling party of Afghanistan before being ousted in 2002, the Northern Alliance that deposed them, and the entire male population, with selected images of still-bearded men in street scenes showing apparent discomfort at some women discarding the burka, the traditional female covering. It is entirely on the basis of this background that Martha judged Reza's behaviour. That he was uneasy in class and at the hospital, he himself confirms; but the explanations for this could be many; and in effect she had no direct evidence arising from the situation itself to support misogyny. In Martha's second encounter with Reza, he explains his reason for discomfort in class and in the hospital as to do with being a newcomer in very difficult social circumstances. His statement about how he left Afghanistan to give his daughter better opportunities also goes against Martha's assumption about his attitude towards his daughter. Indeed, feeling isolated and a member of the Canadian underclass might well make him cautious about his daughter integrating into a society seen from that point of view. The hospital incident is significant because Martha had simply assumed that there was no infrastructure in Kabul. She had also assumed that there were no Afghans who had the social sophistication to deal with their own identity – that this was the exclusive domain of Western society.

All of these assumptions about Martha and Reza are, of course, grey areas and in the realm of rough generalizations. However, it is not difficult to imagine that a major reason why Martha saw Reza as a bigoted misogynist was that he did not respond to her strategy to reconstruct him. In effect, he was neither a misogynist nor in need of reconstruction. In terms of a methodology for understanding, she did indeed observe him closely, but her observation may have been clouded by a certain prejudice.

Communication

The disciplines within this theme need to focus on our awareness of the images from our own society which influence they way we see other people. This takes us further into the need for us to research ourselves (Unit A2.2). Taking heed of the experience in this unit, when communicating with others, we therefore need to do the following (see other disciplines listed previously).

15. Be aware of the media, political and institutional influences in our own society which lead us to see people from other cultural backgrounds in a certain way.
16. See through these images and fictions when we encounter people from other cultural backgrounds, and always try to consider alternative representations.

Task A3.1.1   Thinking about Reza

➤ Think of a situation you have been in that is like the Reza example and describe it in similar detail.
➤ Explain how what happens in the situation can be understood in terms of the types of images and representations described in the Deconstruction section and Figure 7.
➤ Explain what you therefore need to know in order to understand people like Reza better. Refer to the disciplines listed.
➤ What can you learn from this about intercultural communication?

COMPLEX IMAGES
We have no idea how deeply we get things wrong

UNIT A3.2

Experience and deconstruction

In this unit we will look more deeply at some of the profound errors of representation of the foreign Other within our own society. The images we show will present a familiar picture; but what we need to do is fathom the unfamiliar which they hide. We will not present a description of one event, but instead a series of descriptions of different media events. These really took place, but they are of course our personal impressions of them, coloured by our desire to undo essentialism. The examples all come from British or American television, radio and publications; but we are purposely not revealing their origin and are also changing one or two key aspects which do not change the overall significance in order to maintain anonymity. As in previous units, the examples are presented as vignettes. This unit also combines the Experience and Deconstruction sections, which will allow us to deal with each example in turn. The first example speaks for itself.

Example A3.2.1 Indian or British art?

There is a television discussion programme about the arts in India. The discussants include two women writers from India, a writer and a film-maker who are both British Asian women, an academic and a presenter who are both white British. The point being made by the majority of the speakers is that Indian art is being changed by new art produced by British Asians. The two British Asians try to counter this idea by insisting that their art is *not* part of Indian art at all, but contributes to a growing multicultural British art form. However, they fail to make any impact in the discussion.

'British Asian' is commonly used in Britain to refer to people who have an ethnic origin in India, Pakistan, Bangladesh and Sri Lanka. We use the term 'white' to refer to British people who have their ethnic origin in the British Isles. It is important, however, to note that these are shifting and politically charged labels.

This television discussion might not seem particularly problematic to the majority of viewers, who would most probably see things in the same way as the majority of the discussants – that British Asian art *is* part of Indian (or perhaps Pakistani or Bangladeshi) art. The programme did not make this clear to the audience; but let us presume that the two British Asian women come from families which emigrated from India (rather than what is now Pakistan or Bangladesh) a generation ago, so that the issue is not to do with a confusion between Indians and other people from the subcontinent. What is then evident is that the inability of the discussants to respond to the idea that the art of these two British Asians could be considered British rather than Indian is because it does not conform to a dominant discourse – that all people and what they do can somehow be traced to India as part of 'Indian culture'. The following definitions are our own.

- Dominant discourses are ways of talking and thinking about something which have become naturalized to the extent that people conform to them without thinking.
- Discourse, in this sense, is a way of using language which promotes a particular view of the world.
- Naturalization occurs when a social phenomenon becomes sufficiently routine and natural to be internalized into everyday 'thinking-as-usual'.

Naturalization is very similar to institutionalization (where new behaviour becomes established practice in an institution), reification (where something which is only an idea is considered real) and routinization (where new behaviour becomes a routine). All these processes can happen by themselves as part of the natural way in which society works, or be socially engineered by managers, spin doctors, governments, the media, political parties or anyone who has influence over other people.

An example of *a discourse* might be sexist discourse, where phrases which reduce women (e.g. 'the woman's place is in the kitchen', 'women can't be managers') are used in such a way that the ideas behind them are promoted as normal for the group who use them. Discourses can thus be associated with group identity and exclusivity. Anyone who has had to mix socially or work with a group of people who use sexist language as the norm, and who has found that not joining with the discourse would mean being excluded, will understand how discourses work. Sexist discourse becomes *dominant* when it begins to rule over other discourses in a larger group or society. The media can play a significant role in promoting discourses and making them dominant. At the time of writing there is a discussion in the British media about how certain national newspapers are promoting a particular 'way of talking about' people from other countries who are seeking political asylum – 'asylum seekers' – which demonizes them. There is a fear that this discourse will become dominant. The people who speak against it are promoting a *counter discourse* which is trying to prevent it from being naturalized.

Dominant discourses can be so *naturalized* that people become unaware of them (Fairclough 1995). In Example A3.2.1 the dominant discourse is such that the argument of the two British Asian women does not seem to be opposed so much as simply not heard. This may be because the ideas the British Asian women express do not correspond with what the other discussants normally think about. In other words, their ideas do not conform to the thinking-as-usual of the other people. Thinking-as-usual is a term used in sociology to mean what people have got used to thinking of as being normal. It is an essentialist dominant discourse which insists that once born in India, simplistic notions of national culture will follow even the adult activities of one's children who are born and brought up elsewhere. The women writers from India might have had their own interests in colluding with the dominant discourse and seeing British Asian art as theirs. In Britain, this dominant discourse is connected with the tendency to explain all activities of perceived immigrants in terms of an ethnic-national culture (Table 1 cell ix).

The next example shows how the media can feed dominant discourses about cultural stereotypes. It is in two parts, the first looking at a travelogue and the second seeing a probable effect of this.

Example A3.2.2 Middle East travelogue

Part 1

A well-known television travel correspondent is doing a series of programmes on Middle Eastern countries. At the end of her programme on Turkey, she is filmed standing on the Syrian border and announcing that her next programme would take her to 'fundamentalist' Syria. The next programme on Syria fronts images of men in kufiyahs and women in abayahs (traditional Arab women's dress) in the old quarters of Damascus and Aleppo.

Part 2

Matthew recently visited Damascus with a group of colleagues, all of whom were well-travelled and sensitive to issues of otherization. Nevertheless, he found himself on the edge of a discussion of how the dress code for women visitors might be relaxed because there was 'now' a new president. The implication was that 'now' Syrian society might be more modern ('equals liberal' 'equals less fundamentalist' 'equals allowing women to cover less'). He had been in Damascus fifteen years before when the previous government had prohibited university students from wearing Islamic hejab (the head cover for Muslim women) and *abayahs* on the campus; but he did not feel it appropriate to bring this up on the edge of this casual conversation as they were getting on the conference bus. He thus allowed the dominant discourse to rule.

The views of Matthew's colleagues, who were not at all familiar with Syria, were fed by news items and documentaries of the type described in the first part of Example A3.2.2. It would not be surprising if the correspondent in the example did not purposely *choose* to *select* only the images which would support the notion of 'Arab country', 'therefore Muslim', 'therefore fundamentalist', 'moreover anti-Israel', 'therefore anti-West' – hence images of people who *looked* like the people one sees in media images of men and women with covered heads throwing stones at Israeli soldiers. The dominant discourse is so strong that the correspondent probably did not notice the other images, which prevail in Damascus, of young men and women, intensely conscious of high European fashion, which they integrate into their own styles, walking by elegant boutiques and sitting in restaurants. And of course it might well not occur to someone with these dominant views that people wearing the traditional dress of the region might not be fundamentalist at all, and might not even be Muslim but Christian. A very similar dominant discourse is present in the next example.

Example A3.2.3 Traffic problems

In a popular tourist guide series, which has the reputation of being progressive and culturally sensitive, there is a reference to traffic problems in Tehran. It is commented that the inhabitants of this country are just beginning to learn to use traffic lights.

The reference to traffic lights is motivated by what appears to the writers of the guide to be a less improper use of traffic lights than might have been observed elsewhere. It is indeed true that the use of traffic lights in Tehran is different to their use in, say, Britain. One can observe, for example, that motorcyclists will sometimes position themselves in front of motorists, in front of the line at which motorists have stopped; and indeed the line itself might be interpreted liberally by some motorists. It might also be true that in recent years the practice has become more like that of, say, Britain. It is however factually inaccurate to say that Iranians are just learning to use traffic lights. The culture of traffic-lights use is as long-standing as it is in any Western country, but different. The rules for use are as sophisticated, but being mysterious to the British observer, they are depicted as being primitive. If there *is* a change in the behaviour at traffic lights, it might be more a result of globalization than anything else.

As tourism to more 'exotic' locations becomes more accessible to the West, tourist guides become a more influential part of the media which influences the way in which we see each other. As with the case of Matthew's well-travelled colleagues in Example

A3.2.2, a significant twist in first part of Example A3.2.3 is the intended intellectual sensitivity of the text, which is thus all the more likely to draw the discerning reader into the discourse. The issue of tourism in a postcolonialist discourse is taken up in Unit B2.4.

The next example moves us into the more politically sensitive domain of the Arab–Israeli conflict, which has become more emotionally charged since the events of 11 September 2001 in New York and the subsequent 'war on terrorism'.

Example A3.2.4 Israeli schoolchildren

There is a short piece on a news programme about how children in an Israeli school are coping with the atmosphere of terrorism surrounding the Palestinian–Israeli conflict in the spring of 2002. The school and the children look affluent and middle class. Those who are interviewed speak calmly and articulately. This is followed by a scene of Palestinians throwing stones at Israeli soldiers in a West Bank urban setting with dust, rubble and unfinished building sites.

This is a very complex case. One of the authors' major feelings at the time of seeing these news items was how easy these contrasting images made it for a middle-class viewer like himself to identify with the (to him) familiarly middle-class image of the Israeli school children, who seemed 'normal', 'calm' and (presumably) therefore more 'civilized', than of the stone-throwing Palestinians. In fighting this seduction he also wondered why we in the West do not see comparable images of middle-class Palestinians in the media, which might help to break the dominant discourse of 'them as terrorists and funda-mentalists' – very similar to that discussed in Example A3.2.2 generated by Syrian street scenes. On the other hand, there are complex issues of identity here. Who are *we* to presume the images by which *we* would like other people to be represented simply in order for me to undo *our* reductive preoccupations?

The final two examples are also sensitive in that they are connected with the emotions surrounding personal abduction and abuse. Each case deals with a serious issue which it is the responsibility of the media to reveal. In Example A3.2.5 the women and children in question are clearly suffering. The question is, how is the cause of their suffering represented and is it a simple one-sided matter?

Example A3.2.5 Abducted children

A television documentary tells a story of a group of British (Anglo-Christian) women travelling to a Middle-eastern country to see their children who have been 'abducted' by their Middle-eastern ex-husbands. The men are characterized as despotic; they do not respect prior agreements; they will imprison their children; women and children in their society have no rights.

The real anguish of the women in this example has to be respected. However, the documentary is one-sided in that there is no discussion of the complex cross-cultural history of each relationship which must have led up to this state of affairs. There is no discussion of the point of view of the husbands, who are rarely heard to speak. Some or all of the traits of the Middle-eastern husbands might have been true in some or all of the cases in the documentary, but there was no exploration of the possibility that they might not. Exploration of any of these issues would have implied a diversity in 'their' foreign society perhaps as diverse as 'our' own society – which the discourse of otherization does not allow (Table 1 cell ix). Thus, the essentialist packaging of the Middle-eastern Other is perpetuated. It seems strange that the level of sophisticated analysis one might expect of the British documentary was suspended in this case.

There is also a degree of sensationalism present in Example A3.2.5. A media message is sensational when it exaggerates particular features in order to appeal to the emotions. There was perhaps no *intention* in this documentary to be sensational. Indeed, the emotions connected with the abduction of children are real and do not need to be exaggerated. However, if we consider Edward Said's arguments about how the West constructs an imaginary exotic image of the East (see Unit B2.1), the documentary could be criticised for exoticizing and sensationalising the Middle-eastern husbands as distant and alien imprisoners of women and their children, instead of as ordinary men with different principles and laws governing child custody.

Our final example demonstrates a similar case of 'Eastern' people being exoticized sensationally as imprisoners of women.

Example A3.2.6 Abuse of women

An item about the abuse of British women by their husbands appears on a radio discussion programme. However, it quickly becomes apparent that the focus of the item is Hindu and Muslim Asian families. Another radio discussion features a British Asian academic who makes the point that outsiders to 'British culture' might well think that it is characterized by paedophilia, given the quantity of discussion of this issue in the British media.

This was an important item in that such abuse should be revealed and its causes discussed. It may or may not be the case that such abuse is more common within Asian families than within other British families. However, the phrase 'in Islam' was used in such a way as to imply that abuse of women was a default feature of Islam. 'Arranged marriages' were also referred to; and one immediately sees how the packaging of this particular 'foreign' Other begins to be formed. Otherization of the Asian community might have been far from the agenda of the journalist involved, but it was deep in the discourse of the item. There are perhaps parallels in British society whereby arranged marriages also exist in an Anglo-Christian community where money, property and dynasty are at stake. Some of our soap operas pivot around this fact. Neither will it draw attention to the fact that 'arranged marriage' might not be a bad thing, or that not all Muslim marriages are arranged, because these facts are not part of the packaging. A friend of Adrian Holliday's (author of Section A of this book) from Leeds commented that the radio story did not sit easily with the 'liberated young Asian women who jump on the bus with me each morning'. They are not part of the package either. Perhaps we feel that they are not 'real Asians', or that they are 'Westernized' (like Parisa in Unit A1.1). It is the second news item in Example A3.2.6 which shows us the reality of this reductive distortion. 'We' Western people would not like to think that 'they' could so easily reduce 'us' to a 'British culture' in which children are abused.

Communication

In this final unit in Theme 3 Representation, it is important to build on the advice of Unit A3.1 and look deeper into some of the origins of essentialist prejudice in the media. We can see from all the examples in this unit that it is important to think about dominant discourses, which continue from other disciplines listed in Section A.

17. Be aware of dominant discourses which are easily perpetuated by the media, and which lead us to 'think-as-usual' that familiar images of the foreign Other are 'normal'.

From Examples A3.2.2 and A3.2.3 especially, we can see how prejudice is sometimes hidden behind intellectual sensitivity.

18. Be aware that even images projected by sensitive, intellectual sources can seduce our own sensitivities and intellects into thinking that they are 'true'.

From Examples A3.2.5 and A3.2.6 especially, we can see that there is often a hidden sensationalism.

19. Although sensationalism in the media is something we know about and guard against, we need to appreciate how deeply it exists in our traditional views of the foreign Other.

Task A3.2.1 Thinking about representation

➤ Think of a situation you have been in or observed that is like one of the examples presented in this unit and describe it in similar detail.
➤ Provide an example of naturalization in the description and try to link it with a dominant discourse.
➤ Thinking about the disciplines listed, consider how far we really do need to search out hidden forces.
➤ What can you learn from this about intercultural communication?

DISCIPLINES FOR INTERCULTURAL COMMUNICATION

As we reach the end of Section A it is now possible to put together all the disciplines covered in Table 4. These disciplines have been derived from analysis of the situations discussed throughout the section. The right-hand column provides a summary which clarifies their relationship with each of the three themes that run throughout the book. Along with further discussions connected with the readings presented in Section B, these disciplines will be taken forward to Section C, where they will be realized in research projects.

Table 4 Disciplines

Discussion	*Statement*	*Summary*
	Identity	
Unit A1.1 page 6	1. Respond to people according to how you find them rather than according to what you have heard about them.	Seek a deeper understanding of individual people's identity by:
	2. Avoid easy answers about how people are. Bracket – put aside simplistic notions about what is 'real' or 'unreal' in your perception of 'another culture'.	a) avoiding preconceptions
	3. Appreciate that every society is as complex and culturally varied as your own.	b) appreciating complexity
	4. Learn to build up thick descriptions of what happens between you and others – to work out how to communicate as you go along.	c) not overgeneralizing from individual instances.
Unit A1.2 page 10	5. While respecting whatever people say about their own culture, take what they say as evidence of what they wish to project rather than as information about where they come from.	Achieve this by employing *bracketing* to put aside your preconceptions, *thick description* to enable you to see complexity, and an appreciation of *emergent data* to signal the unexpected.
	6. Take what people say about their own culture as a personal observation which should not be generalized to other people who come from the same background.	
Unit A1.3 page 16	7. Understand how people are creating and indeed negotiating their cultural identity in the very process of communicating with us.	
	8. Appreciate that you are creating and negotiating your own cultural identity in the process of communicating with others.	
	9. Appreciate that the creation and negotiation of cultural and personal identity are the same thing.	

Table 4 (continued)

Discussion	Statement	Summary
	Otherization	
Unit A2.1 page 21	10. Avoid falling into the culturist trap of reducing people to less than they are – in the same way as we must avoid racist and sexist traps.	Seek a deeper understanding of the prejudices, preoccupations and discourses which lead you to otherize.
Unit A2.2 page 25	11. Be aware that what happens between yourself and others is influenced very much by the environment within which you are communicating and your own preoccupations.	Use this to enable bracketing and to manage your own role in communication.
	12. Become aware of your own preoccupations in order to understand what it is that people from other backgrounds are responding to.	
Unit A2.3 page 30	13. Avoid being seduced by previous experience of the exotic.	
	14. Monitor our own language and be aware of the destructive, culturist discourses we might be conforming to or perpetuating.	
	Representation	
Unit A3.1 page 36	15. Be aware of the media, political and institutional influences in our own society which lead us to see people from other cultural backgrounds in a certain way.	Seek a deeper understanding of the representations of the foreign Other which are perpetuated by society.
	16. See through these images and fictions when we encounter people from other cultural backgrounds, and always try to consider alternative representations.	
Unit A3.2 page 41	17. Be aware of dominant discourses which are easily perpetuated by the media, and which lead us to 'think-as-usual' that familiar images of the foreign Other are 'normal'.	
	18. Be aware that even images projected by sensitive, intellectual sources can seduce our own sensitivities and intellects into thinking that they are 'true'.	
	19. Although sensationalism in the media is something we know about and guard against, we need to appreciate how deeply it exists in our traditional views of the foreign Other.	

Although for the most part the disciplines relate directly to the substantive knowledge required for successful intercultural communication, there is also a research methodology, focused on bracketing, thick description and emergent data, which comes directly from mainstream qualitative research. This will be the main approach presented in Section C.

SECTION B
Extension

Units in Section B are centred on texts concerned with issues introduced in Section A, which will also be explored further in Section C of the book. Each unit comprises an introduction, one or more texts accompanied by tasks, and a commentary in which we point to related issues and perspectives of other writers. At the end of each unit there are suggestions for further reading.

Units B0.1 and B0.2 serve as an introduction to Section B. They are concerned with a number of issues which we will explore in more depth later in the section and which were introduced in Section A – for example:

- how our understanding of ourselves and different people, and of the relationships and communication between these individuals, is often framed by the language (or 'discourse') that we use when we speak or write
- how we tend to group people together under simplistic labels, while not considering the implications of doing so
- how the language we use all too often exaggerates the differences between people rather than the similarities
- how the mass media often engages in simplifying issues and exaggerating differences
- how the ways 'cultures' and 'communities' are referred to, and talked and written about, often serve particular vested interests.

Units B1.1 to B1.5 explore different aspects of and approaches to identity and consider what identity might mean for the individual, as well as how the individual may construct identity, in the contemporary world.

Units B2.1 to B2.5 are concerned with otherization, and with how images of the Other, in both the literal and metaphorical sense, continue to dominate both understandings of, and interaction with, people of different cultural identities.

Units B3.1 to B3.5 focus on representation of different individuals and groups in the mass media and in academic discourse.

We have employed a number of criteria when selecting texts for inclusion, as follows:

- Accessibility – the capacity of texts to be accessible to the reader who may not have specialist knowledge of issues being discussed.
- Richness – the capacity of texts, on the other hand, to introduce key concepts and raise important issues in terms of the themes of the book: identity, otherization, and representation.
- Relevance – the capacity of texts to introduce concepts and raise issues which are of relevance to readers studying or working in a range of disciplines or fields.
- Variety – the capacity of texts to provide a variety of perspectives, and to be taken from a variety of genres.

As research in various sub-fields in the related disciplines of cultural studies, media studies and applied linguistics has demonstrated, the selection of a text is in itself significant, and reflects a certain personal standpoint. The texts in Section B do indeed reflect our own interests and, in some cases, our own experiences, and we have sometimes included personal reflections in introductory sections and commentaries.

Taken together, the texts reflect our belief that it is by engaging with the ideas of others that plays an important part of understanding ourselves and our own contextual realities. 'Engagement' does not necessarily involve 'agreement'; we do not expect you to agree with all the ideas in the texts, and we do not do so ourselves.

With regard to the tasks designed to accompany texts, these are designed as a way of helping you to consider the implications and applications of issues raised, and per-spectives provided, in the texts, and to consider them particularly as they relate to yourself. We, like anyone else writing tasks to accompany texts, are open to accusa-tions of leading you towards certain conclusions and positions. We have tried to avoid doing so, and have deliberately made tasks generally open-ended, but we are aware that the very questions we have asked you to consider will inevitably reflect our own preoccupations and concerns.

Introduction

UNIT B0.1
'CULTURE' AND 'COMMUNITY' IN EVERYDAY DISCOURSE

The first text in Unit B0.1 was written by the social anthropologist Ulf Hannerz, who is particularly concerned with how the term 'culture' is used in everyday discourse, and emphasises the need to 'keep a critical eye on the varieties of culturespeak both among ourselves and in society at large' (1999:396).

Ylanne-McEwen and Coupland (2000:210) state that 'studies aiming to describe "intercultural" communication should ideally be linked to studies of how individuals and social or cultural groups define themselves and others'. The second text, by sociologist Gerd Baumann, is an extract from such a study, which was the result of extensive ethnographic research carried out in Southall in west London, England.

Before you read Text B0.1.1, do Task B0.1.1 below.

 Task B0.1.1

The word 'culture' is used in many different ways (often in combination with other words) and with a variety of different meanings.

➤ Note down a number of different uses of the word 'culture' (as well as 'cultural') which you have come across recently in the mass media and everyday use.

TEXT B0.1.1
U. Hannerz

Hannerz, U. (1999) 'Reflections of Varieties of Culturespeak', *European Journal of Cultural Studies*, 2:3 pp. 393–407 (extracts)

A sunny morning a few years ago, at my summer house in southern Sweden, with a national election season approaching, I found a leaflet in my mail box. In blue letters against a yellow background (the colors of the Swedish flag), an extremist group in a nearby town argued that the country had turned from a folkhem, a 'home of the people', into a 'multicultural inferno'.

One could reflect that this suggests two things about the place of the culture concept in contemporary discourse. One is that 'culture' is no longer a notion occurring mostly among the well-educated, within the confines of their scholarly, intellectual, and esthetic preoccupations. Increasingly it, and other concepts deriving from it, seem to be just about everywhere, from public commentary and political agitation through organizational consultancy to commerce and advertising. And there are no real barriers separating different uses and different users. Researchers and policy makers now share the term 'multiculturalism' with ethnic minority

U. Hannerz

politicians, as well as with the xenophobia activists claiming to represent a silent majority. One has to be sensitive, consequently, to those refractions of meaning which may occur as a vocabulary of culture moves between contexts.

The other thing to note, with regard to that suggestion of a 'multicultural inferno', is that while 'culture' in the past was probably a term with mostly consensual and positive overtones, it now very often shows up in contexts of discord – 'culture clash', 'culture conflict', 'culture wars'; and perhaps also, at a different level, 'culture shock'. A major reason for this, no doubt, is that culturespeak now very often draws our attention to what are taken to be the interfaces between cultures; a tendency which in its turn has much to do with that polymorphous global interconnectedness through which such interfaces become increasingly prominent in human experience.

Scrutinizing culturespeak

. . . Cultural study is not only a summarizing label for all those inquiries we conduct into the wide range of things we consider cultural, but also (not least in the present period) a study of popular theories, prototheories and quasitheories of culture.

Cultural fundamentalism is only one of these. They may develop in different contexts, shaping themselves to meet different requirements, and they need not all be malignant. I mentioned above the concept of 'culture shock', diffusing widely in the late 20th century as a way of referring to the kind of emotional and intellectual unease that sometimes occurs in encounters with unfamiliar meanings and practices. Rather facetiously, I have also occasionally referred to the growth of a 'culture shock prevention industry'. The proper term for its practitioners, I should quickly note, is 'interculturalists' – a new profession of people working commercially as trainers and consultants, trying to teach sensitivity toward cultural diversity to various audiences through lectures, simulation games, videos, practical handbooks and some variety of other means. From an academic vantage point one may be critical of certain of the efforts – they may seem a bit trite, somewhat inclined toward stereotyping, occasionally given to exaggerating cultural differences perhaps as a way of positioning the interculturalists themselves as an indispensable profession.

. . . It would seem helpful to make more continuously visible how both persistence and change in culture depend on human activity; and how in contemporary, complex social life, the combined cultural process, and the overall habitat of meanings and practices in which we dwell, is the outcome of the variously deliberate pursuit by a variety of actors of their own agendas, with different power and different social and spatial reach, and with foreseen or unanticipated consequences. Such an approach to cultural process would be a challenge to each of us, layperson or scholar, to try and work out what ingredients go into situations that may puzzle us or annoy us. . . .

The attention to processes and people may also help unpack the assumption of the unitary, integrated culture which may not be unique to cultural fundamentalism but which goes well with it. We have an old habit of speaking about 'cultures', in the plural form, as if it were self-evident that such entities exist side by side as neat packages, each of us identified with only one of them – this is indeed a time-worn implication of at least one 'anthropological culture concept'. And the notion of 'cultural identity' often goes with it. It may well be that some considerable number of people really live encapsulated among others who share most of the same experiences, ideas, beliefs, values, habits, and tastes. Nonetheless, it appears increasingly likely that many people have biographies entailing various cross-cutting allegiances – they share different parts of their personal cultural repertoires with different collections of people. And if there is an 'integrated whole', it may be a quite individual thing. Under such circumstances, people may well value some parts of these personal repertoires more highly than others, identify

U. Hannerz

themselves particularly in terms of them, and identify in collective terms more strongly with those other people with whom they share them. It could also be, on the other hand, that they may resist attempts to categorize them unidimensionally in terms of any single cultural characteristic.

. . . and the point here must be that whatever is most enduring is not necessarily also at any one time most central to people's cultural preoccupations, and to their sense of who they are. There are now surely many different ways of being more or less Christian, more or less Muslim, more or less Confucian; and of being at the same time some number of other things. Most significantly, finally, an emphasis on process may entail a subversion of a kind of mystique of cultural difference which seems to be an important part of cultural fundamentalism.

Task B0.1.2

In the text Hannerz writes that ' . . . while "culture" in the past was probably a term with mostly consensual and positive overtones, it now very often shows up in contexts of discord.'

➤ In looking back at the notes you made in Task B0.1.1 on different uses of the words 'culture' and 'cultural', do the examples you listed reflect Hannerz's view that today the term 'culture' has negative overtones?

Task B0.1.3

In the text Hannerz also writes that 'it would seem helpful to make more continuously visible . . . how in contemporary, complex social life, the combined cultural process, and the overall habitat of meanings and practices in which we dwell, is the outcome of the variously deliberate pursuit by a variety of actors of their own agendas . . .'

➤ What 'actors' and 'agendas' do you think Hannerz is thinking of?

Task B0.1.4

➤ Considering a society you have lived in or are familiar with, which different communities would you say there are, and what makes these communities distinct from other communities?

TEXT B0.1.2
G. Baumann

Baumann, G. (1996) *Contesting Culture: discourses of identity in multi-ethnic London*, Cambridge: Cambridge University Press pp. 1–2, 4–6 (extracts)

Having myself migrated to Britain at the age of twenty-one, I had been puzzled for a long time by the way in which immigrants were portrayed in the British media, in political rhetoric, and,

G. Baumann

not least, in the academic literature . . . in Britain (this) ethnic reductionism seemed to reign supreme, and the greater number even of academic community studies I read seemed to echo it. Whatever any 'Asian' informant was reported to have said or done was interpreted with stunning regularity as a consequence of their 'Asianness', their 'ethnic identity', or the 'culture' of their 'community'. All agency seemed to be absent, and culture an imprisoning cocoon or a determining force. Even their children, born, raised, and educated in Britain, appeared in print as 'second-generation immigrants' or 'second-generation Asians', and, unlike the children of white migrants like me, were thought to be precariously suspended 'between two cultures'.

This latter commonplace in particular I failed to understand. I could not work out why they should be suspended between, rather than be seen to reach across, two cultures. More importantly, which two cultures were involved? Was there a homogeneous British culture on the one hand, perhaps regardless of class or of region, and on the other hand some other culture, perhaps one which was shared with their parents? If so, how were these parental cultures defined: was it on the basis of regional origin or religion, caste or language, migratory path or nationality? Each of these could define a community, a culture, and an ethnic identity in the same breath, it seemed. . . .

. . . The answers to my confusion could, I thought, be found only by fieldwork: I rented a house in the centre of Southall, where I lived for the next six years, and from there involved myself in the life of the suburb. My agenda, as in all fieldwork, was open: live locally, socialize locally, find local things to do, and let yourself in for whatever comes. At the same time, keep a daily research diary, write fieldwork notes, and, not least, keep a personal diary in order not to confuse private concerns with the documentation of other people's doings and sayings.

. . . Adult Southallians were no less relativist than their children in discussing culture and community. Even assuming that community was a matter of birthplace, as the dominant discourse so often does, some Southallians could, among friends, squeeze a laugh out of the absurdities of ethnic classification. 'See me friend Jas here', said Phil, an Englishman, and pointed to his drinking-mate at the Railway Tavern bar, 'he's an Asian, but he's born in Africa, so I'd say he's an African. And me, I was born in Burma, so I'm the Asian here, aren't I. And Winston here, you think he's a West Indian: he's the only one of us born in this town, so he's the Englishman born and bred!' Attributions of culture and community can clearly not be reduced to one factor alone. Rather, all but the most single-minded of adult Southallians, it turned out, regarded themselves as members of several communities at once, each with its own culture. Making one's life meant ranging across them. I did find a few people who said: 'I am a Muslim and nothing else', 'I am a Christian and have no other community', or 'I am an African from the Caribbean, but as African as the people born in Africa' . . . Nevertheless, the vast majority of all adult Southallians saw themselves as members of several communities, each with its own culture. The same person could speak and act as a member of the Muslim community in one context, in another take sides against other Muslims as a member of the Pakistani community, and in a third count himself part of the Punjabi community that excluded other Muslims but included Hindus, Sikhs, and even Christians. In this way, they echoed the awareness of shifting identities that young Southallians had alerted me to. Matters got more confusing, however, as fieldwork progressed. Some Hindu parents would claim that 'all Sikhs are Hindus'; some Sikh parents would dissociate themselves from the Sikh community and describe their culture as 'British-Asian, basically, whatever the religion you're from'; and Muslim friends would argue with pride that the local mosque was in itself a multi-cultural community. Clearly, all these utterances could be discounted as if they were mere figures of speech. But when an ethnographer collects more of them by the week, should one not ask what makes these usages any less important, authentic, or truthful than the usages that equate culture with community; community with ethnic identity; and ethnic identity with the 'cause' of a person's doings or sayings?

. . . The dominant discourse relies on equating community, culture, and ethnic identity, and its protagonists can easily reduce anybody's behaviour to a symptom of this equation. So long as its human objects can be logged under some ethnic identity other than, say, British, German, or American, it can even claim to speak 'for' them, 'represent' them, explain them to others. The ways in which Southallians spoke about each other and about themselves added up to a very different message: culture and community could be equated in some context, but were not the same in others. What the word 'identity' might mean in any one context, was a question of context.

 ### Task B0.1.5

Baumann and Hannerz make similar points concerning how individuals do not see themselves in uni-dimensional terms: Baumann writes that people see themselves 'as members of several communities, each with its own culture', and that 'making one's life meant ranging across them', while Hannerz writes that 'many people have biographies entailing cross-cutting allegiances' and 'share different parts of their personal cultural repertoires with different collections of people'.

➤ Do you agree with Baumann and Hannerz?
➤ If so, what 'communities' do you feel you are a member of, and how does your own life mean 'ranging across' these communities? Or, in the words of Hannerz, which 'cross-cutting allegiances' does your own biography involve? What are the significant different parts of your own 'personal cultural repertoire', and with which 'different collections of people' do you share these?

 ### Task B0.1.6

Baumann refers to 'ethnic reductionism' in the British media, political rhetoric and academic literature which consists of equating community, culture and ethnic identity.

➤ Can you think of examples in the media, political rhetoric, and academic literature where such 'ethnic reductionism' is apparent?

Commentary

We shall be considering what has been written about the concept of 'culture' in more depth in Unit B0.2. The crucial point to come out of both of the texts in this unit is that 'culture' and 'community' (and, indeed, 'cultural identity') are *not* concepts which exist independently, and somehow abstracted from how these terms are used by any individual in society and by the mass media, politicians and academics. Moreover, there are tangible consequences for any society of how such terms are used.

An interesting point made by Hannerz is the use of the term 'multiculturalism' by both 'ethnic minority politicians' as well as 'xenophobia activists'. Even when the intention is to challenge those Hannerz calls 'cultural fundamentalists', who put a negative spin on the term 'multiculturalism', the effect can be to further reinforce the 'ethnic reductionism' Baumann refers to. Watson (2000:51–3), for example, writes of how the British education system has been seen by some as failing to get to grips with 'multiculturalism'; these critics argue that 'the initiatives taken in schools . . . have raised awareness of ethnic minorities in British', but they have done so 'by exoticizing them and hence perpetuating stereotypes of difference, and, ipso facto, inferiority. The phrase frequently used to describe this exoticization is 'steel bands, saris, and samosas' . . . It is, claim the critics, these visible and tangible phenomena which are seized upon time and time again in schools as markers of cultural identity, and by failing to explore the deeper realities of ethnic minority experience schools trivialise other cultures, rendering them entertaining but superficial and periphery. This reduction of ethnic minorities to a limited set of cultural traits is subsequently further endorsed by the media and becomes firmly ensconced in the national mentality, to the point where knowledge of the other is confined to dismissive referential images. Such an approach, termed 'soft multiculturalism' by Watson, is also that of those termed by Hannerz 'interculturalists', trainers and consultants who try to 'teach sensitivity toward cultural diversity', but are 'somewhat inclined toward stereotyping, occasionally given to exaggerating cultural differences . . .'.

A number of writers have been interested in the notion of 'community'. One common reference is to the 'symbolic' community, which is well defined by Cohen (1985:98): 'The community as experienced by its members does not consist in social structure or in "the doing" of social behaviour. It inheres, rather, in "the thinking" about it. It is in this sense that we can speak of the community as a symbolic, rather than a structural construct.' Central to the work of Benedict Anderson (1983) is that communities, and particularly national communities, are 'imagined', while for Barthes (1973) the nation is not so much imagined as represented and projected in terms of 'cultural myths'. Others have been more concerned with what Potter and Wetherell (1987) call 'communities of practice', in which members tend to 'communicate with each other in the same terms'; this leads over time to communities of practice having particular 'interpretative repertoires'. More recently, of course, we are used to 'communities' being described as 'virtual', and we will investigate the impact of the World Wide Web on 'community' and 'identity' in Unit B1.5.

'CULTURE': DEFINITIONS AND PERSPECTIVES

UNIT B0.2

In Unit B0.2 we focus on how the term 'culture' has been defined and interpreted in the academic domain. Much of the debate on 'culture' in the last fifty years or so has been concerned with challenging models of culture which have emanated from the field of anthropology. Such a model is that of Tylor (1871), for whom 'culture' is 'that complex whole which includes knowledge, belief, art, morals, law, customs, and any other capabilities and habits acquired by man as a member of society'. There has been unease with, and debate about, both what culture is seen to 'include' in such a model, and the notion that culture is 'acquired', as we shall see in texts B0.2.1, B02.2 and B02.3.

Extension

The first text in the unit, by Brian Fay, provides a summary of differences between 'standard' and 'complex' views of culture. In the second, Celia Roberts and Srikant Sarangi discuss how a 'standard' view has tended to dominate the fields of applied linguistics and intercultural communication studies. In the final text Adrian Holliday, the author of Section A of this book, offers an alternative to the 'standard' view of culture in his discussion of 'small cultures'.

Before you read Text B0.2.1, do Task B0.2.1 below.

 Task B0.2.1

Read the definitions of 'culture' below, then answer the questions that follow.

1. A culture is 'a text the vocabulary and grammar of which its members learn' (Fay 1996:55).
2. 'Culture is a verb' (Street 1991).
3. Culture is 'an evolving connected activity, not a thing' (Fay 1996:62–3).
4. 'Believing . . . that man is an animal suspended in webs of significance he himself has spun, I take culture to be those webs' (Geertz 1973:5).

➤ What do you think the writers mean by their descriptions?
➤ Which, if any, of the descriptions do you feel successfully captures the *complete* or a *partial* meaning of 'culture'?

TEXT B0.2.1

B. Fay

Fay, B. (1996) Contemporary Philosophy of Social Science: A Multicultural Approach, Oxford: Blackwell pp. 55–60 (extracts)

According to a standard view, a culture is a complex set of shared beliefs, values, and concepts which enables a group to make sense of its life and which provides it with directions for how to live. This set might be called a basic belief system (note that such a belief system can include items which are fully explicit and others which are not, and can include matters of feeling and deportment as well as discursive claims about the world). In perhaps the most influential variant of this standard view, culture is pictured as a text the vocabulary and grammar of which its members learn. Indeed, in this view, becoming a member of a particular culture is a process of enculturation conceived as learning to read the culture's basic text and making it one's own.

This standard view asserts the further claim that in becoming the carriers of a specific cultural tradition individuals become the people they are. That is, by internalizing a particular belief system and its attendant forms of feeling and interaction a person acquires the basics of his or her identity. A culture penetrates its individual members mentally (so that they possess a certain mind-set), physically (so that they possess certain basic bodily dispositions), and socially (so that they relate to one another in certain characteristic ways). This penetration produces in them their distinctive capacities and characteristics. In this holistic way identity is a function of enculturation . . .

So far I have been speaking as if culture consisted of a coherent set of beliefs (a 'text'). But this is a mistake. Any culture complex enough to warrant the name will consist of conflicting beliefs and rules which offer mixed, contested, and ambiguous messages to its followers. The reason for this derives in part from what I have already said about cultural rules and agency:

rules require interpretation, and interpretation requires reflexive analysis and judgment on the part of agents. Besides, cultural beliefs and ideals apply to people in differential positions of power. The meaning of a rule for a powerful member of an elite often will not be the same for, nor will it have the same outcome on, a member of a group who is on the periphery. Moreover, cultural norms and ideals result from histories of struggle in which significant voices are silenced. As a result, various members in a cultural group will have heterogeneous histories, divergent interests, and antagonistic interpretations. Far from being coherent unities uniformly distributed throughout a society, cultures are rather tense loci of difference and opposition . . .

Another important fact about cultures is that they are essentially open. Cultures are ideational entities; as such they are permeable, susceptible to influence from other cultures. Wherever exchange among humans occurs, the possibility exists of the influence of one culture by another. (Even when such influence does not occur it is because those in one culture consciously reject the foreign or strange culture: but this rejection is itself another way the alien culture interjects itself into the home culture.) Human history is in part the story of the ways different cultural groups have rearranged cultural boundaries by expanding contacts, tolerating outsiders, and fashioning interactive arrangements. Even the creation of stricter boundaries involves mutual impact. The human world is not composed of a motley of independent, encapsulated, free-floating cultures; rather, it is one of constant interplay and exchange . . .

. . . consider the deeper cultural rhythms by which you live. Your conceptions of time, of space, of power, of beauty, of agency, of sociality, of knowledge have all been deeply affected by importing, responding to, transforming, and borrowing the cultural meanings and values of others different from you.

B. Fay

Task B0.2.2

➤ How do you think 'the cultural meanings and values of others different from you' that Fay refers to have affected your own conceptions of:

- ■ time
- ■ space
- ■ beauty
- ■ knowledge?

Roberts, C. and Sarangi, S. (1993) '"Culture" Revisited in Intercultural Communication', in Boswood, T., Hoffman, R. and P. Tung (eds), *Perspectives on English for International Communication*, Hong Kong: Hong Kong City Polytechnic pp. 97–102 (extracts)

TEXT B0.2.2
C. Roberts and
S. Sarangi

(Note: AL is an abbreviation for Applied Linguistics; ICC is an abbreviation for Intercultural Communication)

Within AL and ICC, many researchers regard culture as a preference for certain patterns of communicative behaviour, though such patterns can only be interpreted at a higher level of abstraction. In the functionalist tradition, 'culture' is seen as background and resource, where the human subject is only seen in his/her role of executor of functions. 'Culture' thus comes to be viewed too simply as either behaviour (e.g. x people don't smile in public), or as fixed values and beliefs, separated from social interaction and socio-political realities (e.g. x culture values

C. Roberts and
S. Sarangi

the elderly). Such reductionism is characteristic of AL and ICC studies where ethnicities and cultural identities have been reduced according to Hewitt (1989, pp. 6–9), to 'a list of strange linguistic and interactional elements arranged in academic display, dislocated from the sources of their generation, from human agency, intelligence, politics and from the possibility of change'.

There is no sense of culture as symbolically ordered in its own right or constitutive to any degree. Nor is there any sense of the human subject as an agency constituted through culture.

It is not surprising therefore that in analytic terms, culture has thus become the 'residual realm left over after all forms of observable human behaviour have been removed' (Wuthnow et al., 1984). Especially in the context of interactional studies, this has amounted to explaining behaviour away. Such characterisations of culture as social behaviour and/or shared values leave the notion of 'culture' itself intact as an impressionistic explanation for understanding differences and difficulties in communication in multi-ethnic societies.

Hinnenkamp (1987:176) quite rightly observes:

> Culture as adapted in most linguistic sub-disciplines has unfortunately become a passé-partout notion; whenever there is a need for a global explanation of differences between members of different speech communities the culture card is played – the more 'distant' in geographic and linguistic origin, the more 'cultural difference'!

This leads us to highlight the problem both in theoretical studies of AL and ICC and in applications such as education and training programmes. There are three major difficulties here: firstly that the nature of these studies and programmes means that the focus is on problems and difficulties and so 'culture' or what we might call the 'cultural principle' is used in a 'celebration of miscommunication'. Secondly, 'culture' is conceived of in a limited way to refer to resources, behaviour patterns and fixed values. And finally, 'culture' in the limited way described above becomes the necessary and sufficient explanation of intercultural encounters. Within ICC studies, it is generally assumed that things go wrong because two cultural groups behave differently, which makes communication between them problematic. This means that within such a view, 'culture' is seen as creating and maintaining an unfavourable climate for ICC. So 'culture' becomes a negative term rather than a positive term . . .

Task B0.2.3

➤ Think of your own experiences studying foreign or second languages, history or the social sciences. Have the ways you have been encouraged to view other cultural groups in such studies been characterised by the kind of 'ethnic reductionism' highlighted by Roberts and Sarangi?

TEXT B0.2.3
A. R. Holliday

Holliday, A. R. (1999) 'Small Cultures', *Applied Linguistics*, 20:2 pp. 237–264 (extracts)

Two cultures

On asking both academics and non-academics what they mean by 'culture', one will invariably find that they first refer to 'large' entities such as British, Indonesian, Western or European cultures. However, at other times one may also hear people referring to 'small' entities such as hospital, research, family, office or organisation cultures. When asked how these two types

A. R. Holliday

of culture relate to each other, some people say that the 'large' usage is the correct one and that the 'small' usage is metaphorical. Others say that the small cultures are 'sub-cultures'. Casual observation thus gives the impression that when asked, people will state 'large' culture, but will often use 'small' culture as an unmarked form . . .

Two paradigms

The notion of small culture does not . . . relate simply to something smaller in size than large ethnic, national or international cultures, but presents a different paradigm through which to look at social groupings. The small culture paradigm, set against the large culture paradigm is summarised in [Table 5]. The idea of small cultures (central column) is non-essentialist in that it does not relate to the essences of ethnic,[1] national or international entities. Instead it relates to any cohesive social grouping with no necessary subordination to large cultures. [Table 5] also distinguishes a research orientation for each paradigm. 'Research' is used here in the broadest sense, as any academic or non-academic process of learning about culture. Non-academic cultural research is naturally carried out by anyone 'approaching' an unfamiliar social grouping in the sense of Schutz' 'stranger', 'who has to place in question nearly everything that seems unquestionable to the members of the approached group' (1962:96). In cultural research, small cultures are thus a heuristic means in the process of interpreting group behaviour. The idea of large cultures (right-hand column), in contrast, is essentialist in that it relates to the essential differences between ethnic, national and international entities. Because the large culture paradigm begins with a prescriptive desire to seek out and detail differences which are considered the norm, and because it aims to explain behaviour in these terms, it tends to be culturist . . .

Table 5 Two paradigms

	Small cultures	Large cultures
Character	Non-essentialist, non-culturist.	Essentialist, culturist.
	Relating to cohesive behaviour in activities within any social grouping.	'Culture' as essential features of ethnic, national or international group.
Relations	No necessary subordination to or containment within large cultures, therefore no onion-skin.	Small (sub)cultures are contained within and subordinate to large cultures through onion-skin relationship.
Research orientation	Interpretive, process.	Normative
	Interpreting emergent behaviour within any social grouping.	Beginning with the idea that specific ethnic, national and international groups have different 'cultures' and then searching for the details (e.g. what is polite in Japanese culture).
	Heuristic model to aid the process of researching the cohesive process of any social grouping.	

---

1 'Ethnic' is as troublesome as 'culture'. It can be argued that it is a product of the same essentialist discourse as large culture (e.g. Baumann (1996), Sarangi (1994, 1995)).

'Small' is therefore not just a matter of size, but of the degree of imposition on reality. Whereas the large culture notion imposes a picture of the social world which is divided into 'hard', essentially different ethnic, national or international cultures, the small culture notion leaves the picture open, finding 'softer' 'cultures' in all types of social grouping, which may or may not have significant ethnic, national or international qualities. In this sense, the focus of a large culture approach is what makes cultures, which everyone acknowledges as existing, essentially different to each other. In contrast, a small culture approach is more concerned with social processes as they emerge . . .

Small cultures: 'A process of making and remaking'

Within the small culture paradigm, 'culture' refers to the composite of cohesive behaviour within any social grouping, and not to the differentiating features of prescribed ethnic, national and international entities. Distant from the large culture approach, which takes ethnic, national and international groupings as the default [Table 5], small cultures can be any social grouping from a neighbourhood to a work group (Beales et al 1967:8). . . .

Small culture is thus a dynamic, ongoing group process which operates in changing circumstances to enable group members to make sense of and operate meaningfully within those circumstances. When a researcher looks at an unfamiliar social grouping, it can be said to have a small culture when there is a discernible set of behaviours and understandings connected with group cohesion. The dynamic aspect of small culture is central to its nature, having the capacity to exist, form and change as required. According to Beales et al., 'the outstanding characteristic of a cultural system is that it is in process; it moves' (1967:5). Small culture is thus 'the sum total of all the processes, happenings, or activities in which a given set or several, sets of people habitually engage' (ibid.:9). Thus, small culture constitutes a social 'tool-kit' which emerges to 'solve problems' when required (Crane 1994:11). Moreover, it involves an underlying competence in which 'people are not passive "cultural dopes"; they are active, often skilled users' (ibid.:11).

Task B0.2.4

➤ In text B0.2.3 Holliday writes that 'small cultures can be any social grouping from a neighbourhood to a work group'. What 'small cultures' can you identify?
➤ Think of one particular small culture. What 'discernible set of behaviours and understandings' is characteristic of this small culture?
➤ How does this 'discernible set of behaviours and understandings' help to make this small culture cohesive?

Commentary

Any study of culture will inevitably be complex and there are no easy off-the-peg definitions. It is, indeed, off-the-peg definitions that prevent a consideration of the complexities of culture, and prevent us approaching culture as a dynamic and interactive process, a key theme in the texts in this unit.

What are the implications of approaching culture as a dynamic and interactive process for individuals who want to carry out research into their own and others' cultures? This is a key concern for Ylanne–McEwen and Coupland (2000:208–9), who ask: 'What are we to make of this orientation to the study of culture? How should we respond to it in research on cultural difference and language? Does it perhaps make the study of "intercultural" relations and communication impossible, even reprehensible, because it fixes the notion of "cultural group" prematurely and in ways that do not reflect how cultural identity is nowadays lived and experienced?' These are questions to which there are no easy answers, and there are relatively few published examples of 'process' approaches to researching culture.

A starting point for any such research is suggested by Alasuutari (1995:135–6), who states that 'the researcher must be able to see beyond the horizon of the self-evident' and needs to 'generate why-questions': 'In an ethnographic study of a foreign culture the why-questions will often stem from the researcher's own failure to understand why the people concerned are living the way they do, or why they think the way they do'; however, 'when you are looking at something that is closely related to your own culture, most things will often appear more or less self-evident or trivial'. Such a view is similar to that of Bauman (1990:15–6), who employs the term 'defamiliarization', a process which 'takes us away from our comfortable, limited, commonly accepted and often unconsidered opinions about what everybody and everything is like and makes us more sensitive to the way that those opinions are formed and maintained. It alerts us to the ways that things which at first sight appear obvious and 'natural' are actually the result of social action, social power or social tradition'. Alasuutari (ibid.:35–6) claims that the best chance of finding answers to the 'why-questions' is through the eclecticism of cultural studies since 'cultural studies has explored the concept of meaning from various angles and studied the mediation of social reality through meanings in different ways'.

SECTION

B

Theme 1
Identity

UNIT B1.1   **IDENTITY AS A PERSONAL PROJECT**

In recent years in the broad field of cultural studies there has been a growing interest in questions of identity. Questions commonly discussed include the following.

■ How is the identity of any one individual created?
■ In the creation of individual identity, what factors are salient and how do these factors interact?
■ To what extent is any one individual's identity a matter of personality and to what extent do influences from the sociocultural context impact?
■ How much commonality of identity is there, first, between two individuals who inhabit the same physical and sociocultural space and, second, between two individuals who inhabit very different physical and sociocultural spaces?
■ How far is identity fixed and stable?
■ If identities do change, what factors are responsible for such change?
■ How far is individual identity influenced by global forces?
■ What is the relationship between language and identity?

The term 'identity' defies precise definition and crosses traditional boundaries between disciplines in the social sciences. Increasingly in recent years there has been an emphasis on the interrelationship of culture and *identity*, as well as on the longer-established emphasis on the interrelationship between culture and *behaviour*.

'Identity' is the focus of the next five units. In this unit we consider a particular aspect of identity which has come to the forefront in recent years: that of identity being a personal project. The first text is by a Peruvian novelist, short-story writer, play-wright and essayist, Julio Ramón Ribeyro, while the second is by Anthony Giddens, an increasingly well-known social scientist.

Before you read the texts, do the following task.

 Task B1.1.1

➤ In what ways might identity be said to be 'a personal project'?

Ribeyro, J. R. (1972) 'Barbara' from *La Palabra del Mundo*, collected short stories, translated by D. Douglas (1986) from *On Being Foreign: Culture Shock in Short Fiction; an international anthology*, Lewis, T. J. and Jungman, R. E. (eds), Yarmouth, Maine: Intercultural Press (extracts)

TEXT B1.1.1
J. R. Ribeyro

Despite the fact that he was a mulatto[1] named Lopez, he longed to resemble less and less a goalie on the Alianza Lima soccer team and increasingly to take on the appearance of a blond from Philadelphia. Life had taught him that if he wanted to triumph in a colonial city it was better to skip the intermediate stages and transform himself into a gringo[2] from the United States rather than into just a fair-skinned nobody from Lima. During the years that I knew him, he devoted all of his attention to eliminating every trace of the Lopez and zambo[3] within him and Americanizing himself before time could sentence him to an existence as a bank guard or a taxi driver. He had had to begin by killing the Peruvian in himself and extracting something from every gringo that he met. From all this plundering a new person would emerge, a fragmented being who was neither mulatto nor gringo, but rather the result of an unnatural commingling, something that the force of destiny would eventually change, unfortunately, for him, from a rosy dream into a hellish nightmare.

But let's not get ahead of ourselves. We should establish the fact that his name was Roberto, that years later he was known as Bobby, but that in the most recent official documents he is listed as Bob. At each stage in his frantic ascension toward nothingness his name lost one syllable . . .

First of all he had to eliminate every trace of the zambo in himself. His hair didn't cause any major problem; he dyed it with peroxide and had it straightened. As for his skin, he mixed starch, rice powder, and talcum from the drugstore until he found the ideal combination; but a dyed and powdered zambo is still a zambo. He needed to know how the North American gringos dressed, talked, moved, and thought: in short, precisely who they were.

In those days we saw him marauding about during his free hours in diverse locales which seemingly had nothing in common, except for one thing: they were usually frequented by gringos . . .

. . . This phase of his plan was for him absolutely perfect. In the meantime, he was able to confirm that the gringos were distinguishable from others by the special way they dressed, which he described as sporty, comfortable, and unconventional. Because of his observations, Roberto was one of the first to discover the advantages of blue jeans, the virile cowboy look of the wide leather belt fastened by an enormous buckle, the soft comfort of white canvas shoes with rubber soles, the collegiate charm of a canvas cap with a visor, the coolness of a flowered or striped short-sleeved shirt, the variety of nylon jackets zipped up in front bearing an emblem of special significance, always influential and distinctive, and worn underneath, a white shirt also bearing an emblem of a North American university.

All of these articles of clothing were not sold in any department store but had to be brought from the United States, a place where he had no contacts. There were North American families who, prior to returning to the United States, announced in the newspaper their intention to sell everything they had. Roberto showed up on their doorstep before anyone else, acquiring in this way a wardrobe in which he invested all of his savings.

With hair that was now straightened and bleached, a pair of blue jeans and a loud shirt, Roberto was on the brink of becoming Bobby.

---

1 'Mulatto' means someone who is a mixture of white and black.
2 'Gringo' is a term used to identify a (white) North American.
3 'Zambo' means someone who is a blend of Native Indian and black.

Task B1.1.2

Ribeyro writes of Lopez 'killing the Peruvian in himself'. This assumes that his identity is in part defined by national culture (in his case, Peruvian culture).

➤ Do you think your own identity is in part defined by one or more national cultures? If so, in what ways and to what extent?

Task B1.1.3

In the extract Lopez attempts to change his identity by changing his name, appearance and social contacts.

➤ Do you think it is possible to change your identity by changing these things? Have any changes you have made to your own name, appearance or social contacts affected your own sense of self-identity?

TEXT B1.1.2
A. Giddens

Giddens, A. (1991) *Modernity and Self-Identity: Self and Society in the Late Modern Age*, Cambridge: Polity pp. 14/ 81; 53–55 (extracts)

Today each of us lives a biography reflexively organised in terms of flows of social and psychological information about possible ways of life. . . . 'How shall I live?' has to be answered in day-to-day decisions about how to behave, what to wear and what to eat, and many other things [14] . . . each of the decisions a person makes every day . . . are decisions not only about how to act but who to be [81].

Self-identity is not a distinctive trait, or even a collection of traits, possessed by the individual. It is the self as reflexively understood by the person in terms of her or his biography. Identity here still presumes continuity across time and space: but self-identity is such continuity as interpreted reflexively by the agent. This includes the cognitive component of personhood. To be a 'person' is not just to be a reflexive actor, but to have a concept of a person (as applied both to the self and others). What a 'person' is understood to be certainly varies across cultures, although there are elements of such a notion that are common to all cultures. . . .

The existential question of self-identity is bound up with the fragile nature of the biography which the individual 'supplies' about herself. A person's identity is not to be found in behaviour, nor – important though this is – in the reactions of others, but in the capacity to keep a particular narrative going. The individual's biography, if she is to maintain regular interaction with others in the day-to-day world, cannot be wholly fictive. It must continually integrate events which occur in the external world, and sort them into the ongoing 'story' about the self. . . .

. . . the 'content' of self-identity – the traits from which biographies are constructed – varies socially and culturally. In some respects this is obvious enough. A person's name, for example, is a primary element in his biography; practices of social naming, how far names express kin relations, whether or not names are changed at certain stages of life – all these things differ between cultures. But there are other more subtle, yet also more important, differences. Reflexive biographies vary in much the same ways as stories do.

Task B1.1.4

➤ Do you see your own identity as a matter of keeping 'a particular narrative going' or would you use another metaphor?

➤ If you do believe identity is a matter of keeping 'a particular narrative going', then what does your own 'narrative' consist of?

➤ If you came up with another metaphor for describing your identity, explain this metaphor.

Task B1.1.5

Giddens writes that although there are commonalities between cultures, 'what a "person" is understood to be' varies culturally. Wetherell and Maybin (1996:221) point to some key assumptions 'which many people in countries such as the UK and USA would see as simply obvious and true, although they may want to add items to or qualify our list'. These are as follows.

1. A person is someone with a self-contained mind and consciousness: a unique individual who is separate and distinct from other people.
2. Each individual has one personality or a consistent set of traits, characteristics, preferences, or abilities which sum up that person's true nature. . . .
3. People own their thoughts and feelings. These are private, self-generated and organized within the inner self. Thoughts, feelings and internal states can, however, be expressed publicly through language, actions and through other symbolic means. Although people might struggle to find the right terms, their words reflect more or less accurately their internal states.
4. People . . . are the centre and source of their experience. Individuals initiate action and try to realize themselves (their plans, beliefs, desires) in the world.

➤ Do you think there is any truth in the assertion by Giddens that 'what a "person" is understood to be' varies culturally? Why?/why not?

If so:

➤ If you live in a country 'such as the UK or USA', do you share and/or recognise the assumptions described by Wetherell and Maybin?

or:

➤ If you live in a country very different from the UK or USA, would you say there are different and contrasting assumptions about individual identity?

Commentary

Giddens believes that whereas the lives of individuals in previous generations were structured around 'life cycles' consisting of 'ritualised passages' (e.g. particular birthdays of significance, festivals and marriage), in contemporary life individuals' lives are 'more and more freed from externalities associated with pre-established ties to other individuals and groups' (1991:147) and are structured around 'open experience thresholds' (i.e. particular events and experiences in the individual's 'biography' which have particular significance). Giddens believes that in contemporary life, 'life-planning' is of particular importance for the individual: 'Life plans are the substantial content of the reflexively organised trajectory of the self. Life-planning is a means of preparing a course of future actions mobilized in terms of the self's biography' (1991:85).

The move away from 'traditional' means of defining identity has for some been a key feature of postmodernism. For Strinati (1997:431), for example, postmodernism has seen 'the gradual disappearance of the traditional long-standing and once legitimate frames of reference in terms of which people could define themselves and their place in society, and so feel relatively secure in their own identities. These traditional sources of identity – social class, the extended and nuclear family, local communities, the "neighbourhood", religion, trade unions, the nation state – are said to be in decline as a result of tendencies in modern capitalism towards increasingly rapid rates of economic, geographical, political and cultural change.' What is more, for Strinati, 'nothing emerges to take the place of the traditional sources of personal and collective identity. No new forms or institutions, no new ideas or beliefs, can now serve to give people a secure and coherent sense of themselves'.

UNIT B1.2 GLOBALIZATION AND IDENTITY

We considered in Unit B1.1 how commentators on contemporary life have tended to emphasize the disappearance of 'traditional' frames of reference by which individuals can identify themselves. In this unit we focus on the processes of globalisation and, in particular, how these processes may be important factors in defining 'identity'.

The first part of the title of the text in this unit is 'Global Culture/Individual Identity'. Before you read the text, do Task B1.2.1.

 Task B1.2.1

➤ How far, and in what ways, would you say your sense of your own identity has been affected by global trends, the flow of goods, people and images around the world, and the increasing possibilities available for global communication?

Mathews, G. (2000) *Global Culture/Individual Identity: Searching for home in the cultural supermarket,* London: Routledge pp. 19–23 (extracts)

TEXT B1.2.1
G. Mathews

The cultural supermarket bears some resemblance to its metaphorical root, the material supermarket. Just as the material supermarket has been transformed as to the scope of its goods in recent years, . . . so too has the cultural supermarket, thanks to television and computers. And just as in the material supermarket shelf space is unequally distributed – products like Coca-Cola being on the middle, easily seen shelves, other, less heavily advertised products being above the customer's head, and less noticeable – so too in the cultural supermarket. Those societies whose material goods are readily available in the world also have greater cultural influence in the world. 'The United States', writes Robert Boock, '. . . has come to epitomize the modern [worldwide] consumer's dreamland', and certainly the world's cultural supermarket has more than its share of American 'goods,' in the influences of movies, music, and sports – America's celebrity culture, spread worldwide.

But the structure of the cultural supermarket is far more complex than this metaphor indicates; in its far-flung intangibility, it is more like a vast library than like a grocery store, more like the internet than like a map of nations of the world. . . .

. . . The information within the cultural supermarket may be categorized by its users in a number of different ways, but the two most readily available are (1) region of origin, and (2) realm of use. For most of the information in the cultural supermarket, we have some idea of where it comes from. This usually corresponds to culture as 'the way of life of a people,' as embodied in national culture: we refer to Indian music, Brazilian samba, French cuisine, and so on, in order to have a shorthand way with which to refer to these entities. These represent aisle signs, often of questionable validity but of considerable convenience, in labeling and dividing up the vast array of materials in the cultural supermarket for consumers' ease. As we will see, these claims may become particularly vital when applied to oneself; claims of 'Japanese' art or 'American' religion or 'Chinese' values may seek to make what may seem a choice from the cultural supermarket into one's underlying essence – they may seek to make a choice not a choice.

There is also the realm of use. We fashion ourselves from the cultural supermarket in a number of areas, among them our choices in home decor, in food and clothing, in what we read, watch, and listen to in music, art, and popular culture, in our religious belief, and in ethnic and national identity itself: whether, in the United States, to identify oneself as Hispanic-American or as American; whether, in Hong Kong, to be Chinese or Hongkongese. These different shapings bear differing degrees of personal significance: one's choice of home decor, for example ('That Buddhist mandala in the living room? No, of course I don't believe in that stuff. I just thought it looked neat'), may be of considerably less significance for one's sense of cultural identity than, for example, one's choice of religion, which may lie at the core of who one senses oneself to be. In this book, we will consistently see that the choices people make in the realms of artistic expression, religious belief, and cultural identity are of deep personal significance: we will find that choices from the cultural supermarket, unlike many choices from the material supermarket, are very often agonized over, for they may be of extraordinary importance to these people in defining what their lives are most essentially about.

The foregoing should not, however, be taken to mean that our choices from the cultural supermarket are free; rather, as earlier noted, our choices are restricted in a number of different senses. There is first of all the differential in receiving equipment for the cultural supermarket. One who is educated and affluent may possess optimal receiving equipment: access to and ability to make use of the repository of human thought contained in libraries, and access to the contemporary repositories of thought in the Internet and in mass media – the world assortment of newspapers, magazines, and compact disks available at key outlets throughout the world.

Extension

G. Mathews

A person with such advantages may make full use of the cultural supermarket, but many of the people in the world cannot – their access to the cultural supermarket is more limited, confined to whatever echoes of the cultural supermarket may reach their particular corner of the world. No doubt more people from rich societies than poor societies, and more people from the upper, affluent, educated classes in every society than the lower, poorer, less-educated classes have this optimal receiving equipment. It may be that the less sophisticated the receiving equipment you have, the more likely that you will be manipulated down the standard paths of Coca-Cola, Marlboro, Rambo, Doraemon, although there are certainly exceptions to this; and as anthropologists often note, how consumers in different societies actually interpret these various products may differ substantially from the plans of marketers.

Beyond this, there is the fact that the choices each of us makes as to cultural identity are made not for ourselves but for performance for and in negotiation with others: we choose ourselves within the cultural supermarket with an eye to our social world. One's cultural identity is performed in that one must convince others as to its validity: one must have the knowledge and social grace to convince others that one is not an impostor. Efforts to this effect may be seen in many different social milieux, . . . from the Japanese salaryman/rock musician who wears a short-hair wig to his office rather than get his hair cut, so that he can convince his fellow rock musicians that he is 'for real,' to the American spiritual seeker who pursues various religions despite the scorn of her husband, snickering that she 'goes through religions like she goes through clothes,' to the mainland Chinese woman in Hong Kong who wears expensive fashions but not with quite enough of a sense of style to disguise her mainland background from the disdainful eyes of Hong Kong people.

A wide range of cultural identities in this world is available for appropriation; but although culturally the world may be wide open, socially it is not. One's cultural choices must fit within one's social world, which is more limited. In a typical middle-class American neighborhood, I could probably become a Buddhist without alarming my neighbors, but I could not become an Islamic fundamentalist; I may study the Mbuti pygmies in an anthropology text, but were I to express beliefs such as theirs to my co-workers, I would at best be seen as eccentric, at worst as a lunatic. One's social world – outside one's mind, and more, as resident within one's mind – acts as a censor and gatekeeper, selecting from the range of possible cultural ideas one might appropriate only those that seem plausible and acceptable within it. One's social world particularly constrains one's choices in terms of such factors as class, gender, and age. The elderly woman who wears a miniskirt and the working-class kid who uses fancy foreign words are likely to learn quite rapidly, if they have any sensitivity at all to the cues of their social world, about the inappropriateness of their cultural choices.

Despite these strictures, there is often the effort to bring into one's social world what Pierre Bourdieu terms 'cultural capital': knowledge from the cultural supermarket that one can display to one's social credit, justifying and bolstering one's social position. One's interest, at least within some segments of American society, in Indian ragas as opposed to top 40 hits, or in Tibetan Buddhist writings as opposed to evangelical Christian tracts, is a way of advertising cosmopolitan discernment: my far-flung tastes may well be the servant of my local strategy of impressing the people around me. The matter of what from the cultural supermarket can provide status in a given social milieu is highly complex. Each social milieu has its rating system for information and identities from the cultural supermarket; individuals seek to attain maximum credit and credibility, not only through consumption within the existing cultural rating system, but also through bringing in new information and identities, whose high status they seek to establish. The criteria for the establishment of such status are thus highly specific and flexible; individuals play the game with an extraordinarily acute sense of its implicit rules and strategies.

But all this is not to claim that there is absolutely no room for individual choice from the cultural supermarket. Why does one person thrill to Bach, another to juju? Why does one person become a Christian, another a Buddhist? Why does one person revel in her ethnicity, while another spurns that ethnicity? Why does one person travel the world while another stays home? Much can be predicted about our choices by considering such factors as social class, educational level, income, gender, and age, as well as our personal histories, but not everything can be predicted. We are not slaves to the world around us, but have (in a social if not a philosophical sense) a certain degree of freedom in choosing who we are. This freedom may be highly limited, but it cannot be altogether denied.

Task B1.2.2

Mathews suggests that 'our choices in home decor, in food and clothing, in what we read, watch, and listen to in music, art, and popular culture' all help to fashion our identities.

➤ Do you think that your own identity has been partly fashioned by such things, and if so, how important are they to your own sense of identity?

Task B1.2.3

Mathews writes that 'class, gender, and age' limit people's choices from the cultural supermarket?

➤ To what extent do you agree with this idea?
➤ In what ways might your own class, gender or age place limits on your own choices from the 'cultural supermarket'?

Task B1.2.4

A key issue raised by Mathews concerns the relationship between consumer objects and individual identity.

Many people have recently expressed concern not just about the negative economic affects of the global domination of such brands as Coca-Cola and McDonald's, but also about the ways in which their global domination swamps individuals' identities, particularly of those in economically disadvantaged areas of the world. Others have suggested that people will always 'appropriate' such products (i.e. interpret and exploit them according to their purposes and advantages), and that to talk of the identities of the most disadvantaged people (who in the words of Mathews have 'less sophisticated receiving equipment') being swamped by them is at best simplistic and at worst racist.

➤ Do you believe that brands such as Coca-Cola and McDonald's, and the values associated with them, do swamp the identities of individuals in different parts of the world?

Commentary

There is no doubt that for many of us our world is very different, in many respects, from that of previous generations. Yet, despite the myriad changes, questions at the core of debate in the social sciences remain unanswered: those of how much freedom individuals have to fashion their own identities (in other words, the degree of agency individuals have), and, on the other hand, of how far individuals' thoughts, values and identities are determined and constrained by the values of the social structures, economic realities and mass media of their cultural milieux. These questions Mathews touches on in the last two sentences of the extract.

A number of writers have made similar links between consumption and identity. In linking consumption with identity, it is not simply a question of identity being formed through the acquisition of consumer goods. As Mathews suggests, it is what objects *mean* to individuals rather than the objects themselves that is significant. Gabriel and Lang (1995:89), in similar vein, write of the 'stories' which the individual 'reads into' consumer objects; for them this is the particular nature of 'Western' consumption so that 'identity becomes vitally and self-consciously enmeshed in stories which are read by consumers themselves into innumerable, relatively mundane, mass-produced objects which they buy, use or own. These unexceptional objects are not so much carriers of meaning, as carriers of vivid and powerful images, enabling us to choose them consciously from among similar ones, promising to act as the raw material out of which our individual identities may be fashioned'. Moreover, such 'vivid and powerful images' are constantly changing and 'the meanings of objects or practices are continually being re-created . . .'

Mathews makes reference to Pierre Bourdieu and his notion of 'cultural capital'. Bourdieu's ideas on consumption and identity have been especially influential, and his theory of 'cultural capital' has been increasingly discussed in relation to education.

UNIT B1.3   DISCOURSE, IDENTITY AND CULTURE

How far people's identities are bound up with how they speak and write, and all the contextual factors that go together with how they speak and write, is the focus of this unit. In his book *An Introduction to Discourse Analysis: Theory and Method* (1999), extracts of which will be the text featured in this unit, Gee writes that 'When we speak or write we always take a particular *perspective* on what the "world" is like. This involves us in taking perspectives on what is "normal" and not; what is "acceptable" and not; what is "right" and not, what is "real" and not; what is the "way things are" and not; what is the "way things ought to be" and not; what is "possible" and not; what "people like us" or "people like them" do and don't; and so on and so forth, again through a nearly endless list' (1999: 2).

The relationship between language and culture has long been a major concern in both anthropology and applied linguistics. The work of North American anthropologists Edward Sapir (e.g. 1947), and later Benjamin Whorf (1956), and their theories of how the languages of particular language communities mirror their particular views of reality, have wielded, and in many quarters continue to wield, considerable influence on debates in the social sciences on the nature of such a relationship. Questions continue to centre on whether, and to what extent, language reflects the world-view of a particular 'culture' or, conversely, whether, and to what extent, language determines the world view of a particular 'culture'.

In recent years, however, the theories of Sapir and Whorf, and the work of those who have applied their theories, have come under increasing scrutiny and a number of reservations have been expressed. Gumperz (1996:376–7), for example, writes that 'The assumption that our social world comes segmented into discrete internally homogenous language/culture areas has become increasingly problematic. Cultures are no longer homogenous and language divisions have become more and more permeable . . . speakers of the same language may find themselves separated by deep cultural gaps, while others who speak distinct languages share the same culture . . . At the same time group boundaries are rapidly changing and less sharply marked. We can thus no longer assume that language and culture are co-extensive and shared understandings can-not be taken for granted. The one to one relationship between language and cultural variability must now be seen as an oversimplification.'

Another issue that has tended to be skirted over when discussion takes place as to the relationship between language and culture is the nature and relative importance of all the different actions and activities that accompany language and help express meaning, as well as what underlies language in terms of such things as values, beliefs, attitudes, intentions, political considerations and historical 'baggage'. These are the concerns of Discourse Analysis and such concerns are explored in text B1.3.1.

Gee, J. P. (1999) *An Introduction to Discourse Analysis: Theory and Method*, London: Routledge pp. 12 –13, 17–18, 37 (extracts)

. . . I want to develop several 'tools of inquiry' (ways of looking at the world of talk and interaction) . . . The tools of inquiry I will introduce in this chapter are primarily relevant to how we (together with others) build identities and activities and recognize the identities and activities that are being built around us. . . . The tools to be discussed are:

(a) 'Situated identities,' that is, different identities or social positions we enact and recognize in different settings.

(b) 'Social languages,' that is, different styles of language that we use to enact and recognize different identities in different settings; different social languages also allow us to engage in all the other building tasks above (in different ways, building different sorts of things).

(c) 'Discourses' with a capital 'D,' that is, different ways in which we humans integrate language with non-language 'stuff,' such as different ways of thinking, acting, interacting, valuing, feeling, believing, and using symbols, tools, and objects in the right places and at the right times so as to enact and recognize different identities and activities, give the material world certain meanings, distribute social goods in a certain way, make certain sorts of meaningful connections in our experience, and privilege certain symbol systems and ways of knowing over others . . .

(d) 'Conversations' with a capital 'C,' that is, long-running and important themes or motifs that have been the focus of a variety of different texts and interactions (in different social languages and Discourses) through a significant stretch of time and across an array of institutions.

(Gee states later in the book that he uses 'Conversation' to mean 'the range of things that count as "appropriately" "sayable" and "meaning-able", in terms of (oral or written) words, symbols, images, and things, at a given time and place, or within a given institution, set of institutions, or society, in regard to a given topic or theme (e.g. schools, women's health, smoking, children, prisons, etc.)' and refers to the work of Foucault (1985) |p. 37|

. . . When you speak or write anything, you use the resources of English to project yourself as a certain kind of person, a different kind in different circumstances. You also project yourself as engaged in a certain kind of activity, a different kind in different circumstances. If I have no idea who you are and what you are doing, then I cannot make sense of what you have said, written, or done.

You project a different identity at a formal dinner party than you do at the family dinner table. And, though these are both dinner, they are none the less different activities. . . |pp. 12–13|

. . . making visible and recognizable *who* we are and *what* we are doing always involves a great deal more than 'just language.' It involves acting-interacting-thinking-valuing-talking (sometimes writing-reading) in the 'appropriate way' with the 'appropriate' props at the 'appropriate' times in the 'appropriate' places.

Such socially accepted associations among ways of using language, of thinking, valuing, acting, and interacting, in the 'right' places and at the 'right' times with the 'right' objects (associations that can be used to identify oneself as a member of a socially meaningful group or 'social network'), I will refer to as 'Discourses,' with a capital 'D' . . . 'Big D' Discourses are always language *plus* 'other stuff.' There are innumerable Discourses in any modern, technological, urban-based society: for example (enacting) being something as general as a type of African-American or Anglo-Australian or something as specific as being a type of modern British young second-generation affluent Sikh woman. Being a type of middle-class American, factory worker, or executive, doctor or hospital patient, teacher, administrator, or student, student of physics or of literature, member of a club or street gang, regular at the local bar, . . . are all Discourses.

The key to Discourses is 'recognition.' If you put language, action, interaction, values, beliefs, symbols, objects, tools, and places together in such a way that others *recognize* you as a particular type of who (identity) engaged in a particular type of what (activity) here and now, then you have pulled off a Discourse (and thereby continued it through history, if only for a while longer). Whatever you have done must be similar enough to other performances to be recognizable. However, if it is different enough from what has gone before, but still recognizable, it can simultaneously change and transform Discourses. If it is not recognizable, then you're not 'in' the Discourse.

Discourses are always embedded in a medley of social institutions, and often involve various 'props' like books and magazines of various sorts, laboratories, classrooms, buildings of various sorts, various technologies, and a myriad of other objects from sewing needles (for sewing circles) through birds (for bird watchers) to basketball courts and basketballs (for basketball players). Think of all the words, symbols, deeds, objects, clothes, and tools you need to coordinate in the right way at the right time and place to 'pull off' (or recognize someone as) being a cutting-edge particle physicist or a Los Angeles Latino street gang member or a sensitive high-culture humanist (of old).

It is sometimes helpful to think about social and political issues as if it is not just us humans who are talking and interacting with each other, but rather, the Discourses we represent and enact, and for which we are 'carriers.' The Discourses we enact existed before each of us came on the scene and most of them will exist long after we have left the scene. Discourses, through our words and deeds, carry on conversations with each other through history, and, in doing so, form human history.

Think, for instance, of the long-running and ever-changing 'conversation' in the U.S. and Canada between the Discourses of 'being an Indian' and 'being an Anglo' or of the different, but equally long-running 'conversation' in New Zealand between 'being a Maori' and 'being an Anglo' (or, for that matter, think of the long-running conversation between 'being a British Anglo' and 'being an American Anglo'). Think of the long-running and ever-changing 'conversation' between creationists and biologists. Think of the long-running and ever-changing 'conversation' in Los Angeles between African-American teenage gang members and the L.A. police. . . . Intriguingly, we humans are very often unaware of the history of these conversations, and thus, in a deep sense, not fully aware of what we mean when we act and talk . . . [pp. 17–18]

Task B1.3.1

At the beginning of Text B1.3.1, Gee refers to 'Situated identities', in other words 'different identities or social positions we enact and recognize in different settings'.

➤ Think of different identities you have enacted and/or might enact in the following settings.

- As a member of the family at a family gathering (e.g. for a wedding, funeral or formal birthday celebration).
- As a witness in a criminal trial in a court of law.
- As a job applicant at a job interview.
- As a sports supporter at a sporting event at which an individual or team shares the same nationality as you and is representing that nation.

➤ What different styles of language did you employ/might you employ in such settings?
➤ What thoughts, actions, patterns of interaction, values, feelings, beliefs were/would be integrated or underlie the language used in these settings?
➤ What symbols, tools and objects accompanied/might accompany the language in such settings?
➤ What long-running 'Conversations' (as defined by Gee in text B1.3.1 Extract 1) do you engage in and draw on in such settings?

Task B1.3.2

➤ Consider how one or more of the following individuals mentioned by Gee might 'pull off' a Discourse and describe what this Discourse comprises: an African-American; an Anglo-Australian; a modern British young second-generation affluent Sikh woman; a middle-class American; a factory worker; an executive; a doctor; a hospital patient; a teacher; an administrator; a student; a student of physics or of literature; a member of a club or street gang; a regular at the local bar.

➤ Consider how someone famous you are familiar with 'pulls off' a Discourse and describe what this Discourse comprises: e.g. a politician; a movie star; a pop star; a writer; an artist; a sports (wo)man.

 Task B1.3.3

Think of a long-running 'conversation' between two Discourses in a cultural context familiar to you. (The examples Gee provides in the text are the long-running 'conversation' in New Zealand between 'being a Maori' and 'being an Anglo', and between 'being a British Anglo' and 'being an American Anglo').

TEXT B1.3.1,
EXTRACT 2
J. P. Gee

Gee, J. P. (1999) *An Introduction to Discourse Analysis: Theory and Method*, London: Routledge pp. 49–50, 68–69, 78 (extracts)

. . . thinking and using language is an *active* matter of *assembling* the situated meanings that you need for action in the world. This assembly is always relative to your socioculturally-defined experiences in the world and, *more or less*, routinized ('normed') through cultural models and various social practices of the sociocultural groups to which you belong. [p. 49–50]

Cultural models

. . . we can distinguish (at least) the following sorts of cultural models:

■ *Espoused models*, that is models which we consciously espouse;

■ *Evaluative models*, that is models which we use, consciously or unconsciously, to judge ourselves or others;

■ *Models-in-(inter)action*, that is models that consciously or unconsciously guide our actions and interactions in the world.

Furthermore, cultural models can be about 'appropriate' attitudes, viewpoints, beliefs and values; 'appropriate' social, cultural and institutional organizational structures; 'appropriate' ways of talking, writing, reading, and communicating; 'appropriate' ways to feel or display emotion; 'appropriate' ways in which real and fictional events, stories, and histories are organized and end, and so on and so forth. Cultural models are com-plexly, though flexibly organised. There are smaller models inside bigger ones. Each model triggers or is associated with others, in different ways in different settings and differently for different socioculturally defined groups of people. And we can talk about 'master models', that is sets of associated cultural models, or single models, that help shape and organize large and important aspects of experience for particular groups of people, as well as the sorts of Conversations we discussed . . . [pp. 68–69]

Cultural models as tools of inquiry

J. P. Gee

Cultural models . . . lead us to ask, when confronted with a piece of talk, writing, action, or interaction, questions like these:

- What cultural models are relevant here? What must I, as an analyst, assume people feel, value, and believe, consciously or not, in order to talk (write), act, and/or interact this way?

- Are there differences here between the cultural models that are affecting espoused beliefs and those that are affecting actions and practices? What sorts of cultural models, if any, are being used here to make value judgments about oneself and others?

- How consistent are the relevant cultural models here? Are there competing or conflicting cultural models at play? Whose interests are the cultural models representing?

- What other cultural models are related to the ones most active here? Are there 'master models' at work?

- What sorts of texts, media, experiences, interactions, and/or institutions could have given rise to these cultural models?

- How are the relevant cultural models here helping to reproduce, transform, or create social, cultural, institutional, and/or political relationships? What Discourses and Conversations are these cultural models helping to reproduce, transform or create? [p 78]

Task B1.3.4

Go back to Section A of this book and re-read one or more of the following examples in the 'Experience' sections: A1.1.1, A1.2.1, A1.3.1, A2.1.1, A2.2.1. Use the 'Cultural models as tools of inquiry' described in Extract 2 from Gee's book to analyse what is described in these examples.

Commentary

Other writers have defined 'Discourse' (and 'discourse') differently to Gee. Jaworski and Coupland (1999:1–3) review the changing definitions of 'discourse' and means of discourse analysis and highlight the increasing importance given to discourse as a means of constructing reality. In doing so they quote a number of writers including Fairclough (1992:28), who is especially concerned with the ideological nature of discourse: '"Discourse" is more than *just* language use: it is language use, whether speech or writing, seen as a type of social practice'; discourse, too, is 'shaped by relations of power, and invested with ideologies'.

The writer whose ideas are often given credit for stimulating an interest in Discourse, and underlie much of the work carried out on Discourse Analysis, is Foucault, to whom Gee makes reference in Text B1.3.1 Extract 1. Foucault is interested in the interrelationship of Discourse and Power, and in particular, the way in which individuals are unaware of how they are 'constituted' by Discourses. He writes that 'Truth is a thing of this world; it is produced only by virtue of multiple forms of constraint. And it induces regular effects of power. Each society has its regime of truth, its "general politics" of truth: that is, the types of discourse which it accepts and makes function as true; the mechanisms and instances which enable one to distinguish true and false statements; the means by which each is sanctified; the techniques and procedures accorded value in the acquisition of truth; the status of those charged with saying what counts as truth' (1980:131).

UNIT B1.4   IDENTITY AND LANGUAGE LEARNING

The learning of a second or additional language, especially when it is 'forced' upon an individual by a (permanent) move to a new-language-speaking community is a process which is inextricably linked to issues of culture and identity. A number of studies have attempted to analyse the processes involved in learning a new language and/or adapting to life in a new cultural context.

A key study is that by Schumann (1976), reproduced in Brown (ed.) (1995). Schumann hypothesizes that two factors are significant in learning an additional language (or in Schumann's terminology, a 'second language'): 'social distance' and 'psychological distance'. For Schumann *social distance* '. . . pertains to the individual as a member of a social group which is in contact with another social group whose members speak a different language'. The degree of 'social solidarity' between the two groups will 'affect how a second language learning group acquires the language of a particular target language group. The assumption is that the greater the social distance between the two groups the more difficult it is for the members of the second language learning group to acquire the language of the target language group' (p. 267).

For Schumann 'psychological distance' in second language learning is determined by how the individual feels in the process of learning the second language. The process involves, first, 'language shock', the severity of which is influenced by how the individual learner reacts when confronted with new words and expressions (e.g. whether the learner feels confused, embarrassed or lost) and how the learner deals with such feelings. The second factor is 'culture shock': 'The learner experiences culture shock when he finds that his problem-solving and coping mechanisms do not work in the new culture. When they are used they do not get the accustomed results. Consequently, activities which were routine in his native country require great energy in the new culture. This situation causes disorientation, stress, fear, and anxiety. The resultant mental state can produce a whole syndrome of rejection which diverts attention and energy from second language learning. The learner, in attempting to find a cause for his disorientation, may reject himself, the people of the host country, the organization for which he is working, and even his own culture.' A third factor in psychological distance for Schumann is 'ego permeability', which is the ability that some people have 'to partially and temporarily give up their separateness of identity' and, as a consequence, be more effective learners of the second language (pp. 272–273).

We have some misgivings about Schumann's notion of 'social distance', and particularly about the way he defines 'social groups' as people who speak the language, and also the implication that speakers of the same language share the same culture. We find Schumann's notion of 'psychological distance', however, a valuable one, although we have some reservations about the way he defines 'language shock' and 'culture shock'. In this unit we consider the psychological processes involved in learning a new additional language at the same time as adapting to life in a new cultural context in light of more recent theories of culture, identity and language learning. We have chosen to focus on a particular autobiographical study of these processes, and a recent interpretation of this autobiographical study. The autobiographical study, written in 1989, is *Lost in Translation: A Life in a New Language* by Eva Hoffman, and the interpretation by Aneta Pavlenko and James Lantolf (2000) (along with interpretations of other similar autobiographical studies by writers originally from Eastern Europe). Pavlenko and Lantolf describe Hoffman's book, in which she details the processes involved in adapting to life in North America and in learning English following her emigration with her family from Poland to North America in 1959, as 'the most detailed and insightful description of second language socialization and acculturation to date' (pp. 163–4).

Pavlenko and Lantolf are particularly interested in how, in Hoffman's account (and in those of the other writers they feature), 'identities are reconstructed and life stories retold' in the process of learning an additional language in a new cultural context. They point to how there are two phases in the reconstruction of identity: 'the initial phase of loss', and 'the phase of recovery and reconstruction'. It is with a more detailed description of these two phases that the text begins.

<table>
<tr><td>Pavlenko, A. and Lantolf, J. P. 'Second Language Learning as Participation and the (Re)Construction of Selves' in Lantolf, J. P. (ed.) (2000) Sociocultural Theory and Second Language Learning, Oxford: Oxford University Press pp. 162–174 (extracts)</td><td>TEXT B1.4.1
A. Pavlenko and
J. P. Lantolf</td></tr>
</table>

The initial phase of loss can be segmented into five stages:

- loss of one's linguistic identity ('careless baptism', according to Hoffman 1989)
- loss of all subjectivities
- loss of the frame of reference and the link between the signifier and the signified
- loss of the inner voice
- first language attrition.

The phase of recovery and (re)construction encompasses four critical stages:

- appropriation of others' voices
- emergence of one's own new voice, often in writing first
- translation therapy: reconstruction of one's past
- continuous growth 'into' new positions and subjectivities.

Second language learning: phase of loss

. . . The first step on the route to self-translation, identified by Hoffman (1989:105), is a name change, often imposed. Due to this 'careless baptism' from Ewa and Alina, the author and

A. Pavlenko and
J. P. Lantolf

her sister become 'Eva' and 'Elaine'. What follows is a shattering loss of their linguistic identity:

> Nothing much has happened, except a small, seismic mental shift. The twist in our names takes them a tiny distance from us – but it's a gap into which the infinite hobgoblin of abstraction enters. Our Polish names didn't refer to us; they were as surely us as our eyes or hands. These new appellations, which we ourselves can't yet pronounce, are not us. They are identification tags, disembodied signs pointing to objects that happen to be my sister and myself . . . [They] make us strangers to ourselves.

At stake in the renaming process is, as Hoffman's commentary especially makes transparent, not merely a phonological problem to be overcome with some practice. It is about the conversion of subjects, actively embedded in their world, into objects no longer able to fully animate that world. In other words, it is about loss of agency in the world – an agency, in large part, constructed through linguistic means.

. . . Loss of agency is not only about severing one's union with the world inhabited by others, it is, and perhaps more profoundly so, about losing the connection to one's own inner world – the world of the mind. This is attested in several of the writers we examined, but it is most explicitly, and painfully, evidenced in the words of Hoffman (1989:107)

> I wait for that spontaneous flow of inner language which used to be my nighttime talk with myself . . . Nothing comes. Polish, in a short time, has atrophied, shriveled from sheer uselessness. Its words don't apply to my new experiences, they're not coeval with any of the objects, or faces, or the very air I breathe in the daytime. In English, the words have not penetrated to those layers of my psyche from which a private connection could proceed.

In the above passage Hoffman seems to be in a semantic twilight zone in which her inner speech in Polish has ceased to function, while the inner speech sparked by English, her new language, has yet to emerge. From a sociohistorical perspective, then, she has no way of organizing and making sense of her experiences.

. . . For a time, Hoffman's heroine is forced to live in a split universe, where the signifier has become severed from the signified. Ewa deeply mourns her inability to describe the world around her; her new words are simple referents without any conceptual systems or experiences to back them up:

> The words I learn now don't stand for things in the same unquestioned way they did in my native tongue. 'River' in Polish was a vital sound, energized with the essence of riverhood, of my rivers, of my being immersed in rivers. 'River' in English is cold – a word without an aura. It has no accumulated associations for me, and it does not give off the radiating haze of connotation. It does not evoke (Hoffman 1989:106).

Often, the inability of the 'new' language to intimately name the world (both inner and outer) is *accompanied by a deterioration* of that same ability in the native language. . . .

. . . The impact of the unraveling of a self is forcefully captured in Hoffman's words:

> Linguistic dispossession is a sufficient motive for violence, for it is close to the dispossession of one's self. Blind rage, helpless rage is rage that has no words – rage that overwhelms one with darkness. And if one is perpetually without words, if one exists in

the entropy of inarticulateness, that condition itself is bound to be an enraging frustration (Hoffman 1989:124).

A. Pavlenko and
J. P. Lantolf

Recovery and (re)construction: second language becoming

The initial step toward recovery and reconstruction of a self, . . . is the appropriation of others' voices. . . . We observe the beginnings of the recreation process in the following excerpt from Hoffman (1989:219–220):

> All around me, the Babel of American voices, hardy midwestern voices, sassy New York voices, quick youthful voices, voices arching under the pressure of various crosscurrents. . . . Since I lack a voice of my own, the voices of others invade me as if I were a silent ventriloquist. They ricochet within me, carrying on conversations, lending me their modulations, intonations, rhythms. I do not yet possess them; they possess me. But some of them satisfy a need; some of them stick to my ribs. . . . Eventually, the voices enter me; by assuming them, I gradually make them mine.

. . . Eventually, a new voice and with it a self gradually emerges. At first the voice is often captured in writing, in many cases in a diary, a private activity conducted in a public language, which grants 'the double distance of English and writing' (Hoffman 1989:121). For Hoffman her diary is a crucial stepping stone toward recovery of agency. It bestows upon her a new, English, 'written self' (*ibid.*). Because this self exists primarily in writing, it is experienced not as a fully agentive self, but as an 'impersonal' and 'objective' self, and even though Hoffman remarks that 'this language is beginning to invent another me' (*ibid.*), she is at first unable to deploy the quintessential indexical pronoun of agency, 'I'. Instead she is 'driven, as by a compulsion, to the double, the Siamese-twin "you" (*ibid.*).' Although at this point in her story, she acknowledges Eva as her public persona, she has not yet identified Eva with 'I' in her private mental domain. . . .

. . . Step by step, Hoffman's Ewa/Eva discovers and inhabits the new cultural space, learning to preserve appropriate distances, read subtle nuances, and act according to new cultural scripts. Slowly Ewa's second voice acquires increasing strength; Eva becomes a person in her own right, arriving at the realization that

> This goddamn place is my home now . . . I know all the issues and all the codes here. I'm as alert as a bat to all subliminal signals sent by word, look, gesture. I know who is likely to think what about feminism and Nicaragua and psychoanalysis and Woody Allen. . . . When I think of myself in cultural categories – which I do perhaps too often – I know that I'm a recognizable example of a species: a professional New York woman . . . I fit, and my surroundings fit me (Hoffman 1989:169–170).

. . . With regard to the bilinguals' narratives considered here, we believe that the problem confronting these individuals is the conflict that arises when they attempt to bring their past into the present. Their personal narratives and, consequently, their 'self' were constructed in a time and place constrained by conventions that differ from conventions of their present time and place. Thus, they have no way of making sense of the present and this, in turn, gives rise to the cognitive and affective dissonances reported in the narratives.

To overcome this difficulty, they are forced to reorganize, and, in some cases, organize anew, the plots of their life stories in line with the new set of conventions and social relationships sanctioned by the new community in which they find themselves. The result is the formation of new ways to mean (i.e. make sense of their experiences and of who they are). Without this restructuring, these individuals would remain on the margins of the new community in which they reside (but do not live). . . .

. . . At one point in her story Hoffman writes that her parents, in their new Anglo cultural setting, express their frustration at no longer knowing how to rear their own children:

> They don't try to exercise much influence over me anymore. 'In Poland, I would have known how to bring you up, I would have known what to do,' my mother says wistfully, but here, she has lost her sureness, her authority. She doesn't know how hard to scold Alinka [Eva's sister] when she comes home at late hours; she can only worry over her daughter's vague evening activities (Hoffman 1989:145).

At another point, Hoffman talks specifically about her loss of past and being trapped in the present and thus being unable to make full sense of her world and her place in it:

> I can't afford to look back, and I can't figure out how to look forward. In both directions, I may see a Medusa, and I already feel the danger of being turned into stone. Betwixt and between, I am stuck and time is stuck within me. Time used to open out, serene, shimmering with promise. If I wanted to hold a moment still, it was because I wanted to expand it, to get its fill. Now, time has no dimension, no extension backward or forward. I arrest the past, and I hold myself stiffly against the future; I want to stop the flow. As a punishment, I exist in the stasis of a perpetual present, that other side of 'living in the present', which is not eternity but a prison. I can't throw a bridge between the present and the past, and therefore I can't make time move (Hoffman 1989:116–17).

 ### Task B1.4.1

➤ How important would you say it is to learn the language, language variety or dialect of any cultural context if you are to fully understand its culture?
➤ Have you had any experience of being in an unfamiliar cultural context in which a language, language variety or dialect unknown or unfamiliar to you was the normal language of communication, and which you needed to learn?
➤ If so, did you:

- experience the same feelings Eva Hoffman describes
- experience the need to 'reconstruct' an identity, and, if so, did this involve the two phases described in the text by Pavlenko and Lantolf?

 ### Task B1.4.2

Pavlenko and Lantolf state the following in the text: 'her inner speech in Polish has ceased to function, while the inner speech sparked by English, her new language, has yet to emerge'.

➤ Do you believe that language consists of 'inner speech', as well as what might be called 'outer speech'?
➤ If so, what are the implications for the learning and teaching of an additional language?

Task B1.4.3

➤ Eva Hoffman writes that 'I know . . . all the codes here. I'm as alert as a bat to all subliminal signals sent by word, look, gesture.' Another account by a writer, Shirley Geok-Lin Lim, who made her life in the United States of America, provides a graphic example of how words, looks and gestures mark one as an outsider, even when you can communicate in the normal language of communication in that context (1996:300–1):

> There are many ways in which America tells you you don't belong. The eyes that slide around to find another face behind you. The smiles that only appear after you have almost passed them, intended for someone else. The stiffness in the body as you stand beside them watching your child and theirs slide down the pole, and the relaxed smile when another white mother comes up to talk. The polite distance as you say something about the children at the swings and the chattiness when a white parent makes a comment. A polite people, it is the facial muscles, the shoulder tension, and the silence that give away white Americans' uneasiness with people not like them.

➤ Think of a particular speech community or ('small') culture that you are a member of or are familiar with. What looks and gestures are specific to this ('small') culture or speech community, what do they mean and how do they mark one as an 'insider' or 'outsider'?

➤ Have you had similar experiences to those described by Shirley Geok-Lin Lim?

➤ What are the implications for those who work with people who need to adapt to life in a new cultural context and, at the same time, need to learn an additional language to function in this cultural context? Consider the following: teachers (in general); language teachers; people working for government and non-governmental agencies (e.g. the police, social services support personnel, health professionals).

Commentary

The discussion by Pavlenko and Lantolf of 'inner speech' that we considered in Task B1.4.2 draws on the work of a number of theorists, including Vygotsky and Bakhtin. A prime interest of Vygotsky is the relationship between thought, meaning and words. In his seminal work *Thought and Language* (1986:218, 251), Vygotsky writes that: 'Thought is not merely expressed through words; it comes into existence through them. Every thought tends to connect with something else, to establish a relation between things. Every thought moves, grows and develops, fulfils a function, solves a problem. . . . Precisely because thought does not have its automatic counterpart in words, the transition of thought to word leads through meaning. In our speech there is always the hidden thought, the subtext.' In text B1.4.1 Hoffman writes that 'this language [i.e. English] is beginning to invent another me'. The notion that language *invents* rather than *defines* a person is an interesting one, and brings to mind the view of Bakhtin (1984:201), who writes that 'when a member of a speaking collective comes upon a word, it is not as a neutral word of language, not as a word free from the aspirations and evaluations of others, uninhabited by others' voices. No, he receives the word from another's voice and filled with that other voice. The word enters his context from another context, permeated with the interpretations of others. His own thought finds the word already inhabited.'

Another interesting interpretation of Eva Hoffman's autobiographical study is by Wierzbicka (1994), who focuses on how 'different cultures have different attitudes towards emotions' (p. 156) and highlights in detail such differences in Polish and 'Anglo' cultures, with examples from Hoffman's book to exemplify these differences. We have reservations, however, about the views expressed by Wierzbicka, and these are similar to our reservations about the theories of Schumann that we stated at the beginning of this unit: is it useful and appropriate to talk of large 'Polish' and 'Anglo' cultures (or even of 'Anglo-American' and 'Anglo-Australian' cultures which Wierzbicka mentions)? Can language itself be responsible for differences in attitudes and orientations towards emotions and feelings? In connection with the first reservation, it is perhaps significant that near the end of the book Eva Hoffman describes herself not in terms of 'Anglo' or 'Anglo-American' culture, but in terms of a much smaller culture: 'When I think of myself in cultural categories – which I do perhaps too often – I know that I'm a recognizable example of a species: a professional New York woman' (pp. 169–170). We will return to the second of these reservations in Unit B2.3.

UNIT B1.5   IDENTITY, COMMUNITY AND THE INTERNET

The Internet has opened up previously unimagined possibilities for communication between individuals and 'communities' (in the broadest sense). Such communication has had an impact upon how we view ourselves and others, and has forced a re-evaluation of what 'communication', 'community' and 'identity' mean. Gergen (1996:132) writes that 'With the proliferation of communication technologies, we are first exposed to an ever expanding vocabulary of being. No longer do we dwell within the boundaries of a single geographically contained community, a region, an ethnicity, or even a culture. We have not a single satisfying intelligibility within which to dwell, but through the process of social saturation, we are immersed in a plethora of understandings – the psychological ontologies of varying ethnicities, class strata, geographic sectors, racial and religious groupings, professional enclaves, and nationalities . . .'.

In this unit two texts are featured: the first, by Burkhalter, is concerned with how racial identity is an important factor in usenet discussions; while in the second, the transcript of part of an interview of Stuart Hall, a key figure in Cultural Studies, the question of what implications the Internet has for the notion of 'community' is discussed.

Burkhalter, B. 'Reading Race Online: Discovering racial identity in usenet discussions' in Smith M. A. and Kollock, P. (eds) (1999) *Communities in Cyberspace*, London: Routledge pp. 63–69, 72–73 (extracts)

TEXT B1.5.1
B. Burkhalter

Racial identity

In face-to-face interaction an individual's physical characteristics, from skin color to vocal patterns, help convey racial identity. Lacking such physical cues on computer networks, one might predict that discrimination on the basis of race, age, gender, sexuality, class, status, and group membership would disappear. Indeed, some participants use the lack of physical cues to claim any identity they want. An SCAA message suggests: 'You are welcome here! Come on in. Would you like a beer or something? The only true color here is the monitor. Here I can be Black, White or Green.'

The sense of freedom when establishing an online racial identity derives from a persistent belief that racial categorization is determined exclusively by corporeal traits. Although much sociologic and anecdotal evidence has challenged this belief, race is still popularly seen as a characteristic of bodies (Spickard 1992). The body does not reveal race irrefutably. Multiracial individuals chronicle incidents in which their physical attributes were variously interpreted. The question multiracial individuals are so often asked – 'what are you?' – displays the problematic relationship between physical characteristics and racial identity. The possibility of passing or being mistaken for a different race in face-to-face interaction is also evidence of the fallible relationship between observable traits and identity (Bradshaw 1992). Of course, answers to the question 'what are you?' must be appropriate to the individual's observable characteristics. Physical characteristics are a resource that permit and limit a range of interpretations, but they are only one medium among a variety of resources.

In online interactions, participants are reduced to textual resources, but these resources can be just as determinant as physical indicators are offline. The posts show that racial identity, although fixed differently than it is offline, is firmly established online. [pp. 63–64]

Identity disputes

Over the course of a single message, authors may racially identify themselves in several ways. In the following message, . . . which generated a small thread over a few days, the author employs a hodgepodge of identity cues:

> Hi. I find that many African-Americans where I live (northern California) tend to act in a way they think they should act, rather than just be themselves. I'm acknowledging this because the reality is, the behavior of the minority completely stands out, as opposed to the behavior of the majority. I must say, that I am part African-American. I don't feel ashamed of this in any way, but I am ashamed of the African-American behavior of many citizens in my area. I am proud of all the ethnicities my gene pool possesses, while at the same time, I am proud of the ethnicities I don't possess. I ACCEPT those who are different from me. Different is good: it is new. It is unique. It is you. It is me. Let me explain more of what hits home for me. I must say that I am extremely proud of my mom: She is African-American and she is an individual. She speaks proper English because she chose to get an education, no matter how difficult that path would be. She's had a tough life; she grew up poor in Michigan; her mother died when she was five; she lived in foster homes her whole life; she was looked down upon because of status and her pigmentation. She is a very beautiful person. There are many more hardships to tell about her, but my point is, she's African-American and she is an individual. I want to let African-Americans know

B. Burkhalter

that they don't have to act 'black'. It doesn't make you more of an 'African-American' to do things you think Blacks should do. I've had friends who felt that acting 'black' was cool, both black and white ones. Did you know much of what many people refer to as being black resulted from their overseers who were known as 'poor white trash'? It's true. They were the ones the slaves learned English from, yet many people don't realize this. Please let me know that the majority of African-Americans are not like the ones I see on Ricki Lake. They don't have attitudes, move their necks from side to side, wave their hands in people's faces, speak loud and improper English, don't listen to what people are saying, don't speak out vulgarly, don't resort to violence because they can articulate how they feel. I'm not trying to put down African-Americans, I want to recognize a problem in the United States. The more people group themselves in simplistic categories, based on skin color, the harder it will be for ALL of us to get along, live as the HUMANS we are . . . Ask me what my culture is and I'll tell you 'I'm American'. [pp. 67–68]

Racial identity and disagreement

. . . identity challenges do not occur often. However, when participants dispute an author's perspective they often challenge the author's identity. Though disagreements come in various forms, one recurrent practice for disputing an author's arguments involves challenges to an author's identity . . . respondents' challenges to an author's identity dispute the social position from which the author makes his/her claim. Instead of arguing with the author's view of the world by presenting a contrasting view, respondents attempt to invalidate the argument by invalidating the author's claimed social position. The first reply to the above post mentions little on the issue of African-Americans acting Black, instead focusing on the author's identity:

I'm acknowledging this because the reality is, the behavior of the minority completely stands out, as opposed to the behavior of the majority. I must say, that I am part African-American. I don't feel ashamed of this in any way, but I am ashamed of the African-American behavior of many citizens in my area.

emphasis on the "part African-American"? why are you ashamed of people you don't personally know? (unless of course, you are referring to the [African-American] folks from your personal lineage?) do you bear the burden for speaking for the race you "partially" belong to?

I am proud of all the ethnicities my gene pool possesses, while at the same time, I am proud of the ethnicities I don't possess. I ACCEPT those who are different from me. Different is good: It is new. It is unique. It is you. It is me.

ummm, excuse me but this little Pollyanna statement just negated the part where you wept tears over the behavior of total strangers. If different is good, you should absolutely love those [African-Americans] that are causing you such embarrassment, doncha think? me thinks you bear more pride for the paler side of your life. perhaps that is who is speaking in this message?

[pp. 68–69]

Consequences for race online

B. Burkhalter

In online discussions, readers treat racial identities as entailing particular perspectives. Offline has a name for the imputation of a characteristic, attitude, belief, or practice based solely on someone's race – 'stereotyping'. An observer may use physical characteristics to impute a racial identity and from that impute a delimited set of beliefs and perspectives. For example, after I confirmed that I was Black in a recent conversation, the talk turned to professional basketball. My co-interactants assumed that a Black male would be interested in basketball. While this stereotyping is not surprising, imagine that, on hearing of their interest in basketball, I had assumed they were Black. This would also be stereotyping, but an unusual variety. Stereotyping in face-to-face interaction follows from an assumed racial identity. Online interaction differs in that the imputation tends to go in the other direction – from stereotype to racial identity.

A discrepancy arises when a person identified as a member of a particular racial group by his or her physical characteristics offers a perspective that is inconsistent with the stereotype of that group. In face-to-face interactions, such an inconsistency can be resolved by modifying the stereotype or seeing the person as an anomaly – rarely are the person's physical racial indicators disputed. In online interactions perspectives resist modification because participants confront an immutable text, whereas racial identifications can be challenged. [pp. 72–73]

Task B1.5.1

Burkhalter states in the text that in face-to-face interaction 'an individual's physical characteristics, from skin color to vocal patterns, help convey racial identity.' Consider:

➤ What physical characteristics, as well as 'skin color' and 'vocal patterns' can help to convey racial identity?

Task B1.5.2

Burkhalter writes in the text that 'the question multiracial individuals are so often asked – "what are you?" – displays the problematic relationship between physical characteristics and racial identity'.

Difficulty in giving a straight answer to this question was experienced by the US golfer Tiger Woods, who on the *Oprah Winfrey Show* in 1997 described himself as 'Cablinasian', a mixture of Caucasian, Black, Indian and Asian. Similar difficulty is highlighted by Claudine Chiawei O'Hearn (1998:xiv), who writes that 'for those of us who fall between the cracks, being "black", being "white", being "Latino", is complicated. . . . Skin color and place of birth aren't accurate signifiers of identity. One and one don't necessarily add up to two. Cultural and racial amalgams create a third, wholly indistinguishable category where origin and home are indeterminate. . . . What name do you give to someone who is a quarter, an eight, a half? What kind of measuring stick might give an accurate estimation?'

Think of other individuals in the public eye and/or people you know personally who also 'fall between the cracks'.

Extension

> How do they define themselves?
> How do others define them?

 Task B1.5.3

Analyse the first usenet message in Text B1.5.1 (beginning 'Hi. I find that many African-Americans . . .'). Burkhalter writes that 'authors may racially identify themselves in several ways. In the following message, . . . the author employs a hodgepodge of identity cues'.

> How does the author of this message identify him/herself? What 'identity cues' does the author employ?

TEXT B1.5.2   Martin Jacques interviews Professor Stuart Hall, Open University, accessed at www.usyd.edu.au/su/social/papers/hall1.html . . . (extracts)

MARTIN: There's a lot of talk of the utopian possibilities opened up by the Internet, of creating a sort of new kind of global community in which people can freely communicate with each other – you can choose what you want to talk about, when you want to talk about it, identities become much more flexible. How do you see all that?

STUART: . . . Let's talk about those two things separately. Obviously the technology does enable linkages to be made across a whole number of barriers and frontiers of language and distance and experience and differences between standards of life and expectations and so on. It allows conversations, sharing of experience across the confines of space. What it does is to transcend space and that's an interesting conception of community because our older conception of community is very, I think, tied to the notion of localities, people living in face-to-face contact with one another. That's what we mean, by communities all huddled together as it were. Actually, of course, there have always been communities which are much wider than that. One's always shared things with people with whom one doesn't live face to face – one shares musical taste with people on the other side of the world – and increasingly because of the media anyway it seems to me, those communities of choice, communities of taste, communities of interest have been growing. What you call symbolic communities have been growing alongside the communities of space and residence and I think the Internet and all that's associated with the new information technology sort of expands in a multiple way the possibilities of sharing the conversations across these different divides. I think a second element of community does have to do with the degree of the knowledge base or information base. My own feeling at the moment is that the Internet is much more useful in terms of information than it is in terms of ideas. My e-mail contains hardly any ideas at all, but it contains lots of information, some of which is useful. So that is empowering for communities, communities that you know have been locked into their own histories, their own economies, their own cultures and can only reach out . . . where they have access to alternative models . . . I know exciting things that are going on in which people in inner cities in Los Angeles are talking to people in inner cities in Johannesburg, and sharing what is common about living in inner cities now. Of course, these two peoples are not the same but they have a common background, some cultural and historical background which they've never spoken about to one another cos they've never had access to a technology which enables them to communicate in that way . . . but

I don't think one should assume just because one's talking in a rather informal and familiar and open way to a lot of different people that one is getting at the deeper complexities of experience which, you know, may have historical roots or unconscious roots or symbolic roots etc., which would take a long time to explore . . . When one talks about sharing a culture, nine-tenths of that is shared unconsciously, it's how you know how to speak the language with somebody, it's not because you know the rules of the grammar. I think the Internet may or may not lead us to be able to share in depth in that way but I don't think it necessarily does and I don't think a lot of the conversations that are being talked about now are really of that quality.

MARTIN: What do you see as the relationship over time between the traditional sense of a community that you were describing earlier and the community of choice – for example, the Internet?

STUART: . . . We are moving more towards belonging to multiple communities, symbolic communities, communities of choice, and further and further away from belonging to communities of traditional location . . . what I think we are going to see is . . . many fewer traditional communities existing of the kind that we've had before, much less closure, much less homogenous identification. What I mean by that is where all your identities overlap; your identity as a parent, as a worker, in your leisure time, in your love life, in your intellectual interests, are all found in the same community, and I think increasingly we'll belong to a variety of communities and we'll learn to manipulate ourselves, reflexively, very differently, the different parts of ourselves for these different conversations. The Internet is in a way, a kind of mirror in cyberspace of the multiplicity of identity, the weakening of homogenous identities, and the multiplicity of identities which we are able to live in and inhabit. . . .

Task B1.5.4

Stuart Hall expresses his belief that the Internet is 'much more useful in terms of information than it is in terms of ideas', and that it is not yet able to really help people to get at 'the deeper complexities of experience' and to 'share in depth'.

➤   What do you think Hall means?
➤   Do you share his views?

Task B1.5.5

Stuart Hall says in the interview that 'We are moving more towards belonging to multiple communities, symbolic communities, communities of choice, and further and further away from belonging to communities of traditional location . . . what I think we are going to see is . . . many fewer traditional communities existing of the kind that we've had before . . .'

➤   What 'multiple communities, symbolic communities, communities of choice' do you think he has in mind?
➤   Do you think that in your own cultural context there will be 'fewer traditional communities' in the future?

Commentary

In Text B1.5.2 Stuart Hall cautions against jumping to too hasty conclusions about the changes the Internet can bring in terms of 'community'. Jones and Kucker (2001: 221) believe that the very word 'community' is not an appropriate word to apply to the Internet, since the 'speed with which we move from place to place online renders any traditional notions of community obsolete' and 'it is increasingly difficult, in a medium built (and continuously imagined) for movement, to develop . . . relatively stable communities'.

Such a reflection points to an important wider issue. This is to do with whether existing concepts, and their realisation in language, are adequate to describe and discuss the rapid changes that the Internet has brought. In the introductory section of this unit I highlighted the words of Gergen, that 'With the proliferation of communication technologies, we are first exposed to an ever-expanding vocabulary of being.' Certainly, the rapid emergence of the Internet, and other information technology, has brought rapid changes to the (English) language. This has not just been in the sense that new terminology has emerged to refer to features and processes of this information technology. It has also been in the sense that we have been forced to redefine and broaden our interpretation of such terms as 'identity', 'community' and 'culture' in light of such technological changes.

Theme 2
Otherization

OTHERIZATION: FOCUS ON JAPAN

I refer in Unit B2.4 to the numerous popular guides published for those visiting, living in and working in, 'foreign' cultural contexts. Possibly more popular manuals have been written about visiting, living in and working in Japan than any other country. In Unit B2.1 Text B2.1.2 is an extract from such a manual, written specifically for members of the US business community who are doing business in Japan. Text B2.1.3, written by Japanese social scientist Yoshio Sugimoto, raises interesting issues that relate to the views expressed by the writer of Text B2.1.2, Boye/Lafayette De Mente.

Unit B2.1 is the first unit relating to Theme 2, 'Otherization', a concept that is the concern of Text B2.1.1. In the text reference is made to the work of Said, whose work (1978; 1993) has been largely responsible in both academic and more public circles for focusing attention on the processes in which those nations and their people on the 'peripheries' of the world, and particularly those who have been colonised and domi-nated by one or more of the European powers, have been framed by the Discourses of the colonisers. In *Orientalism* (1978:4) Said states his belief that 'the Orient' is a social construct: 'The Orient is not an inert fact of nature . . . both geographical and cultural entities – to say nothing of historical entities – such locales, regions, geographical sectors, as 'Orient' and 'Occident' are man-made. Therefore as much as the West itself, the Orient is an idea that has a history and a tradition of thought, imagery and vocabulary that have given it reality and presence in and for the West.' In addition, 'Orientalism depends for its strategy on . . . flexible positional superiority, which puts the Westerner in a whole series of possible relationships with the Orient without him ever losing the relative upper hand.' It is the nature of this 'flexible positional superiority' that is the basis of 'Otherization', as Edgar and Sedgwick (1999) suggest in Text B2.1.1.

We will consider 'Otherization' in relation to the other two featured texts in this unit and also focus on a number of further dimensions to the notion in the other four units related to Theme 2.

Edgar, A. and Sedgwick, P. (1999) *Key concepts in cultural theory*, London: Routledge p. 266

The Other

. . . In the context of theories of culture, perhaps the most prominent contemporary use of this notion has been made by Said. In these terms, the Other may be designated as a form of cultural

A. Edgar and
P. Sedgwick

projection of concepts. This projection constructs the identities of cultural subjects through a relationship of power in which the Other is the subjugated element. In claiming knowledge about 'orientals' what Orientalism did was construct them as its own (European) Other. Though describing purportedly 'oriental' characteristics (irrational, uncivilised etc.) Orientalism provided a definition not of the real 'oriental' identity, but of European identity in terms of the oppositions which structured its account. Hence, 'irrational' Other presupposes (and is also presupposed by) 'rational' self. The construction of the Other in Orientalist discourse, then, is a matter of asserting self-identity: and the issue of the European account of the Oriental Other is thereby rendered a question of power.

TEXT B2.1.2

Boye/Lafayette De Mente 'Beware of Using Logic in Japan!' (accessed online at www.executiveplanet.com/community/items/970695928954_en.asp? section= Japan) (extracts)

TOKYO – The cultural canyons between Japan and many Western countries – the United States in particular – remain broad and deep, despite more than half a century of massive interaction on every social, economic and political level.

From an American viewpoint, one of the most irrational and frustrating of these cultural chasms is the difference between the Japanese and American view and use of logic – ronri (roan-ree) in Japanese – a difference that has an especially profound effect on political as well as economic relations between the two countries.

As is well known, Americans and other Westerners pride themselves on thinking and behaving in a logical manner . . .

Still today, few things turn older Japanese off more rapidly and more completely than for someone to take a purely logical approach to personal, business and political relations. They regard positions and presentations that are based on logic as being cold and calculating, as failing to take into consideration the human and spiritual element.

On innumerable occasions, I have sat in on presentations by visiting American business (sic) that were perfect examples of logical reasoning only to see the Japanese side become increasingly uncomfortable and withdrawn, unable to reconcile their own values with the rationale of the Americans.

Japanese logic is based on cultural imperatives that have to do with creating and sustaining the kind of cooperative, harmonious relationships on which their society was based for many centuries . . .

The main point of difference in Western logic and Japanese ronri is that in its Japanese context logic does not necessarily equate with rationalism. It can, in fact, fly in the face of reason so long as it satisfies a human or spiritual element that the Japanese hold dear.

In Japanese dialogue it is perfectly logical to conceal one's real thoughts and intentions (honne/hoan-nay) behind a public facade (tatemae/tah-tay-my) by using words and phrases that are so abstract they are meaningless, or that give a false impression.

In such cases, which are the rule rather than the exception in most formal situations, it is left up to the listener to divine the true meaning or intentions of the speaker – a process that requires comprehensive knowledge of the Japanese language and culture; a skill that the Japanese refer to as haragei (hah-rah-gay-ee) or 'the art of the stomach,' which could be translated into English as reading the other person's mind.

It is also logical in the Japanese concept of things for responsibility to be diffused among a group rather than placed on an individual. . . .

When serious mistakes or criminal activity do occur in a Japanese company or government organization, it is Japanese logic for the head of the group to take responsibility and resign in a symbolic gesture that makes it possible to maintain the facade of harmony in the organization.

TEXT B2.1.2

Misrepresenting things, telling lies and engaging in other cover-up activities are logical in the traditional Japanese environment – logical when their purpose is to protect the group and the system. . . .

The two main sanctions used by the Japanese system to enforce conformity to Japanese logic are bullying and ostracizing. The bullying by coworkers and superiors can be sadistic and continuous. The ultimate tactic is to completely ostracize the guilty party.

Of course, most Japanese are perfectly capable of logical thinking in the Western mold, but their attitudes and behavior are controlled by the groups they belong to, and with rare exceptions they are not brave enough, strong enough or foolhardy enough to break the codes that bind them.

Task B2.1.1

➤ Do you believe that Text B2.1.2 is an example of 'Otherization' as described by Edgar and Sedgwick in Text B2.1.1?

More specifically:

➤ To what extent are the Japanese 'designated as a form of cultural projection of concepts'?
➤ Is there in Text B2.1.2 'a relationship of power in which the Other is the subjugated element'?
➤ Is there any suggestion in Text B2.1.2 that 'irrational' Other presupposes (and is also presupposed by) 'rational' self?

Sugimoto, Y. (1997) *An Introduction to Japanese Society*, Cambridge: Cambridge University Press pp. 1–4, pp. 11–13 (extracts)

TEXT B2.1.3
Y. Sugimoto

Multicultural Japan

Suppose that a being from a different planet arrived in Japan and wanted to meet a typical Japanese, one who best typified the Japanese adult population. Whom should the social scientists choose? To answer this question, several factors would have to be considered: gender, occupation, educational background, and so on.

To begin, the person chosen should be a female, because women outnumber men in Japan: the 1990 census shows that sixty-three million women and sixty million men live in the Japanese archipelago. With regard to occupation, she would definitely not be employed in a large corporation but would work in a small enterprise, since fewer than one in eight workers is employed in a company with three hundred or more employees. Nor would she be guaranteed life-time employment, since those who work under this arrangement amount at most to only a quarter of Japan's workforce. She would not belong to a labor union, because less than a quarter of Japanese workers are unionized. She would not be university educated. . . .

The identification of the average Japanese would certainly involve much more complicated quantitative analysis. But the alien would come closer to the 'center' of the Japanese population by choosing a female, non-unionized and non-permanent employee in a small business without

Y. Sugimoto

university education than a male, unionized, permanent employee with a university degree working for a large company.

When outsiders visualize the Japanese, however, they tend to think of men rather than women, career employees in large companies rather than non-permanent workers in small firms, and university graduates rather than high-school leavers, for these are the images presented on television and in newspaper and magazine articles. Some academic studies have also attempted to generalize about Japanese society on the basis of observations of its male elite sector, and have thereby helped to reinforce this sampling bias. Moreover, because a particular cluster of individuals who occupy high positions in a large company have greater access to mass media and publicity, the life-styles and value orientations of those in that cluster have acquired a disproportionately high level of visibility in the analysis of Japanese society at the expense of the wider cross-section of its population.

While every society is unique in some way, Japan is particularly unusual in having so many people who believe that their country is unique. Regardless of whether Japan is 'uniquely unique' in sociological and psychological reality, it is certainly unique for the number of Japanese pub-lications which propagate the unique Japan argument. The so-called group model of Japanese society represents the most explicit and coherent formulation of this line of argument and remains the most influential framework for interpreting the Japanese and Japanese social structure. Put most succinctly, the model is based upon three lines of argument.

First, at the individual, psychological level, the Japanese are portrayed as having a personality which lacks a fully developed ego or independent self. The best-known example of this claim is Doi's notion of amae which refers to the allegedly unique psychological inclination among the Japanese to seek emotional satisfaction by prevailing upon and depending on their superiors. They feel no need for any explicit demonstration of individuality. Loyalty to the group is a primary value. Giving oneself to the promotion and realization of the group's goals gives the Japanese a special psychological satisfaction.

Second, at the interpersonal, intragroup level, human interaction is depicted in terms of Japanese group orientation. According to Nakane, for example, the Japanese attach great importance to the maintenance of harmony *within* the group. To that end, relationships between superiors and inferiors are carefully cultivated and maintained. One's status within the group depends on the length of one's membership in the group. Furthermore, the Japanese maintain particularly strong interpersonal ties with those in the same hierarchical chain of command within their own organization. In other words, vertical loyalties are dominant. The vertically organized Japanese contrast sharply with Westerners, who tend to form horizontal groups which define their membership in terms of such criteria as class and stratification which cut across hierarchical organization lines.

Finally, at the intergroup level, the literature has emphasized that integration and harmony are achieved effectively *between* Japanese groups, making Japan a 'consensus society'. . . .

At least four underlying assumptions remain constant in these studies. First, it is presumed that *all* Japanese share the attribute in question – be it *amae* or miniature orientation – regardless of their class, gender, occupation, and other stratification variables. Second, it is also assumed that there is virtually no variation among the Japanese in the degree to which they possess the characteristic in question. Little attention is given to the possibility that some Japanese may have it in greater degree while others have very little of it. Third, the trait in question, be it group-orientation or *kanjin*, is supposed to exist only marginally in other societies, particularly in Western societies. That is, the feature is thought to be uniquely Japanese. Finally, the fourth presupposition is an ahistorical assumption that the trait has prevailed in Japan for an unspecified period of time, independently of historical circumstances. . . .

Japanese culture, like the cultures of other complex societies, comprises a multitude of subcultures. Some are dominant, powerful, and controlling, and form core subcultures in given

Y. Sugimoto

dimensions. Examples are the management subculture in the occupational dimension, the large corporation subculture in the firm-size dimension, the male subculture in the gender dimension, and the Tokyo subculture in the regional dimension. Other subcultures are more subordinate, subservient, or marginal, and may be called the peripheral subcultures. Some examples are the part-time worker subculture, the small business subculture, the female subculture, and the rural subcultures.

Core subcultures have ideological capital to define the normative framework of society. Even though the life-time employment and the company-first dogma associated with the large corporation subculture apply to less than a quarter of the workforce, that part of the population has provided a role-model which all workers are expected to follow, putting their companies ahead of their individual interests. The language of residents in uptown Tokyo is regarded as standard Japanese not because of its linguistic superiority but because of those residents' social proximity to the national power center. . . .

. . . the slanted views of Japan's totality tend to reproduce because writers, readers, and editors of publications on the general characteristics of Japanese society belong to the core subcultural sphere. Sharing their subcultural base, they conceptualize and hypothesize in a similar way, confirm their portrayal of Japan between themselves, and rarely seek outside confirmation. In many *Nihonjinron* writings, most examples and illustrations are drawn from the elite sector, including male employees in managerial tracks of large corporations and high-ranking officials of the national bureaucracy.

Core subcultural groups overshadow those on the periphery in inter-cultural transactions too. Foreign visitors to Japan who shape the images of Japan in their own countries interact more intensely with core sub-cultural groups than with peripheral ones. In cultural exchange programs, Japanese who have houses, good salaries, and university education predominate among the host families, language trainers, and introducers of Japanese culture. Numerically small but ideologically dominant, core subcultural groups are the most noticeable to foreigners and are capable of presenting themselves to the outside world as representative of Japanese culture.

Task B2.1.2

➤ What different perspectives on Japanese identity does Sugimoto provide in Text B2.1.3 that differ from those provided by Boye/Lafayette De Mente in Text B2.1.2?

Task B2.1.3

Interestingly, Sugimoto writes that it is not just popular guides published *outside* Japan for those visiting, living in and working in Japan, that 'propagate the unique Japan argument', but numerous Japanese publications as well.

➤ Try to find examples of descriptions of the 'culture' of the country you live in published both in your country, *and* in another country (you will find extracts from such guides on the Internet, as I did in the case of Text B2.1.2).
➤ Do either or both of these guides propagate the argument that your country is 'unique'?
➤ If so, what is the nature of this uniqueness?

Extension

Task B2.1.4

➤ What are the implications of what Sugimoto writes in Text B2.1.3 for how we understand and describe other cultures?

➤ What are the implications for those involved in 'intercultural' training programmes?

Commentary

Billig *et al.* (1988:16) write that 'Many words are not mere labels which neutrally package up the world. They also express moral evaluations, and such terms frequently come in antithetical opposites which enable opposing moral judgements to be made.' We will investigate this issue further in Units B3.4 and B3.5; suffice it to say for now that the lexical choices made in Text B2.1.2 to describe the Japanese are good examples of how 'moral evaluations' and 'moral judgements' are expressed.

'Intercultural' training is a rapidly growing field in many parts of the world, and often, as Hannerz suggested in Unit B0.1 Text B0.1.1, the efforts of those involved in carrying out such training, who may have the best of intentions, may be misdirected since they propagate stereotypes and myths of national identity through, at best, simplistic representation and, at worst, divisive otherization. The ways in which other cultures are represented in such training, and in the materials and activities that are designed to aid this training, are of vital importance not only to how people view individuals from and in other cultures, but also to how they act when in communication with them.

UNIT B2.2   IMAGES OF THE OTHER

In this unit we focus on 'image', both in its literal sense of visual representation, and in its broader sense of what Miriam Cooke terms 'preconception built on the weak and resilient foundations of myth and [visual] image'. In Text B2.2.1 Cooke explores how our preconceptions intervene in how we perceive and communicate with each other, and writes specifically about the images held in 'the West' of Muslim women.

We live in a time when most of us are surrounded by visual images, both static and moving, in different forms of the mass media. Some go so far as to say that 'we have moved from a *logocentric* (word-centred) to an *occulocentric* (image-centred) world' (Berger AA (1995:79)); Baudrillard (1993:194) goes even further and claims that the world 'is caught up in a mad pursuit of images'.

Yet until fairly recently, when compared with the number of studies on the role of the word in helping to construct reality, there had been relatively few investigations of the part played by images, and particularly of photographs. This is perhaps because, as Bignell (1997:102) suggests, 'photographs appear to denote the things they show, and simply record what is in front of the camera without the intervention of language and culture'; however, this view is misguided since 'there can be no such thing as a purely "denotative" photograph'.

In Text B2.2.2 we go on to consider the discussion of Solomos and Back on how in advertising – and, particularly, the advertising of Benetton clothes by Oliviero Toscani – visual images of racial identity are made deliberately ambiguous, and visual images of racial difference used for particular effect.

Cooke, M. (1997) 'Listen to the Image Speak', *Cultural Values* 1: 1 pp. 101–2, 104, 105, 106 (extracts)

TEXT B2.2.1
M. Cooke

. . . I argue that the major block to respect of and communication with the unknown is preconception built on the weak and resilient foundations of myth and image.

Images are flat impressions that provide pieces of information. They are like photographs that frame and freeze a fragment of the real and then project it as the whole. What was dynamic and changing becomes static. Just as a snapshot provides a true, if partial, picture, so these cultural images contain some truth. That is why they are so hard to change. Just as the image of the amoral, free-living American woman epitomizes for many pious Muslims all that is wrong with Western culture, so the image of the veiled woman encapsulates for the Western observer all the coercion imagined to mark Islamic culture. Women are easily turned by outsiders into emblems of their culture, for within the culture itself women are often made into custodians of their culture's values. No matter how many non-promiscuous, modest Western women the Muslim may meet, no matter how many assertive, independent, unveiled Muslim women the Westerner may meet, there is a possibility that the basic image will not change as these individuals come to be seen as exceptions to a rule that they thereby serve to reinforce. These images are the context of a first encounter between two people who know little if anything about each other.

Images we have of each other are always part of the baggage that we bring to dialogue. Sometimes we are at the mercy of the image our addressee has of us or chooses to invoke. Sometimes we hide behind the image. Sometimes we act *as though* neither of us had an image of the other. Sometimes, those ideal times, the image disappears and the contact is unmediated by the myth. Then we can act as individuals between whom messages pass easily regardless of the contact, code or context.

In September 1996, the Aspen Institute Berlin invited me to participate in a conference entitled 'The Images of Muslim Women in the West'. . . . Throughout the summer I wondered why the image of Muslim women as passive and oppressed has so much power. I have come to believe that this is probably the case because 'Muslim Women' refers not only to a specific group but also to a general category. They are only sometimes both Muslim and women; they are often fused into a single category – Muslims in general and even so nebulous a concept as 'Islam', a term covering both the religion and the culture. However, regardless of whether the reference to 'Muslim Women' is specific women who happen to be Muslims, or slips seamlessly into the general (women who represent a faith and a culture), their look is the same: they are more or less exotic, more or less veiled, more or less armed. The meanings attached to their uniform appearance will differ depending on whether it is the Muslim or the woman who is being considered – a victim of patriarchy or a symbol of a fanatic faith. Since the general association with Islam is the most common, and Islam has long been negatively portrayed in the West, it is not surprising that its key emblem, women, should also be subject to sensationalist misrepresentation.

Most Muslim women and men live in Asia and Africa, hence they are not only Muslim but also Asians and Africans. When we think about them, try to represent them, and teach about them, we run the risk of confounding geographic, linguistic, racial, ethnic, religious and cultural categories. Thus, the fact that they are Syrian, Indonesian, Nigerian, Pakistani and American women, who speak dozens of languages and derive from a great many ethnic roots, becomes less significant than that they happen to practice a particular faith. After all, we can more easily identify as Muslim, rather than Egyptian or Pakistani, a woman we see in some form of *purdah*. The faith position overrides all other particularities to become the primary identity.

Journalists and scholars in the USA are fascinated by this assumed homogeneity of the Muslim world. Far from wanting to complicate this image, many seem intent on reinforcing it. The image is an object of desire. As Bhabha writes (1994:75), the stereotype 'gives access to an "identity" which is predicated as much on mastery and pleasure as it is on anxiety and defense, for it is a form of multiple and contradictory belief in its recognition of difference and disavowal of it'.

Task B2.2.1

Cooke writes in the second paragraph of Text B2.2.1 that: 'No matter how many non-promiscuous, modest Western women the Muslim may meet, no matter how many assertive, independent, unveiled Muslim women the Westerner may meet, there is a possibility that the basic image will not change as these individuals come to be seen as exceptions to a rule that they thereby serve to reinforce. These images are the context of a first encounter between two people who know little if anything about each other.'

➤ Do you agree with Cooke that, when we meet a person for the first time, the images (i.e. preconceptions) we have of people of a similar background will partly determine how we react to, and interact with, that person?

➤ How important a part do you think visual images we have come across of people of a similar background play in these preconceptions?

➤ Can you think of an occasion in your own experience on which an individual from a different background has been seen by you or by someone else as an 'exception to a rule'?

Task B2.2.2

Cooke writes that in the case of Muslim women, 'The faith position overrides all other particularities to become the primary identity.'

➤ Can you think of other groupings of people whose 'faith position' is seen as their 'primary identity'?

➤ Can you think of other examples of how in our perception of others the following 'positions' might be the 'primary identity'?

■ geographic
■ linguistic
■ racial
■ ethnic

■ gender
■ class

Task B2.2.3

Before reading Text B2.2.2, look carefully at Figure 8, a photograph of a Benetton advertisement.

Figure 8 Benetton's 'Angel and Devil' advertisement

➤ What is your overall reaction to the image in the advertisement?
➤ What messages, if any, does the image convey to you about race?
➤ Now read what Oliviero Toscani says about this advertisement:

'It took me one year to find these two children because I wanted them to look just like that . . . in the history of painting angels are blonde, devils are black. So it's a stereotype . . . but it's up to you to look deeper than that.'

What do you think about what Toscani says?

Solomos, J. and Back, L. (1996) *Racism and Society*, London: Macmillan pp. 186–190 (extracts)

TEXT B2.2.2
J. Solomos and
L. Back

. . . what we have seen in recent times is an attempt by some multinational corporations to develop a transnational advertising aesthetic. Perhaps the best and most perplexing example of this is the clothes manufacturer Benetton. Through the camera of Oliviero Toscani, Benetton have attempted to promote a message of human unity and harmony in their advertising. Starting in 1984 they attempted to represent the world's diverse people and cultures as synonymous with the many colours of Benetton's produce. Since then their campaigns have provoked unparalleled controversy, winning them awards and adulation alongside accusations of hypocrisy and opportunism.

Figure 9 A Benetton billboard poster, 1991

One of the striking features of the Benetton campaigns is the degree to which their message of transcultural unity is predicated upon absolute images of racial and cultural difference. The initial campaigns alluded to past and present conflicts through the presentation of arche-typal images of Jews and Arabs embracing the globe. What is intriguing about this move is that Benetton's products do not have to be shown in order to convey meanings about the brand quality; the message is simply resolved by the motif juxtaposed over the images of boundaries and conflicts. The 'United Colors of Benetton' becomes the antithesis of conflict, the expression of unity, the nurturer of internationalism (Back and Quaade 1993). However, what is more troubling about this strategy is the degree to which it is reliant on racism's very categories of personhood and the stereotypes which run from these. The example reproduced here (Figure 9) shows three young people poking their tongues out at the viewer. This advertisement was used in a poster campaign in 1991. The message of transcendence encapsulated in Benetton's slogan only makes sense if it is superimposed on a representation of clear difference. These three figures are coded through a grammar of absolute racial difference: the blue-eyed blond white Aryan figure, flanked respectively by a 'Negroid' black child and an 'Oriental' child. This message of unity can only work if it has a constitutive representation of absolute racial contrast. The danger with such representations is that they rely on a range of racial archetypes that are themselves the product of racism and as a result make racial atavism socially legitimate forms of common-sense knowledge: the concept of race is left unchallenged.

J. Solomos and
L. Back

One of the most interesting things about Toscani's photography is the ways in which he plays with ambiguity. The most dramatic example of this included a picture showing the hands of two men, one black and the other white, handcuffed together; and a picture of the torso of a black woman breast-feeding a white baby released in 1989. The reaction to these ads varied according to national context. In the United States, they were withdrawn following public complaint. The later image conjured the historical experience of slavery and the position of black woman within a gendered and racialised system of exploitation, including their designation as objects of white sexual desire. In the United States and Britain, the image of handcuffed hands evoked notions of black criminality; far from suggesting two men united in incarceration. The advertisement was associated with the daily reality of young black men arrested by predominantly white law enforcement agencies. . . .

While Benetton were very much in the vanguard of this type of imagery during the 1980s, other companies have also embraced the idea of imbuing their brand quality with a transnational ethos. In 1995, British Airways ran a newspaper campaign that presented two brides, a Danish woman in a white long dress alongside an Indian woman in a bride's red sari. The caption read: 'There are more things that bring us together than keep us apart'. The assertion of cultural translation and commensurability – the common reference being that despite ritual differences these two women were both brides – is harnessed to the airline's capacity to bring people together physically. This bears all the hallmarks of the Benetton campaigns of the mid 1980s. One could replace the British Airways' caption with Benetton's and the advertisement would work with equal effect. This intertextual quality can be found in the imagery of other companies too. Philips uses a blond-haired white girl and a black boy alongside the caption 'The universal language of Philips'. Again the two children are united through their consumption of the commodity, with a black and a white thumb sharing the control panel. This advertisement actually appeared in the newspaper that Benetton produced called *Colors*. *Colors* is an extra-ordinary publication because it effectively turns news items into Benetton advertising (Back and Quaade 1993). The intertextual reference made within this advertisement produces a kind of corporate multiculturalism that trades on images of human diversity in order to produce an aesthetic that satisfies and appeals to a global market. This move can be identified within companies as diverse as the drinks magnate Coca-Cola and the Reebok sports shoe manu-facturer, reflecting the way in these companies have embraced a transnational ethos within their imagery to fit in with their global markets. What is common to these campaigns is that they all, in various ways, espouse common humanity and harmony while reinforcing cultural and racial archetypes. At worst they steer a symbolic course that is perilously close to a legacy of crude racist images and associations. . . .

We are making two related points. First, what we have referred to as corporate multi-culturalism possesses a dual quality. While it espouses the goal of transcultural unity it does so through reinforcing crude cultural and racial archetypes. These images operate within what Stuart Hall (1981) called a 'grammar of race'. The overpowering reference point is that race is real: racial archetypes provide the vehicle for the message, and racial common sense is overbearingly present such that the reality of race is legitimated within this media discourse. Second, the valuation and repackaging of cultural difference within contemporary media result in little more than a process of market-driven recolonisation, where the fetish for the exotic reaffirms these various 'global others' as distinct and separate types of humankind. In this context the veneration of difference need not be in any contradiction with white supremacy. Quite the contrary: it can be integrally connected with the formation of contemporary cultures of racism. Yet, we also want to argue that these shifts do create important ambivalences and tensions which can unsettle the valence of racism within popular culture.

Task B2.2.4

➤ Do you agree with the interpretation by Solomos and Back of the advertisement in Figure 9?

➤ Think of contemporary advertisements in different forms of the mass in your own cultural context, which might be said to produce trade on 'images of human diversity in order to produce an aesthetic that satisfies and appeals to a global market'. Do you believe that these advertisements reinforce 'cultural and racial archetypes' at the same time as espousing common humanity and harmony?

Commentary

The view of Solomos and Back that much 'transnational' advertising espouses 'common humanity and harmony while reinforcing cultural and racial archetypes' is an interesting one. Could any advertising which for its effect attempts to depict different racial and national groups ever do so in a way that does not draw on and reinforce some partial and stereotypical perspectives? Or does the very nature of advertising mean that easily grasped images and stereotypical portrayals of racial and other groups of people will continue to be the norm?

It is Cooke's view that many 'journalists and scholars in the USA . . . seem intent on reinforcing' the image of 'the assumed homogeneity of the Muslim world'. If many advertisers, too, while paying lip-service to a multicultural ethos, are intent on 're-inforcing cultural and racial archetypes' then the prospects for a mass media which truly 'espouse common humanity and harmony' is a distant prospect.

UNIT B2.3 ## ABSENCE AND INVISIBILITY IN OTHERIZATION

In this unit we are concerned with notions of 'absence' and 'invisibility' in representation. Two perspectives are provided: first that of Richard Dyer, who points to the absence of 'whiteness' when racial identity and representation are considered; and second, that of Renato Rosaldo, who writes of how 'cultural invisibility' is a dominant position in contrast to the 'cultural visibility' of subordinate groups.

Notions of 'presence' and 'absence' are important issues in textual analysis. Fairclough (1995:5), for example, writes that 'Textual analysis can often give excellent insights about what is in a text, but what is absent from a text is as significant.'

Pennycook (1998:55) provides another perspective on absence when he refers to how lands in previous centuries were often represented as being empty of people, or of 'civilisation', and therefore ripe for the populating or civilizing effects of colonization.

After considering the views of Dyer and Rosaldo, we go on to refer to notions of 'difference', 'presence' and 'absence', key concepts in the work of Jacques Derrida, which have had widespread influence on the work of others, in a number of related fields, who are interested in questions of signification, representation and otherization.

Dyer, R. (1997) *White*, London: Routledge pp. 1–4 (extracts)

TEXT B2.3.1
R. Dyer

Racial imagery is central to the organisation of the modern world. At what cost regions and countries export their goods, whose voices are listened to at international gatherings, who bombs and who is bombed, who gets what jobs, housing, access to health care and education, what cultural activities are subsidised and sold, in what terms they are validated – these are all inextricable from racial imagery. . . . Race is not the only factor governing these things . . . but it is never not a factor, never not in play.

. . . There has been an enormous amount of analysis of racial imagery in the past decades, ranging from studies of images of, say, blacks or American Indians in the media to the deconstruction of the fetish of the racial Other in the text of colonialism and post-colonialism. Yet until recently a notable absence from such work has been the study of images of white people. Indeed, to say that one is interested in race has come to mean that one is interested in any racial imagery other than that of white people. Yet race is not only attributable to people who are not white, nor is imagery of non-white people the only racial imagery. . . .

As long as race is something only applied to non-white peoples, as long as white people are not racially seen and named, they/we function as a human norm. Other people are raced, we are just people.

There is no more powerful position than that of being 'just' human. The claim to power is the claim to speak for the commonality of humanity. Raced people can't do that – they can only speak for their race. But non-raced people can, for they do not represent the interests of a race. The point of seeing the racing of whites is to dislodge them/us from the position of power, with all the inequities, oppression, privileges and sufferings in its train, dislodging them/us by undercutting the authority with which they/we speak and act in and on the world.

The sense of whites as non-raced is most evident in the absence of reference to whiteness in the habitual speech and writing of white people in the West. We (whites) will speak of, say, the blackness or Chineseness of friends, neighbours, colleagues, customers or clients, and it may be in the most genuinely friendly and accepting manner, but we don't mention the whiteness of the white people we know. . . .

. . . for most of the time white people speak about nothing but white people, it's just that we couch it in terms of 'people' in general. Research – into books, museums, the press, advertising, films, television, software – repeatedly shows that in Western representation whites are overwhelmingly and disproportionally predominant, have the central and elaborated roles, and above all are placed as the norm, the ordinary, the standard. Whites are everywhere in representation. Yet precisely because of this and their placing as norm they seem not to be represented to themselves as whites but as people who are variously gendered, classed, sexualized and abled. At the level of racial representation, in other words, whites are not of a certain race, they're just the human race.

We are often told that we are living now in a world of multiple identities, of hybridity, of decentredness and fragmentation. The old illusory unified identities of class, gender, race, sexuality are breaking up; someone may be black *and* gay *and* middle class *and* female; we may be bi-, poly- or non-sexual, of mixed race, indeterminate gender and heaven knows what class. Yet we have not yet reached a situation in which white people and white cultural agendas are no longer in the ascendant. The media, politics, education are still in the hands of white people, still speak for whites while claiming – and sometimes sincerely aiming – to speak for humanity. . . . We may be on our way to genuine hybridity, multiplicity without (white) hegemony, and it may be where we want to get to – but we aren't there yet, and we won't get there until we see whiteness, see its power, its particularity and limitedness, put it in its place and end its rule. This is why studying whiteness matters.

Extension

Task B2.3.1

Dyer says: 'We (whites) will speak of, say, the blackness or Chineseness of friends, neighbours, colleagues, customers or clients, and it may be in the most genuinely friendly and accepting manner, but we don't mention the whiteness of the white people we know.'

> ➤ Does his description reflect your experience of how white people speak?
> ➤ Do you think the same point applies to how other groups in power speak of others less powerful?

Task B2.3.2

> ➤ Do you agree with Dyer's views, and specifically his views below? If so, can you think of concrete examples that support his views?

> Whites are everywhere in representation. Yet precisely because of this and their placing as norm they seem not to be represented to themselves *as* whites but as people who are variously gendered, classed, sexualized and abled. At the level of racial representation, in other words, whites are not of a certain race, they're just the human race.

> We have not yet reached a situation in which white people and white cultural agendas are no longer in the ascendant.

TEXT B2.3.2
R. Rosaldo

Rosaldo, R. (1993) *Culture and Truth: The Remaking of Social Analysis*, London: Routledge pp. 202–204 (extracts)

Although the notion of 'difference' has the advantage of making culture particularly visible to outside observers, it poses a problem because such differences are not absolute. They are relative to the cultural practices of ethnographers and their readers. Such studies highlight cultural forms that diverge from (tacitly normative) North American upper-middle-class professional ones. Social analysts commonly speak, for example, as if 'we' have psychology and 'they' have culture. . . .

In practice, the emphasis on difference results in a peculiar ratio: as the 'other' becomes more culturally visible, the 'self' becomes correspondingly less so. Social analysts, for example, often assert that subordinate groups have an authentic culture at the same time that they mock their own upper-middle-class professional culture. In this view, subordinate groups speak in vibrant, fluent ways, but upper-middle-class people talk like anaemic academics. Yet analysts rarely allow the ratio of class and culture to include power. Thus they conceal the ratio's darker side: the more power one has, the less culture one enjoys, and the more culture one has, the less power one wields. If 'they' have an explicit monopoly on authentic culture, 'we' have an unspoken one on institutional power. This ratio's dark side underscores the urgency of rethinking social analysis in such a manner that at once considers the interplay of culture and power and makes 'ourselves' more culturally visible.

The cultural invisibility within which the North American upper-middle-class hides itself from itself has been vividly portrayed by journalist Frances FitzGerald. Her recent book on intentional communities shows how four quite different groups have attempted to make their lives conform with a particular version of the 'American dream.' These communities share utopian fantasies about making new beginnings and living in a world without precedents. The retirement village of Sun City, for example, appears extraordinary more because of the past and present homogeneity of its residents than because it has succeeded, as its own mythology would have it, in erasing cultural diversity. 'Sun Citians,' FitzGerald writes, 'are a remarkably homogeneous group; in particular, those who live in Sun City proper occupy a far narrower band on the spectrum of American society than economics would dictate. . . . The men are by and large retired professionals. . . . Most of the women were housewives. . . . Most Sun Citians are Protestants. . . . Politically, they are conservative and vote Republican.' Yet the sources of this uniformity remain largely invisible to Sun Citians. To themselves, Sun Citians appear to be so many self-made, rootless monads whose social origins are quite diverse. For them, their current circumstances have produced their cultural transparency.

One Sun City couple affably remarked on how its residents live in the present and appear to have erased their pasts: '"No one gives a hang here what you did or where you came from,"' Mrs. Smith said. 'It's what you are now that matters.' Later, in a different context, her husband said much the same thing, adding that the colonels refused to be called 'Colonel.' In remarking on the irrelevance of social origins, the Smiths failed to notice the striking absence of working-class people, blacks, Chicanos, Puerto Ricans, and Native Americans in Sun City. In this North American rootless Utah pie, some pasts evidently matter more than others.

The attempt of Sun Citians to become transparent and erase their pasts, to make themselves postcultural and post-historical, bears a striking resemblance to objectivism's efforts to make the detached observer omniscient, innocent, and invisible. In both cases, the people involved are largely white, upper-middle-class professionals whose myth of detachment conceals their dominant class position. In North America, this group rarely knows itself as ethnic, cultural, or powerful. Much as nobody in Sun City uses titles, classic social analysis pretends to speak either from a position of omniscience or from no position at all. Yet even lone monads who claim to succeed on their own lead lives that are just as culturally shaped as people with more collective senses of identity.

Task B2.3.3

➤ Do you agree with Rosaldo's argument that 'the more culture one has, the less power one wields'?

Task B2.3.4

➤ Think of a cultural context familiar to you.

➤ Do one or more groups in positions of power seek to erase their own cultural identity while emphasizing the 'culture' of one or more subordinate groups?
➤ If so, how is the 'culture' of the subordinated group(s) emphasized?

Extension

 Task B2.3.5

➤ What are the implications of what Dyer and Rosaldo write for the following.

 ■ How we research our own and other cultures?
 ■ How we write about our own and other cultures?

Commentary

In Derrida's work (1982:213) notions of 'difference', 'presence' and 'absence' are central; he emphasizes how 'Western culture' has tended to promote the dominant poles of a system of binary distinctions to the exclusion of the other, terming this 'metaphysics'.

> Metaphysics – the white mythology which reassembles and reflects the culture of the West: the white man takes his own mythology, Indo-European mythology, his own *logos*, that is, the *mythos* of his reason, for the universal form of that he must still wish to call Reason.

A key notion of Derrida's is that of '*difference*', which Gergen (1999:27) summarizes thus:

> Language is not like a flowing stream, but is divided into discrete units (or words). Each word is distinct from all others. Another way of talking about these differences is in terms of binaries (the division into two). That is, the distinctiveness of words depends on a simple split between 'the word' and 'not the word.' The meaning of 'white,' then, depends on differentiating it from what is 'non-white' (or 'black' for instance). Word meaning depends, then, on differentiating between a *presence* and an *absence*, that which is designated by the word against what is not designated. To make sense in language is to speak in terms of presences, what is designated, against a backdrop of absences . . . the presences are privileged; they are brought into focus by the words themselves; the absences may only be there by implication; or we may simply forget them altogether. But take careful note: these presences would not make sense without the absences. Without the binary distinction there is no meaning . . .

What is more, as Hall (1997:235) writes:

> For Derrida there are very few neutral binary oppositions. One pole of the binary, he claims, is usually the dominant one, the one which includes the other within its field of operations. There is always a relation of power between the poles of a binary opposition.

'Deconstruction' is a complex term used by Derrida which has been employed in different ways in linguistic, literary and cultural studies. For Denzin (1994:196) 'deconstruction is an effort to penetrate the world of lived experience where cultural texts circulate and give meaning to everyday life. It is necessary to show the gap that separates the world of everyday meaning from the worlds that are inscribed about that world by various cultural authorities, including newsmakers, social scientists, novelists, and filmmakers.' For Fay (1996:130–3) 'deconstruction' is the 'critical procedure by which this supposed other is unearthed and shown to be an operative if invisible element in an ongoing scheme of meaning', and involves 'making people's self-understandings clearer than they can be to themselves by showing that these self-understandings are illusory, contradictory, wrongheaded or narrow'. A crucial issue, however, is that attempts to somehow demonstrate how such self-understandings do display such characteristics 'can easily degenerate into ideological assertions themselves, unconstrained by empirical evidence'. Thus it is essential to 'illuminate the self-understandings of a group of people', and this is 'dependent upon interpretation of what the group is doing from its own vantage point even as it transcends this vantage point'.

THE OTHER AND THE TOURIST GAZE

UNIT B2.4

In this unit we focus on Otherization in the travel brochure and travel literature. In both texts featured there are references to Said, whose ideas were introduced in Unit B2.1. The writer of the first, Alastair Pennycook, is primarily concerned with Said's ideas as far as they relate to stereotyping, while Jess Olsen, the author of Text B2.4.2, is interested in Said's notion of Orientalism, and particularly its 'sexual mythologies concerning the dominating of the erotic, exotic, female'.

Olsen also refers to 'postmodernism', a term we considered in Unit B2.3 in relation to personal identity; he is particularly interested notions of 'style' and 'pastiche' in the imagery of the travel brochure (see the reference to Baudrillard in Unit B2.2), of 'fragmentation' and 'diversification', and of 'shrinkage of physical space' and 'compression of time'. Such notions are common in definitions of postmodernism; Sarup (1996:95–6), for example, writes that postmodernism is characterised by 'an acceptance of ephemerality, fragmentation, discontinuity', an 'intense distrust of all global or "totalising" discourses', and a 'rejection of metanarratives, of large-scale interpretations, of universal application'. 'Depth models' are 'replaced by a conception of practices, discourses, textual play, surfaces and textuality' and 'history is not as the real but as representation, as pastiche . . .' For Strinati (1997:422), too, 'popular cultural signs and media images increasingly dominate our sense of reality, and the way we define ourselves and the world around us'. Postmodernism is for Strinati intimately bound up with 'a media-saturated society': 'The mass media . . . were once thought of as holding up a mirror to, and thereby reflecting, a wider social reality. Now that reality is only definable in terms of the surface reflections of the mirror. It is no longer even a question of distortion since the term implies that there is a reality, outside the surface simulations of the media, which can be distorted, and this is precisely what is at issue.' As for questions of space and time, Strinati writes that 'Because of the speed and scope of modern mass media communications, because of the relative ease and rapidity with which people and information can travel, time and space become less stable and comprehensible, more confused, more incoherent, more disunified' (424).

Extension

For Pennycook (1998) travel literature on China, which he analyses in Text B2.4.1 is far from 'postmodern' or 'postcolonial'; instead he sees a 'remarkable continuity with colonial discourse' (180) in such writing. Pennycook suggests that 'rather than disappearing, these discourses have remained fairly constant and indeed are enjoying a period of rejuvenation in conjunction with the continued global expansion of English' (130).

TEXT B2.4.1

A. Pennycook

Pennycook, A. (1998) *English and the Discourse of Colonialism*, London: Routledge pp. 171–2, 174–5, 180 (extracts)

Just as Said (1978) identified a range of stereotypes dealing with the Arab world – the eternal and unchanging East, the sexually insatiable Arab, the feminine, exotic, the teeming marketplace, mystical religiosity, corrupt despotism, and so forth – it is possible to outline a similar series of stereotypes in writing on China: the exotic and eternal, the underdeveloped and backward, the paradoxically juxtaposed old and new, the crowded, dirty and poverty-stricken life, the smiling or inscrutable exterior hiding either bad intentions or misery, the passive Oriental and the despotic leader, the dullness of life under socialism, the uncaring nature of the Communist government, and so on. Such constructions occur across a broad range of writing, from textbooks to encyclopaedias. One domain in which they have a particular salience, and in which they have shown a remarkable resilience over time, is in travel writing. . . .

. . . I would like to look at Paul Theroux's (1988) *Riding the Iron Rooster: By Train through China*. Theroux is, of course, an old and respected hand at travel-writing: 'The world's pre-eminent travel-writer' (*Time*, 16 May 1988); one of 'the best of today's travel writers' (*The Economist*, 1988). And yet, as Salzman discusses in his review of the book, there are many problematic passages:

[At the railway station at Baoji] everyone hawked, everyone spat, sometimes dribbling, sometimes in a trajectory that ran like candle-wax down the side of a spittoon . . . They walked scuffingly, sort of skating, with their arms flapping, with narrow jogging shoulders, or else hustling petlike, with their limbs jerking. They minced, they plodded, they pushed, keeping their hands out – straight-arming their way – and their heads down. They could look entirely graceless – unexpected in Chinese.

Mr Tian [his guide and translator for most of the trip] shrugged, shook my hand, and without another word walked off. It was the Chinese farewell: there was no lingering, no swapping of addresses, no reminiscence, nothing sentimental. At the moment of parting they turned their backs, because you ceased to matter and because they had so much else to worry about.

It seemed to me that the Chinese . . . had no choice but to live the dullest lives and perform the most boring jobs imaginable – doing the same monotonous Chinese two-step from the cradle to the grave . . .

Such descriptions can be commonly found in writing on China. It is interesting to observe here how Theroux on the one hand dwells on practices such as spitting, and on the other, manages to make vast generalizations about Chinese life: 'the Chinese farewell', the 'monotonous Chinese two-step' and so on. . . .

Chinua Achebe has remarked that travellers with closed minds can tell us little except about themselves (1975:40). I would suggest that he is right up to a point here. Travellers and travel writers may indeed tell us more about themselves than the place they are travelling in, but that telling about the Self is a telling that is discursively constructed. We do not, therefore, learn much about the lived realities of other contexts, but we do learn a great deal about how the Other is constructed in Western discourses. What I think by now must be manifestly clear – a point that I have perhaps belabored somewhat – is that there are a series of dominant discourses on China which, with a remarkable continuity with colonial discourses, constantly construct China in a very particular way, dichotomizing and essentializing to create a stereotyped vision denying any lived experience of Chinese people.

Task B2.4.1

Much travel writing shares similar characteristics to those highlighted by Pennycook in the passages from Theroux's book.

➤ Do you believe the very nature of travel writing makes it possible for a travel writer to give an account of what Pennycook calls the 'lived experience' of people and the 'lived realities of other contexts'?
➤ If so, what will this account consist of?

Task B2.4.2

In recent years how readers respond to texts is, for some, as important as the actual content of the texts themselves. Thompson (1995:213–214), for example, writes that '. . . whether mediated messages are ideological will depend on the ways in which they are taken up by the individuals who receive them and incorporated reflexively into their lives. Texts and media programmes which are replete with stereotypical images, reassuring messages, etc., may in fact be taken up by recipients and used in quite unexpected ways . . . one must consider the ways in which these messages are incorporated into the lives of recipients.'

Watson (1997:90), on the other hand, believes that 'Readers . . . actively interpret texts but cannot interpret them in just any way they wish. The texts themselves contain "instructions" which yield strongly preferred readings.'

➤ What is your point of view?
➤ Do you believe, for example, that descriptions in travel, and other, literature, such as those written by Theroux and highlighted by Pennycook, 'yield strongly preferred readings' or could they be 'taken up by recipients and used in quite unexpected ways'?
➤ If they 'yield strongly preferred readings' what might be the implications for how the Other is perceived?
➤ If they could be 'taken up by recipients and used in quite unexpected ways', what might these 'unexpected ways' be and what might be the implications?

TEXT B2.4.2
J. Olsen

Olsen, J. 'Through White Eyes: The packaging of people and places in the world of the travel brochure', *Cultural Studies from Birmingham* 2:1 (1998) accessed online at http://artsweb.bham.ac.uk/bccsr/issue L/olsen.htm (extracts)

The holiday brochure is a significant element of popular culture which has become so naturalized within society as a way to fill 'leisure time' that its existence as a constructed commodity is largely ignored. Certainly, the travel brochure, with its eloquent marketing philosophy, perpetuates a certain 'way of seeing' (Berger 1972). This makes it important to explore how these 'ways of seeing' are constantly naturalised and re-naturalised within our psyche. . . .

The tourist industry and the role of the brochure in the 20th century

In contemporary society the tourist industry operates according to a systematic structure which views a holiday as a commodity that must be sold to ensure economic survival. The image is vital to the sale of the commodity and the key to successful imagery lies in the enticing pages of the tourist brochure. Travel brochure imagery appears to operate on different levels; On the one hand the brochure needs to present itself as a geographical manual, detailing potential holiday destinations. On the other hand, as Burns and Holden (1995:111) suggest, '. . . the operator aims to reaffirm to the consumer through sophisticated brochure imagery that the holiday on offer can address the perceived needs of the tourist.' Thus, the photograph must accentuate the emotional expectation of the holiday – be it quality family time, a romantic break for two or the opportunity for exotic social encounters. What needs to be questioned is whether or not these realist representations in the brochure offer little more than an arbitrary configuration of the ability of the various technological processes and discourses of knowledge to materially produce 'reality' and 'emotional satisfaction'. If the tourist brochure constructs a version of reality through surface images then it is useful to employ the term postmodernism to explore this fascinating space.

The postmodern characteristics of the travel brochure

Postmodern styles and the tourist industry have much in common. It is possible to view the tourist brochure as a constant and frequently contradictory flow of consumer images and spectacles which are often fragmented and overemphasized in order to create a heightened, intense surface style. Brochure photography tends to promote a plurality of meaning, encompassing instantaneity, pastiche, time and space compression and elements from different historical periods which all serve to blur the distinctions between both social and cultural and subject and image.

Fragmentation and diversification

Postmodernism is anti-elitist and based on popular pleasures. I suggest that travel brochures adhere to this through the fragmentation of the boundaries between high and popular culture. . . .

. . . The postmodern fragmentation of boundaries and frontiers between countries is also characterized by the travel brochure due to its 'pick and mix' format. The consumer can simultaneously experience not only the delights of Tunisia and Turkey at a flick of the page but also view the same standardised sun, sand and sea image in virtually every location. The ubiquity of these photographic representations constitutes a shrinkage of physical space and a compression of time. The world, according to the travel brochure may, thus, be semiotically appropriated and consumed without leaving the comfort of the armchair. These postmodernist tendencies may be both empowering in that they allow for an increase in the amount and speed of cultural exchange and also enlightening in that they allocate greater freedom to the consumer to explore the world with the greatest of ease.

Additionally, the fragmentation and diversification of a marketable product is a feature of postmodernism which I suggest that both travel brochures and tourist boards use to their advantage. . . .

. . . This fragmentation and diversification may also extend to reality itself. The tourist brochure can promote fabricated images as reality and I suggest this is in accordance with what the tour operators perceive the desires within the tourist imagination to be. Thus, as Albers and James (1988:136) note, '. . . tourists rely on stereotyped photographs as measures for their own visualization.'

Postcolonialism, Orientalism and historical frameworks of power

I suggest that Orientalism continues to manifest itself in contemporary society. In my view, Western popular cultural texts, such as travel brochures, partake in the perpetuation of Orientalist imagery. Said (1993:229) explains; 'When you can no longer assume that Britannia will rule the waves forever, you have to reconceive reality as something that can be held together by you the artist, in history rather than in geography. Spatiality becomes, ironically, the characteristic of an aesthetic rather than of political domination.' Certainly, within the world of the travel brochure there remains a powerful nostalgic feeling toward earlier colonial periods. . . .

. . . Historical legacies of power are also reformulated through contextual exclusion and inclusion of the native . . . holidaymaking is depicted as white, heterosexual, and nuclear. The black Britons or indigenous tourists simply do not exist. However, the tourist brochure has the power to include the Other according to its own marketing strategy. Although it must emphasise the contrast between the local and the tourist in order to invoke the idea that the holiday will place the tourist in a position of lavish superiority, it must also address the image of the demonised Other as perpetuated by the majority of the Western press.

Figure 10 is startling in that the model who is dressed in exotic clothing, in order (I suggest), to represent the destination of Thailand, is Western. This may suggest a perpetuation of a kind of 'safety' within this strange foreign land. Paradoxically, the image provides the fantasy that the reality of the holiday will be intrinsically linked with what is familiar within the Western imagination, thus, distorting the boundaries of fantasy and reality.

Certainly, these images tend to call upon subconscious colonial knowledges; however, most disturbingly, I suggest that the frameworks of power manifest in the images extend beyond unhistorical legacies of geographical domination and serve to reformulate Orientalist, sexual mythologies concerning the dominating of the erotic, exotic female who is often fantasized and objectified under the tourist gaze.

Task B2.4.3

Olsen makes a number of assertions concerning the tourist brochure. From your experience (and/or analysis) of such brochures, do you agree with the following points?.

➤ 'Holidaymaking is depicted as white, heterosexual, and nuclear.'

- ■ 'The postmodern fragmentation of boundaries and frontiers between countries is . . . characterized by the travel brochure.'
- ■ 'Within the world of the travel brochure there remains a powerful nostalgic feeling toward earlier colonial periods.'

Figure 10 A photograph from a tourist brochure for Thailand

 Task B2.4.4

The points made by Olsen relate as much to what has been written about *tourism* itself, as to the *tourist brochure*, particularly 'the contrast between the local and tourist' with the tourist being placed in 'a position of lavish superiority' and the objectification of locals 'under the tourist gaze'.

> How far do you believe that tourism perpetuates such contrast, division and objectification?
> Do you have personal experience of such contrast, division and objectification as a tourist or of being 'under the tourist gaze'?
> What are the effects on and consequences for intercultural understanding and communication of such contrast, division and objectification in tourism?

Commentary

Olsen makes an important point when he writes that economic factors and the 'systematic structure' of the tourist industry play an important part in the content and style of the tourist brochure: 'In contemporary society the tourist industry operates according to a systematic structure which views a holiday as a commodity that must be sold to ensure economic survival. The image is vital to the sale of the commodity and the key to successful imagery lies in the enticing pages of the tourist brochure.' Kellner (1995:9) writes that 'Inserting texts into the system of culture within which they are produced or distributed can help elucidate features and effects of the texts that textual analysis alone might miss or downplay.' Such a consideration is increasingly important in a world where the production of culture is controlled by ever larger corporations and conglomerates. Ironically, while postmodernists emphasize the 'fragmentation' and 'diversification' of the world, the mass media are characterized by increasing merger and homogenization.

'UNDEMONIZING' THE OTHER

UNIT B2.5

We start this unit with an extract from Christopher Hope's novel *Darkest England*, the overall comic effect of which is created by parodying the 'image of the demonized Other' characteristic of anthropological texts and indeed, some literary texts, of the late nineteenth and early twentieth centuries, which Olsen believes 'is perpetuated by the . . . Western press' (Unit B2.4). Hope in effect is involved in an attempt to 'deconstruct' such an image, or in Denzin's words (1994:196), 'to show the gap that separates the world of everyday meaning from the worlds that are inscribed about that world by various cultural authorities, including newsmakers, social scientists, novelists, and filmmakers'. In doing so he parodies anthropological and literary texts of an earlier time, and in particular a novel written in the early part of the 20th century, *Heart of Darkness* by Joseph Conrad, an extract from which is included as Text B2.5.2. Indeed, our understanding of the fact that it is parodying previous texts is because of intertextuality, which is concerned with how 'the interpretation that a particular reader generates from a text will . . . depend on the recognition of the relationship of the given text to other texts' (Edgar and Sedgwick 1999:197). The concept of intertextuality relates to the notion of 'presence' and 'absence' in the work of Derrida and, in particular, the ideas of Bakhtin (Bakhtin and Medvedev1978:120): 'Not only the meaning of the utterance but also the very fact of its performance is of historical and social significance, as, in general, is the fact of its realisation in the here and now, in given circumstances, at a certain historical moment, under the conditions of the given social situation.'

In the third text Littlewood and Lipsedge consider how the Other continues to be demonized, sometimes being perceived as 'sick or subhuman', and point to how 'outsiders are part of our definition of ourselves'. In doing so, they suggest that Otherization is not a relic of previous times, but a continuing and pervasive presence which has implications for all of us in our everyday dealings and relationships.

TEXT B2.5.1
C. Hope

Hope, C. (1996) *Darkest England*, London: Macmillan (extracts)

It was an awesome journey, that expedition into the heart of London. As you travel you might be like the even tinier creatures who live on a water-spider, floating haphazardly down a stream. You feel you are in the world as it was in its primeval beginnings. Every so often we would stop at stations and a group of young warriors, male and female, would board in a kind of explosion, a whirl of white limbs, a mass of hands clapping, of feet stamping, of bodies swaying, of eyes rolling.

I was delighted to have a chance to note the peculiar characteristics of the natives as we rolled slowly southward. The females are notable for the small development of the mammary organs. Few have small waists. Both sexes pierce their ears. Some of the young warriors cut their hair, as do those of the peace tribe, so that it commands their heads like an axe-blade, which they colour with a variety of strong hues. Often they employ scarification, and amongst the most popular of the clan-marks is a stippled line along the temporal lobes from the external edges of the eyebrows to the middle of the cheeks or the lower jaws.

With each stop, a fresh invasion. The chants went up anew, and I felt as if prehistoric man was cursing us, praying to us, welcoming us – who could tell? Their cries were incomprehensible. My friend interpreted for me, saying that some commented on the failures of the French, or the deformities of foreigners generally. I should not be in the least bit afeared, as this was a perfectly normal practice – bands of sport lovers travelling abroad to support their country.

Love of country among these young men was unashamed, as they repeatedly chanted the beloved name of their sceptred isle, which they pronounced with a curious double beat, accentuating both syllables, ENG-LAND! ENG-LAND! Many carried flags. Not only was the proud standard waved at every opportunity, but many of them had made clothes of the national emblem and wore it as a shirt, or as a scarf or even as trousers. Some flew the flag on the tips of their stout black boots, or had tattooed tiny eaglets on each knuckle. One fine young buck, clearly a super-patriot, had emblazoned the beloved red, white and blue on his shaven skull, and the precious emblem flew wonderfully against the granite gleam of bone. Another had taken matters a step further and, perhaps because he was a great singer, he bellowed out 'God Save the Queen' in a rough baritone, showing, as he did so, that each of his teeth had been stained red, white and blue. This display of what we might call dental patriotism impressed me deeply.

None the less, I had to confide in my mentor that the sight left me secretly appalled, as a sane man would be before an enthusiastic outbreak in the madhouse.

On catching sight of me, they became very excited. Some leaped from their seats, lifting their arms and scratching in their armpits as if troubled by furious itching; some threw monkey nuts in an artillery barrage of shells, ending with a large banana which struck me on the forehead to the accompaniment of loud cheers. They howled, they leapt and spun and made horrid faces. Ugly? Yes, it was ugly enough, but I felt in me a faint response to the terrible frankness of that noise. It was something that we, so far from the night of the First Ages, find so hard to comprehend, that someone from another part of the world should be traditionally saluted with fruit and nuts.

C. Hope

Task B2.5.1

Consider the following questions in relation to Text B2.5.1.

➤ How does your interpretation of Text B2.5.1 'depend on the recognition of the relationship of the given text to other texts'?
➤ What particular characteristics of the 'natives' are described in the text?
➤ What effect does the description of the 'natives' have?

Task B2.5.2

Consider the role of the narrator in Text B2.5.1.

➤ Is the narrator an objective or subjective observer?
➤ What is the nature of this subjectivity/objectivity?
➤ Can any implications be drawn for how we might observe and describe people in cultural contexts we are unfamiliar with?

Conrad, J. (1902) *Heart of Darkness*, London: Penguin p. 96

TEXT B2.5.2
J. Conrad

When next day we left at noon, the crowd, of whose presence behind the curtain of trees I had been acutely conscious all the time, flowed out of the woods again, filled the clearing, covered the slope with a mass of naked, breathing, quivering, bronze bodies. I steamed up a bit, then swung downstream, and two thousand eyes followed the evolutions of the splashing, thumping, fierce river-demon beating the water with its terrible tail and breathing black smoke into the air. In front of the first rank, along the river, three men, plastered with bright red earth from head to foot, strutted to and fro restlessly. When we came abreast again, they faced the river, stamped their feet, nodded their horned heads, swayed their scarlet bodies; they shook towards the fierce river-demon a bunch of black feathers, a mangy skin with a pendant tail – something that looked like a dried gourd; they shouted periodically together strings of amazing words that resembled no sounds of human language; and the deep murmurs of the crowd, interrupted suddenly, were like the responses of some satanic litany.

Task B2.5.3

➤ How does the description of the 'natives' in Text B2.5.2 compare to the description of the 'natives' in Text B2.5.1?
➤ In what ways does your interpretation of Text B2.5.1 depend on the 'recognition of the relationship' with such texts as Text B2.5.2? In what ways is there intertextuality between Texts B2.5.1 and B2.5.2?

Extension

Littlewood, R. and Lipsedge, M. (1997, 3rd edition) *Aliens and Alienists: ethnic minorities and psychiatry*, London: Routledge pp. 27–28 (extracts)

However we conceive of our group, whether a class, nation, or a race, we define it by those we exclude from it. These outsiders are perceived as different from ourselves. They may have different languages, different customs or beliefs. They may look different. We may even regard them as sick or sub-human. However we define them we perceive them as an undifferentiated mass with no individual variations.

Outsiders always pose a threat to the status quo. Even if they are not physically dangerous, they are threatening simply because they are different. Their apartness is dangerous. It questions our tendency to see our society as the natural society and ourselves as the measure of normality. To admit a valid alternative is already to question the inevitability of our type of world. We forget that outsiders are part of our definition of ourselves. To confirm our own identity we push the outsiders even further away. By reducing their humanity we emphasize our own . . .

. . . Successful belief systems pre-empt the possibility of change by apparently describing all possible alternatives in the restricted form of the outsider. He is always necessary: he is part of our beliefs and his presence legitimates our institutions. He is the model for all challenges to the accepted order.

Outsiders' characteristics must be contrasted unfavourably with our own. They are nature: we are culture. Excessive cruelty and sexuality is attributed to groups which are technologically less developed than ourselves (too little discipline), while the technologically more advanced are seen as mindless automatons (too much discipline). Some groups are paradoxically both. We delineate the features of the outsider and avoid seeing ourselves in this mirror of our own deficiencies; his evident peculiarities become the scale by which we measure our own conformity. To many communities, including Europeans, the outsider appears dirty and bestial, aggressive but matriarchal, treacherous but stupid, and frequently with an enormous sexual appetite. Some societies perceive their neighbours as cannibals or witches or lunatics – the standardized nightmares of the community.

Outsiders in our midst also have to be identified and isolated. Because they are so close and yet are difficult to distinguish they may be even more dangerous than the outsider from abroad: heresy and witchcraft are contagious . . .

. . . Both internal and external aliens have a role in our society: they demonstrate to the average individual what he should avoid being or even avoid being mistaken for – they define for him the limits of his normality by producing a boundary only inside which he can be secure.

 Task B2.5.4

➤ How do the points made by Littlewood and Lipsedge in Text B2.5.3 relate to the content of Texts B2.5.1 and B2.5.2?

 Task B2.5.5

➤ How far is the view of Littlewood and Lipsedge that 'Outsiders in our midst also have to be identified and isolated':

  ■ borne out by a study of history
  ■ relevant to current national, regional and international events and contexts?

Commentary

For Denzin (1997:33) '. . . the worlds we study are created through the texts that we write . . . we do not study lived experience; rather we examine lived textuality . . . Real-life experiences are shaped by prior textual representations.' The extract from Christopher Hope's novel (Text B2.5.1) achieves comic effect partly because the majority of 'prior textual representations' have, in Dyer's terms, represented certain groups (like the English) as the 'norm' and therefore, in Rosaldo's terms, 'culturally invisible' (see Unit B2.3).

Comic effect is also achieved by the way in which the narrator in the novel extract describes the experience. There is a serious point to be made about the narrator's description, however, which is not only to do with how we describe, but also how we research and observe other cultures. This is to do with the narrator's position. Berg and Smith (1985:9) write that in any social investigation 'we have to make a choice about where we will position ourselves . . . Whatever our choice, the position we take is still a position. And what we look at, what we see, what we encode, what we make sense of, are all a function of that positioning . . . every piece of research . . . must constantly monitor the relationship between the researcher and the researched.'

Not only should we be aware of this relationship, but also we should always be aware that the notion of culture is not a simple nor a simplistic one. Clifford Geertz, whose metaphor for 'culture' we considered in the first unit of Section B, writes of the importance, when researching culture, of 'thick descriptions' that capture 'the multiplicity of conceptual structures, many of them superimposed upon or knotted onto one another, which are at once strange, irregular, and inexplicit' (1973:10).

Theme 3
Representation

REPRESENTATION IN THE MASS MEDIA: THE CASE OF 'ASYLUM SEEKERS'

Despite the proliferation of news about national and international issues in a burgeoning variety of mass media, there is arguably no corresponding broadening of perspective. Noam Chomsky's view (1992:6) that the news media provide us with 'a very narrow, very tightly constrained and grotesquely inaccurate account of the world in which we live' is one which is shared by a number of commentators. In this unit we focus on the often narrow ways that those in the mass media, sometimes unconsciously, represent others. In particular, we focus on the representation of those commonly described in the mass media as 'asylum seekers'. We start by considering a single sentence in the recent novel *By the Sea* by the British-based writer Abdul Razak Gurnah (2001), a sentence which suggests that the language we use to describe those seeking refuge or asylum plays an important part in how we perceive them (see Task B3.1.1). This is also the concern of the first longer text, an extract from an article by Stephen Moss in the British newspaper the *Guardian*, also written in 2001. In Text B3.1.2, Teun van Dijk, who has written extensively about the ideological nature of discourse and about 'critical' approaches to discourse analysis, describes the role of discourse in a 'new' form of racism and analyses specific techniques used in the mass media which help to promote it.

 ## Task B3.1.1

In a passage near the beginning of Abdul Razak Gurnah's novel *By the Sea*, an individual who is fleeing his own country, has no visa or permission to enter the United Kingdom, and is hoping to be given permission to stay in the UK, arrives by air at Gatwick Airport, near London. The story is narrated by the new arrival:

> I am a refugee, an asylum-seeker. These are not simple words, even if the habit of hearing them makes them seem so (p. 4).

➤ Consider in what ways 'refugee' and 'asylum seeker' are *not* 'simple words'.
➤ What does the narrator mean when he says that the 'habit of hearing' the words 'refugee' and 'asylum seeker' makes them seem simple?

Moss, S. 'Mind your language: the semantics of asylum', *Guardian* 22 May 2001

TEXT B3.1.1
S. Moss

'Asylum seeker' is a term that gained currency in the 90s. In 1990 references in the *Guardian* to 'refugees' outnumbered references to 'asylum seekers' by 10 to one. Last year it was less than two to one. This year the ratio is even closer. In 1999, across all papers, the ratio was six to one in favour of refugees. In 2000 references to refugees halved, while references to asylum seekers doubled.

It is not easy to identify when the change occurred, though two stories in the *Guardian* on women displaced by the war in ex-Yugoslavia suggested a change in usage in the first half of the 90s. The unquestioned 'refugee' of 1993 had become the 'asylum seeker' of 1994 . . . bureaucratic unease about growing numbers claiming to be refugees had produced the new category of asylum seeker, and the media quickly latched on to the change of nomenclature. Significantly, it will enter the online version of the Oxford English Dictionary later in the year.

The term 'asylum seeker' was first used in the *American Political Science Review* in 1959 and was a Cold War creation: most asylum seekers were political dissidents from the Soviet Union. Refugees were quite different: people displaced in large numbers by war or famine. 'Refugee' is a word that evokes immediate sympathy; 'asylum seeker' is a colder, more bureaucratic term, and it is convenient for the Home Office[1] that the latter is now increasingly favoured.

Task B3.1.2

Consider the pairs of words and phrases below, all of which might be used in everyday talk or in the mass media to describe or discuss those seeking to be given, or who have been given, permission to stay in a particular country after they have fled their own (and, indeed, to describe or discuss other categories of people and individuals).

aggressive	assertive
overwrought	hysterical
unforthcoming	quiet
determined	stubborn
to claim financial assistance	to scrounge
to receive a handout	to receive financial assistance
to open the door to	to grant asylum to
to mislead	to lie to
to fail to adapt to the culture	to reject the culture

➤ Would you say that both words or phrases in each pair have a similar connotation?
➤ If not, which of the pair would you say has the more positive, and which the more negative connotation?
➤ Can you think of other pairs of words or phrases which might be used in everyday talk or in the mass media to describe or discuss those seeking to be given, or who have been given, permission to stay in a particular country after they have fled their own?

---

1   The Home Office is the term used to describe that ministry of the government of the United Kingdom which is responsible for such issues as law and order, immigration and domestic security.

Task B3.1.3

Find at least one report from the mass media which focuses on those seeking to be given, or who have been given, permission to stay in a particular country after they have fled their own.

➤ What words and phrases used in the report(s) to describe such people and to discuss related issues could be said to have negative or positive connotations?
➤ What other devices, in addition to the choice of words, are used in the reports which help to represent such people in a negative or positive light?

TEXT B3.1.2
T. A. Van Dijk

Van Dijk, T. A. 'New(s) Racism: A discourse analytical approach' second short draft (July 1998) accessed online at www.hum.ura.nl/2teun/racpress.htm of chapter to be published in Cottle, S. (ed.) (2000) *Ethnic Minorities and the Media* Buckingham: Open University Press (extracts)

The New Racism

In many respects, contemporary forms of racism are different from the 'old' racism of slavery, segregation, apartheid, lynchings, and systematic discrimination, of white superiority feelings, and of explicit derogation in public discourse and everyday conversation. The New Racism (Barker 1981) wants to be democratic and respectable, and hence first denies that it is racism. Real Racism, in this framework of thought, only exists among the Extreme Right. In the New Racism, minorities are not biologically inferior, but different. They have a different culture, although in many respects there are 'deficiencies', such as single-parent families, drug abuse, lacking achievement values, and dependence on welfare and affirmative action – 'pathologies' that need to be corrected of course . . .

The role of discourse

Especially because of their often subtle and symbolic nature, many forms of the 'new' racism are *discursive*: they are expressed, enacted and confirmed by text and talk, such as everyday conversations, board meetings, job interviews, policies, laws, parliamentary debates, political propaganda, textbooks, scholarly articles, movies, TV programs and news reports in the press, among hundreds of other genres. They appear 'mere' talk, and far removed from the open violence and forceful segregation of the 'old' racism. Yet, they may be just as effective to marginalize and exclude minorities. They may hurt even more, especially when they seem to be so 'normal', so 'natural', and so 'commonsensical' to those who engage in such discourse and interaction. . . .

Discourse analytical approaches

Discourse analytical approaches systematically describe the various structures and strategies of text or talk, and relate these to the social or political context. For instance, they may focus on overall topics, or more local meanings (such as coherence or implications) in a *semantic* analysis. But also the *syntactic* form of sentences, or the overall *organization* of a news report may be examined in detail. The same is true for variations of *style, rhetorical* devices such as metaphors or euphemisms, *speech acts* such as promises and threats, and in spoken discourse also the many forms of *interaction*. . . . These structures of text and talk are systematically related to elements of the social *context*, such as the spatio-temporal setting, participants and their various social and communicative roles, as well as their goals, knowledge and opinions.

T. A. Van Dijk

The role of the media

There is no need to argue here the overall power of the media in modern 'information' societies . . . the power of the media is primarily *discursive* and *symbolic*. Media discourse is the main source of people's knowledge, attitudes and ideologies, both of other elites as well as of ordinary citizens. Of course, the media do this in joint production with the other elites, primarily politicians, professionals and academics. Yet, given the freedom of the press, the media elites are ultimately responsible for the prevailing discourses of the media they control.

This is specifically also true for the role of the media in ethnic affairs, for the following reasons:

(a) Most white readers have few daily experiences with minorities
(b) Most white readers have few alternative sources of information about minorities
(c) Negative attitudes about minorities are in the interest of most white readers
(d) More than most other topics, ethnic issues provide positive but polarized identification for most white readers, in terms of Us and Them
(e) The media emphasize such group polarization by focusing on various Problems and Threats for Us, thus actively involving most white readers
(f) Minority groups do not have enough power to publicly oppose biased reporting
(g) The dominant (media) discourse on ethnic issues is virtually consensual
(h) In particular there is little debate on the 'new' racism
(i) 'Anti-racist' dissidents have little access to the media.

In sum, when power over the most influential form of public discourse, that is, media discourse, is combined with a lack of alternative sources, when there is a near consensus, and opponents and dissident groups are weak, then the media are able to abuse such power and establish the discursive and cognitive hegemony that is necessary for the reproduction of the 'new' racism. Let us now examine in some more detail how exactly such power is exercized in news and newsmaking.

News structures

. . . on ethnic issues, for which alternative sources of information are scarce, news on TV or in the press often provides the first 'facts', but at the same time the first 'definitions of the situation' and the first opinions – usually those of the authorities or other white elites.

Topics

Interestingly, whereas there are a large number of types of topic in the press, news about immigrants and ethnic minorities is often restricted to the following kind of events:

(1) New (illegal) immigrants are arriving
(2) Political response to policies about (new) immigration
(3) Reception problems (housing etc.)
(4) Social problems (employment, welfare etc.)
(5) Response of the population (resentment etc.)

(6) Cultural characterization: How are they different?
(7) Complications: Negative characterization: How are they deviant?
(8) Focus on Threats: Violence, crime, drugs, prostitution
(9) Political response: Policies to stop immigration, expulsion, etc.
(10) Integration conflicts.

In each of these cases, even potentially 'neutral' topics, such as immigration, housing, employment or cultural immigration, soon tend to have a negative dimension: Immigration may be topicalized as a threat, and most ethnic relations represented in terms of problems and deviance if not as a threat as well, most typically so in news about crime, drugs and violence minorities are associated with. On the other hand, many topics that are also part of ethnic affairs occur much less in the news, such as migrants leaving the country, the contributions of immigrant workers to the economy, everyday life of minority communities, and especially also discrimination and racism against minorities. Since topics express the most important information of a text, and in news are further signalled by prominent headlines and leads, they are also best understood and memorized by the readers. In other words, negative topics have negative consequences on the 'minds' of the recipients.

In general what we find is a preference for those topics that emphasize Their bad actions and Our good ones. On the other hand, Their good actions and Our bad ones are not normally emphasized by topicalization (and will therefore also appear less in headlines or on the front page, if reported at all). This general *strategy of positive self-presentation and negative other-presentation* is prevalent in most dominant discourse about immigrants and minorities . . .

Local meanings

Derogatory words in racist discourse are well known, and need not be spelled out here. The new racism, as described above, however, avoids explicitly racist labels, and uses negative words to describe the properties or actions of immigrants or minorities (for instance, 'illegal') Special *code-words* (such as 'welfare mothers') may be used, and the readers are able to interpret these words in terms of minorities and the problems attributed to them. And it needs no further argument that attitudes about groups and opinions about specific events may influence the *lexical choice* of such words as 'riot' on the one hand, or 'urban unrest', 'disturbance' or 'uprising' on the other hand, as is also the case for the classical example of 'terrorist' vs. 'rebel' vs. 'freedom fighter'. Thus, most mentions of 'terrorists' (especially also in the US press) will stereotypically refer to Arabs. Violent men who are our friends or allies will seldom get that label. For the same reason, 'drug barons' are always Latin men in South America, never the white men who are in the drugs business within the USA itself. In other words, when there are options of lexicalization, choosing one word rather than another often has contextual reasons, such as the opinions of the speaker about a person, a group or their actions.

Modern linguistics and discourse analysis, however, goes beyond the study of isolated words, and also studies the *meaning of sentences* or sequences of sentences and their role in the text as a whole. Thus, sentence meanings also show what specific *roles* participants have, for instance as responsible agents, targets or victims of action. What we find in such an analysis is in line with the general strategy mentioned above: minorities are often represented in a passive role (things are being decided, done, etc. for or against them), unless they are agents of negative actions, such as illegal entry, crime, violence, or drug abuse. In the latter case their responsible agency will be emphasized.

Much of the information in discourse, and hence also in news reports, is implicit, and supplied by the recipients on the basis of their knowledge of the context and of the world. Also in news and editorials about ethnic affairs, thus, many meanings are merely *implied or presupposed* and not explicitly stated. Because of social norms, and for reasons of impression management, for instance, many negative things about minorities may not be stated explicitly, and thus are conveyed 'between the lines'. For instance in a sentence like 'The rising crime in the inner city worried the politicians', it is presupposed, and not explicitly stated, *that* there is rising crime in the inner city, as if this were a known 'fact'.

Task B3.1.4

In Text B3.1.2 Van Dijk writes that 'news on T.V. or in the press often provides the first "facts", but at the same time the first "definitions of the situation" and the first opinions'.

➤ Analyse news reports on TV, in newspapers and on the Internet. How far do these reports provide definitions of situations, and opinions, as well as factual accounts?

Task B3.1.5

In light of the events of 11 September 2001, and the ongoing situation involving Israel and Palestine, Van Dijk's assertion that 'most mentions of "terrorists" . . . will stereotypically refer to Arabs' is particularly topical.

➤ Analyse reports in the mass media which focus on the events of 11 September 2001, and its aftermath and repercussions, and on the ongoing situation involving Israel and Palestine.
➤ How far do these reports demonstrate the 'New' Racism' that Van Dijk refers to in Text B3.1.2?

Commentary

In recent years considerable work has been done on devising techniques for analysing the ways the news is presented in the mass media, and the factors that lead to certain events 'becoming' news. Stuart Hall, whose views on the effect of the Internet on the notion of 'community' we considered in Unit B1.5, is one who has written extensively on the mass media, and is particularly concerned with its ideological dimensions. He is interested in how news stories are constructed so that they will be 'comprehensible' to a particular audience (1996:425). This involves bringing events 'within the horizon of the "meaningful"' and this entails 'referring unusual and unexpected events to the "maps of meaning" which already form the basis of our cultural knowledge, into which the social world is *already* "mapped"'. Hall believes that such a process is ideological because particular 'maps of meaning' have become universal maps which are imposed: 'Because we occupy the same society and belong to roughly the same "culture", it is assumed that there is, basically, only *one* perspective on events: that provided by what is sometimes called *the* culture, or *the* central value system.'

T. A. Van Dijk

REPRESENTATION: SPORT AND STEREOTYPING IN THE MASS MEDIA

International sporting events, such as the Olympic Games, which today are covered extensively, and in some people's opinions, ad nauseam, in the press and on TV world-wide, offer the best opportunity (with the possible exception of war and international conflict), for press and TV journalists to draw on and reproduce certain perspectives, or myths, of how nationality and/or race are linked to particular physical characteristics, qualities, personality types, emotional tendencies, beliefs and historical events, a point emphasized by O'Donnell, the writer of Text B3.2.2.

In this unit, we first consider the nature of and processes involved in stereotyping, and then focus on the stereotyping of nationality, race and gender in the international press in relation to what is the only other international sporting event which receives a comparable level of media coverage to the Olympic Games, the Football World Cup.

Stereotyping

What processes does stereotyping involve? Hall (1997:268) writes that stereotypes get hold of the few 'simple, vivid, memorable, easily grasped and widely recognized characteristics about a person, reduce everything about that person to those traits, exaggerate and simplify them, and fix them without change or development to eternity'. Moreover, stereotyping both reflects and promotes particular perspectives; O'Sullivan in Text B3.2.1 refers to the historical dimension to stereotypes and to the 'power relations, tensions and conflicts' which underlie them.

TEXT B3.2.1
T. O'Sullivan,
J. Hartley,
D. Saunders,
M. Montgomery
and J. Fiske

O'Sullivan, T., Hartley, J., Saunders, D., Montgomery, M. and Fiske, J. (1994) *Key Concepts in Communication and Cultural Studies*, London: Routledge pp. 299–300

Stereotyping is:

> the social classification of particular groups and people as often highly simplified and generalised signs, which implicitly or explicitly represent a set of values, judgements and assumptions concerning their behaviour, characteristics or history.

In the field of social psychology stereotyping:

> has been defined as a particular extension of the fundamental cognitive processes of categorisation, whereby we impose structure and make sense of events, objects and experience. The process in itself requires the simplification and organisation of diverse and complex ranges of phenomena into general, labelled categories. In so doing attention is focused on certain similar identifying characteristics or distinctive features, as opposed to many other differences. Stereotypes, however, not only identify general categories of people: national populations (e.g., the Irish), races (e.g., the Latin race), classes (e.g., the working class), genders (i.e. men or women), occupations (e.g., accountants) and deviant

groups (e.g., drug takers), etc., they are distinctive in the way that they carry *undifferentiated judgements* about their referents. Whilst they may vary widely in terms of their emotional appeal and intensity, they generally represent underlying power relations, tensions or conflicts (i.e. the 'stupid' Irish, the 'excitable' Latins, the 'cloth cap' image, the 'dumb blond', the 'boring' accountant, the 'evil' junkie and so on). In short, they operate to define and identify groups of people as generally alike in certain ways – as committed to particular values, motivated by similar goals, having a common personality, make-up and so on. In this way stereotypes encourage an *intuitive belief* in their own underlying assumptions, and play a central role in organising common sense discourse . . .

Task B3.2.1

Consider the following questions.

➤ Is your nationality commonly stereotyped in the mass media both within your own country and in other countries (e.g. in newspapers and magazines, on television, in films, and in advertising)?
➤ What particular 'characteristics or distinctive features' are focused on, exaggerated and simplified?
➤ Do you think stereotypical representations of your own nationality are indicative of 'underlying power relations, tensions or conflicts'? If so, what are these underlying power relations, tensions and conflicts'?

Task B3.2.2

Look carefully at Figure 11 on the next page.

➤ What particular 'simple, vivid, memorable, easily grasped and widely recognized' characteristics of the six nationalities are drawn on by the cartoonist?
➤ What particular 'simple, vivid, memorable, easily grasped and widely recognized' characteristics of women and men are drawn on by the cartoonist?
➤ In what ways can the stereotypical images in the cartoon be said to fix national and gender characteristics 'without change and development to eternity'?
➤ Can the national stereotypes in the cartoon be said to represent a set of values and assumptions concerning the behaviour, characteristics or history of the people in the cartoon? (Think about both the nationalities depicted and the genders.)

Evening Standard 10 June 1998

Figure 11 Cartoon from the London *Evening Standard* 10 May 1998

TEXT B3.2.2
H. O'Donnell

O'Donnell, H. 'Mapping the Mythical: A geopolitics of national sporting stereotypes' *Discourse and Society*, 5:3 pp. 345–80 (1994) Sage, reproduced in O'Sullivan, T. and Jewkes, Y. (1997) *The Media Studies Reader* London: Edward Arnold (extracts)

The Germans

When European sports journalists refer to Germany, the dominant stereotype of national character combines the idea of strong mental control with discipline, efficiency, reliability and hard work: the central elements of what Spain's best-selling daily El Pais (3 November 1993) calls 'the German legend'. This stereotype is found throughout the European media, and is at times reflected in the German press itself. Thus, talking of the German football team's national coach during Euro '92, the German weekly magazine Stern (25 June 1992) wrote: 'Discipline, order, punctuality – national trainer Berti Vogts leads his team in the tried and tested Teutonic tradition.'

In the terms of this stereotype, the Germans have, above all, the right mental 'attitude': a confidence in their ability to get the job done, and total commitment to the task in hand. In 1992, as Germany overcame Sweden 3–2 in the semi-final of Euro '92, the Norwegian tabloid *Dagbladet* (22 June 1992) wrote: 'Their attitude is the Germans' strongest weapon. A winning instinct and self-confidence their greatest quality.' The Norwegian quality daily *Aftenposten* (26 June 1992) agreed, supplying an anecdote to support its point of view. 'German self-confidence in football knows no bounds. The Germans were the only team to book their hotel rooms in Gothenburg for the European Championship final in advance.'

H. O'Donnell

During the 1990 World Cup (Italia '90) the leading Swedish quality daily *Dagens Nyheter* (16 June 1990) described the German football team as a 'machine team', a phrase which would reappear verbatim in the Swedish tabloid *Aftonbladet's* coverage of Euro '92 (21 June 1992). The nation of mechanical efficiency accompanies German sportsmen and sportswomen across a range of sports.

The Southern Europeans

In sports reporting on Mediterranean countries, the dominant stereotype is clearly that of the temperamental Latin, a stereotype which also extends to South America. This is one of the most deep-rooted stereotypes in northern European culture, its main elements being passion, hot temper, frivolity, sensuality, even hedonism.

This stereotype finds one of its most widespread expressions in reporting on football. The absence of Mediterranean teams during Euro '92 meant that, in footballing terms at least, it was in the reporting of Italia '90 that such stereotyping achieved its greatest expression, its main European bearers being the Italians. Thus the then Soviet daily *Pravda* (21 June 1990) assured its readers that 'the Italian team . . . reflected the explosive nature of its people'. The ultimate symbol of fiery Italianness during Italia '90 was to be Vesuvius, representing the allegedly volcanic nature of the Italian temperament. When Italy was eliminated by Argentina in the semi-final, *Bild* (4 July 1990) wrote: 'Vesuvius, Naples and all of Italy weeps'. 'The Italians . . . went to Naples and at the edge of Vesuvius were burned by the molten lava', added the Basque daily *Deia* (4 July 1990).

The South Americans

The 'fieriness' of the Latins carries with it notions of unpredictable, even uncontrolled creativity. For all its entertainment value however, this creativity – which is often described as 'magic', particularly in the case of Latin Americans – is viewed unfavourably if it does not bring results. Thus, when AC Milan defeated PSV Eindhoven in the Champions' League in 1992, PSV's Brazilian player Romário da Souza Faria (commonly known simply as Romário) had, according to the Flemish-language Belgian daily *Gazet van Antwerpen* (10 December 1992), 'conjured up a few magic tricks out of his Brazilian shuffle, but lacked any sense of efficiency'.

It is in relation to South America in particular that the ultimately damaging effect of such stereotypes comes most fully into view. Their inherent ambivalence, on the one hand, facilitates their routine reproduction, since their positive side allows their inclusion in areas of journalistic production where any suggestion of direct prejudice would be discouraged and perhaps even censored. But their negative underside – seldom expressed directly though always present in a submerged mode – is an indissociable part of the stereotype and is triggered by implication when any element of the stereotype is used. In this way apparently inoffensive characterizations contribute to the maintenance and reproduction of prejudice in a powerful but elusive form.

If flair and creativity are the positive pole of the Southern stereotype, its negative pole brings tougher notions of indiscipline; irrationality and recklessness. In the case of the Latin Americans, 'temperament' usually deteriorates into supercharged emotions and complete irresponsibility. Thus the Soviet daily *Izvestia* (26 June 1990) reported of the Brazilians:

Suffice it to say that on those days when there are matches in which the national team is taking part the number of heart attacks doubles . . . In the waiting room of a hospital in São Paulo a female patient died of a stroke – all the medical staff were enthusiastically watching the match between Scotland and Costa Rica. And while Maradona joyously waved the green-yellow strip of his defeated Brazilian opponent above his head, fourteen criminals managed to escape from the grounds of a prison also in São Paulo, taking advantage of the inconsolable grief of the guards. No one was particularly surprised: it's football . . .

Beneath its superficial humour, this report tells of social acquiescence in collective professional negligence.

The Africans

During Italia '90, an unexpectedly exogenous recipient of at least parts of the Latin stereotype was to emerge: the Cameroonians. Indeed, with the early exit of Brazil from the competition, they came to be presented as 'the Brazilians of Africa' (*El Pais*, 13 June 1990), displaying, according to the German weekly *Sport-Bild*, 'Brazilian artistry' (20 June 1990). Their links with the Latin stereotype are immediately apparent, though the details of the stereotype are visibly more extreme. Thus, they are seen as sharing the 'magic' of the Latins – for the *Hannoversche Allgemeine Zeitung* (9 June 1992) they were 'football magicians', for *Bild* (16 June 1992) 'the magicians from Africa' – but in this case it is, in the words of the Italian daily *Corriere della Sera* (15 June 1992), 'black magic', suggesting even more unenlightened forms of religiosity than those conventionally associated with Latins.

Another feature of the Latin stereotype which they share is 'temperament', but again its expression externalizes elements of the stereotype which are often left unsaid. Thus, not only did the *Hannoversche Allgemeine Zeitung* (29 June 1990) describe the Cameroonians as personifying 'African temperament' (which it contrasted with the 'Siberian chill' of their Soviet trainer!) and as being themselves 'bundles of temperament', but *L'Équipe* (25 June 1990) even described their football as a 'victory for the irrational'. . . .

Modern sport provides an international arena in which symbolic national confrontations are played out at times before audiences of hundreds of millions. Sport is now also deeply commercialized, and, as just another form of commercial enterprise, it functions on an international level as a site in which advanced countries can and must act out their preferred myths through self-and-other stereotypes, and celebrate those qualities which, in their own eyes, make them more modern, more advanced, in short *superior* . . . This process routinely involves downgrading other national groups. The salience of widely disseminated schematic discursive models such as stereotypes in this process is encouraged not only by the ritualistic framework of the sporting confrontations, but also by both the demonic nature of much sports reporting and the pressure to produce dramatic reportage under which sports journalists work (Goldlust 1987:94); these circumstances combine to enhance the use-value of totemic reductionism, packing pre-formed and easily absorbed narratives into off-the-shelf formulations. And since sport . . . continues to constitute an area of social activity in which overt emotional engagement remains publicly acceptable in ways in which this would be unthinkable in other contexts (at least in Western societies), the sports section of a newspaper is one in which a level of national sentiment and a corresponding density of highly charged national stereotypes are to be found which it is difficult (at least under peacetime conditions) to imagine elsewhere.

 ### Task B3.2.3

➤ Compare the stereotypical images found in Text B3.2.2 by O'Donnell of the Germans, Italians and Cameroonians to the stereotypical images of these nationalities in Figure 11.

Task B3.2.4

The title of the article by O'Donnell includes the words 'national sporting stereotypes'. However, in the article itself O'Donnell in some cases considers specific nationalities (the Germans are the nationality focused on in the edited extract in Text B3.2.2) and, in other cases, considers nationalities in sections under the headings of races or groups of nations (the 'Southern Europeans', the 'South Americans', and the 'Africans').

➤ Consider the effect this has.

Task B3.2.5

O'Donnell writes that sport is like any other commercial enterprise and, as such, 'functions on an international level as a site in which advanced countries can and must act out their preferred myths through self-and-other stereotypes, and celebrate those qualities which, in their own eyes, make them more modern, more advanced, in short *superior*'.

➤ Do you agree with O'Donnell that sport is like any other 'commercial enterprise' in this respect?
➤ Can you think of ways in which your own nation acts out through sport and related activities its 'preferred myths through self-and-other stereotypes' and celebrates certain qualities which make it seem 'superior'?
➤ Can you identify other fields apart from sport in which nations act out their 'preferred myths through self-and-other stereotypes' and celebrate certain qualities which make them seem 'superior'?

Task B3.2.6

➤ Find examples of the stereotyping of your own and other nations from the sports sections in newspapers available in your own context. Are the results of your analysis similar to what O'Donnell found?

Commentary

In Text B3.2.2 O'Donnell writes that sport 'functions on an international level as a site in which advanced countries can and must act out their preferred myths'. The mention of 'myth' brings to mind the work of Roland Barthes, much of whose early work was concerned with myths of nationality, particularly French nationality. For Barthes (1973:142–3) myth has a naturalising effect: 'myth is constituted by the historical loss of the quality of things; in it, things lose the memory that they were once made. . . . The function of myth is to empty reality . . . Myth does not deny things, on the contrary, its function is to talk about them; simply it purifies them, it makes them innocent, it gives them a natural and eternal justification.' Such ideas have been influential to the work of those who have investigated how national and racial identity is constructed. Benedict Anderson (1983) is one such figure and writes that : 'Communities are to be distinguished by the style in which they are imagined.' Smith (1990:109) refers, too, to the need in nation building for a 'common depository of myths, heroes, events, landscapes and memories which are organised and taken to assume a primordial quality'.

For Hall (1996:613) 'A national culture is a discourse – a way of constructing meanings which influences both our actions and our conceptions of ourselves.' The means by which national identity is constructed through discourse, and specifically that of Austria, is examined in detail by Wodak *et al.* (1999).

UNIT B3.3

THE REPRESENTATION OF IDENTITY: PERSONALITY AND ITS SOCIAL CONSTRUCTION

In this unit we return to the question of individual identity, and particularly the question of personality. You can hardly open a more 'popular' magazine and newspaper without coming across some questionnaire designed to analyse some aspect of your personality or behaviour. Often conclusions of a flippant nature are made about your personality based on the answers that you give to questions on how you behave as a consumer, lover or driver.

While we learn not to take such questionnaires seriously, the constant references to personality traits in various genres in the mass media, whether they are applied to individuals or, as we saw in Unit B3.2, to nationalities or races, suggest that personality is what Gee describes a key 'cultural model' (Unit B1.3) in many contexts. Vivien Burr, whose views on personality we will explore in more detail in this unit, writes that 'The notion of personality is so firmly embedded in our thinking in contemporary Western society that we hardly, if ever, question it' (1996:17). Indeed, not only do we rarely question the 'Western' model of personality, but we often assume that it can be universally applied to, and be a useful mechanism for understanding, individuals in all cultures.

The processes through which we perceive a person's personality are described by Sarah Hampson in Text B3.3.2, and we explore their implications for our perceptions of individuals and their behaviour across different cultural contexts.

Text B3.3.1 also introduces an important concept, which has implications for how we both view the world around us and the people within it. This is 'social constructionism'. We will explore this concept further, together with the related notion of 'social representation', in Unit B3.4.

Task B3.3.1

➤ Before you read Text B3.3.1, write down (in about ten sentences) a description of the personality of a good friend.

Burr, V. (1996) *An Introduction to Social Constructionism*, London: Routledge
pp. 21–28 (extracts)

TEXT B3.3.1
V. Burr

Problems with the traditional view of personality

. . . the idea of 'personality' is one that we use in our everyday lives in order to try to make sense
of the things that we and other people do. 'Personality' can then come to be seen as a theory
(one held very widely in our society) for explaining human behaviour, and for trying to anticipate
our part in social interactions with others. We could say that in our daily lives we act as if there
were such a thing as personality, and most of the time we get by reasonably well by doing so.
But it is a big leap from this to saying that personality really exists (in the sense of traits
inhabiting our mental structures, or being written into our genetic material).

Another weak point in the 'personality really exists' argument is this. If personality does really
exist in this way, then we are describing part of human nature. We should expect to find
'personality' as we know it in all human beings, no matter what part of the world they inhabit or
what period of history they may have occupied. But it is clear that all peoples do not subscribe
to our western view. In some cultures, people account for their actions by reference to invisible
spirits and demons and would find our idea that behaviour originates in personality a very
strange one. . . .

The uniqueness and private nature of much of what we mean by 'personality' is also not a
feature of all cultures. For example, we tend to think of our emotions as private events that are
bound up with the kind of people we are. A person with a 'depressive' personality might be
expected to feel 'sadness' often. We imagine a 'caring' person to have 'loving' feelings. These
feelings or emotions are thought of as the internal, private experience of individuals, and are
intimately connected to the type of person they are. For example, anger is something we feel
inside us, and which is manifested in the things we say and do. However, as Lutz (1982, 1990)
has pointed out, this is not the case in all cultures. For the Ifaluk (Samoan and Pintupi Aborigine),
emotion words are statements not about people's internal states but about their relationship
to events and other people. The Ifaluk talk of song, which in translation comes out as something
like 'justifiable anger'. This justifiable anger is not a privately owned feeling, but a moral and
public account of some transgression of accepted social practices and values.

Of course we could claim that these cultural differences are due to differences in education
and understanding. We could suggest that non-western cultures (and those of previous historical
periods) do not have the benefit of our knowledge. What we would be doing then is making a
claim about the truthfulness of our own view as opposed to the falsity of theirs. We would be
saying, 'We know that in fact people have personalities, and that the way people behave is heavily
influenced by their personality. People in other cultures have not realised this yet, and they
therefore hold a false view of reality.' This is to state the case rather strongly, but it makes the
point that unless we have complete confidence in the 'personality really exists' view, we have to
accept that personality may be a theory which is peculiar to certain societies at appertain point
in time . . .

As I mentioned earlier, one of the fundamental assumptions of the common-sense view of
personality is that personality is stable across situations and over time. However, this does not
stand up to scrutiny when we examine our own day-to-day experience. Do you behave in the
same way when you are in the pub with your mates and when you are taking tea with Great-uncle
Eric? (I'm sure you can find your own equivalents.) Do you talk to your closest friend in the same
way as to your bank manager? Do you feel confident, outgoing and 'on the ball' when you are at
a party with people you know? What about when you go for a job interview? These examples may
look trivial and you will probably already be coming up with explanations for the differences.
But the overall message is an important one. We think and feel differently depending on whom
we are with, what we are doing and why . . .

Extension

V. Burr

The social construction of personality

What might it mean, then, to say that personality is socially constructed? One way of looking at this is to think of personality (the kind of person you are) as existing not within people but between them. This is hard to conceptualize at first, so I will give you some illustrative examples. Take some of the personality-type words we use to describe people: for example, friendly, caring, shy, self-conscious, charming, bad-tempered, thoughtless. If you like, make your own list of words you could use to describe the people you know. I would predict that most of them will be words which would completely lose their meaning if the person described were living alone on a desert island. Without the presence of other people, i.e. a social environment, can a person be said to be 'friendly', 'shy' or 'caring'? The point is that we use these words as if they referred to entities existing within the person they describe, but once the person is removed from their relations with others the words become meaningless. They refer to our behaviour towards other people. The friendliness, shyness or caring exists not inside people, but in the relation between them . . .

Next, think of a person you know, someone with whom you are more than just slightly acquainted. Think about how you are when you are with that person. Perhaps you feel that when you are with her or him you are level-headed and rational. She or he always seems to be leaping from one crisis to another and seems to be in awe of your apparent ability to take the world in your stride. The nature of the relationship between you is one of counsellor and client, or 'the strong one' and 'the weak one'. Now think of someone else with whom you are just the opposite. With this person you always seem to be pouring out your troubles, asking advice and taking the lead from him or her. Perhaps this particular example does not fit you, but you will be able to think of comparable ones. The point is that it makes no sense to ask which of these is the real you. They both are, but each version of 'you' is a product of your relationships with others. Each 'you' is constructed socially, out of the social encounters that make up your relationships . . .

Task B3.3.2

➤ Read the description you wrote down of your friend' s personality in Task B3.3.1. Does your description include in it any indication that your friend's personality might vary depending on: the situation your friend might be in; the different people your friend might be with; any reference to events, actions or behaviour that involve your friend?

➤ Consider the description of your friend's personality in light of what Burr writes in Text B3.3.1. How is your friend 'constructed socially'?

TEXT B3.3.2

S. E. Hampson

Hampson, S. E. 'The Social Psychology of Personality' in Cooper, C. and Varma, V. (1997) *Processes in Individual Differences*, London: Routledge pp. 77–80 (extracts)

. . . The following discussion of the observer in personality construction is organized according to a three-stage model of personality perception. . . . In brief, the process of personality construction from the observer's perspective involves (1) the identification of behaviour, (2) the categorization of behavioural acts, and (3) the attribution of personality. These three stages are usually, but not necessarily, sequential. Whether or not processing proceeds from stage 1 to stage 2, or from stage 2 to stage 3, depends upon the goals of the perceiver/observer. Many social interactions can take place without going beyond behaviour identification, and many more can be quite satisfactory without engaging in personality attribution . . .

Personality traits can be used by observers/perceivers to describe (categorize) behaviour, or to describe personality. Each use of traits involves different processes. However, psychologists are not always clear on this distinction, and there can be confusion if a study of act categorization is interpreted as if it were looking at trait attribution, or vice versa. In act categorization (stage 2), traits are used to describe behaviour. Instead of identifying behaviour (e.g., Jane is carrying John's shopping bag), we use a descriptive category (a trait adjective) to describe it (e.g., Jane is being helpful). The behaviour is categorized as an instance of a particular trait category. In person categorization, the trait is applied to the person performing the behaviour, not just the behaviour itself (e.g., Jane is helpful). In everyday language, we may blur the distinction between the two uses of traits with no adverse consequences. Indeed, the tendency to use traits to describe persons when we really only mean to categorize behaviours may be another manifestation of the fundamental attribution error, which is the tendency to explain behaviour in dispositional terms and to ignore the part played by the situation . . .

Stage 1: Behaviour identification

The first step in person perception is to identify what it is that a person is doing. Behaviour identification precedes either use of the trait concept. For example, is the person running or walking? Is Jane carrying something? . . .

Stage 2: Act categorization

Act categorization can only occur after behaviour identification. It involves further identification of the behaviour as a member of a trait category . . .

Behaviours are composed of three kinds of features: behavioural (the actions that occur), situational (the context in which they occur) and motivational (the underlying motive they reflect), and these features vary in their prototypicality with regard to different trait categories. Motivational features are often key to categorizing behaviour and, because motivations have to be inferred from the context and other information, they can be the cause of miscategorizations. A behaviour may appear to be a good member of one category (e.g., Jane carrying John's shopping is a good instance of the trait category helpful); however, if we knew more about the relationship between Jane and John, we might more correctly categorize Jane's behaviour as submissive.

Stage 3: Personality attribution

Personality attribution involves the application of the trait concept to the person performing the behaviour. For example, we describe people as helpful, submissive or altruistic. . . . Unlike act categorization, we do not usually make personality attributions based on just one piece of behaviour (although we may).

In addition, more specific theories can be developed for the conditions under which particular traits will be attributed to persons. . . . For positive moral traits such as honesty, many behavioural instances are required to convince the observer that the person is truly honest, whereas for dishonesty, the observer may use just one behaviour to make a trait attribution. If you observe a pickpocket at work in a crowd, you are likely to make an immediate person categorization (dishonest thief). This is an example of where a person categorization is made simultaneously with the behaviour categorization.

Task B3.3.3

Hampson's belief that 'the observer may use just one behaviour to make a trait attribution' in the case of a 'negative moral trait' was recently the experience of one of the authors of this book. He saw a man walking standing in the street in front of his house apparently talking heatedly to himself and gesticulating animatedly, and categorized the man in the street as being 'off his head'. Only when the man turned round did the author see that the man was using was a hands-free mobile phone and realized that he had made a false trait attribution on the basis of misinterpreting just one behaviour.

➤ Can you think of occasions when you have made false trait attributions on the basis of misinterpreting single instances of behaviour?

 Task B3.3.4

The processes involved in behaviour identification and act categorization as described by Hampson are also salient when considering how we otherize individuals who are different to us. This point is made by Gandy (1998:53) in the passage below.

> We categorize those we believe are different from us into category systems that have less variety than the systems we use for people we think are more like us. In addition, after we have categorized a person as a member of a particular group, that classification affects how we characterize their behavior. The same behavior performed by a member of another group will be characterized in different ways on the basis of the structure of beliefs we have already developed about these groups.

➤ Reread Examples A2.3.1 and A3.1.1 in Section A. How far are Gandy's comments borne out in these examples?

 Task B3.3.5

➤ What are the implications of what Burr and Hampson write in Texts B3.3.1 and B3.3.2, and of Gandy's comments, for how we perceive and interpret the behaviour and personalities, and how we ourselves behave, when we come into contact with individuals in or from cultures which are unfamiliar to us?

Commentary

The fact that Burr focuses on the question of personality at the very beginning of her book, an extract of which was featured in Text B3.3.1, is interesting, and reflects the concern in social constructionism with questions of identity. Burr also refers in the text to how emotions are also socially constructed, and this again is a key interest of others in this field. Strongman (1996:220) writes that 'Theory deriving from social constructionism . . . has it that emotions (or at least adult human emotions) come from the culture or social concepts. . . . The strong form of the social constructionist view of emotion is that *all* human emotions are socially constructed – i.e. they are based on beliefs and shaped by language, and ultimately stem from culture. The weaker view is preferred by most in this camp – i.e. that some emotions are socially constructed and some are more socially constructed than others. Interest then centres on how any social construction occurs.' For Strongman it is also important to consider roles and situations and how in any one 'macro' culture there will be a complex interplay between different factors: '. . . cultural and institutional roles carry implicit and explicit prescriptions about what emotions should be *expressed* and *experienced* in particular situations, and to what degree these emotions should be *displayed*' (p. 223).

SOCIAL CONSTRUCTIONISM AND SOCIAL REPRESENTATIONS

UNIT B3.4

In this unit we consider, in another extract from Burr's readable and accessible introduction to the issue, in more detail how our perceptions of the world might be said to be 'socially constructed' (Text B3.4.1), and also consider a related notion, that of 'social representations'. Serge Moscovici, who is credited with introducing the concept of 'social representations', documented how terms used in the field of psychology, and specifically in psychoanalysis and psychotherapy, had come to be used by French people in describing and explaining everyday behaviour and events (1976). Hewstone and Augoustinos (1998:62) provide their own definition: 'Culturally agreed upon explanations eventually come to be regarded as common-sense explanations. Each society has its own culturally and socially sanctioned explanation or range of explanations for phenomena such as illness, poverty, failure, success, violence crime, etc. People therefore do not always need to engage in an active cognitive search for explanations for all forms of behaviour and events. Instead, people evoke their socialized processing or social representations for expected and normative behaviour and events.' Crucially, social representations have a historical dimension; Moscovici (1998:242) writes that they are 'the product of a whole sequence of elaborations and of changes which occur in the course of time and are the achievement of successive generations. All the systems of classification, all the images and all the descriptions which circulate within a society . . . imply a link with previous systems and images, a stratification in the collective memory and a reproduction in the language, which invariably reflects past knowledge, and which breaks the bounds of current information.' Sperber, who writes that 'To explain culture, then, is to explain why and how some ideas happen to be contagious' (1996:1), attempts to construct his own model of social representations, which we shall consider in Text B3.4.2.

TEXT B3.4.1
V. Burr

Burr, V. (1996) *An Introduction to Social Constructionism*, London: Routledge pp. 2–5 (extracts)

There is no one feature which could be said to identify a social constructionist position. Instead, we might loosely group as social constructionist any approach which has at its foundation one or more of the following key assumptions (from Gergen 1985). You might think of these as something like 'things you would absolutely have to believe in order to be a social constructionist':

1 A critical stance towards taken-for-granted knowledge

Social constructionism insists that we take a critical stance towards our taken-for-granted ways of understanding the world (including ourselves). It invites us to be critical of the idea that our observations of the world unproblematically yield its nature to us, to challenge the view that conventional knowledge is based upon objective, unbiased observation of the world. It is therefore in opposition to what are referred to as positivism and empiricism in traditional science – the assumptions that the nature of the world can be revealed by observation, and that what exists is what we *perceive* to exist. Social constructionism cautions us to be ever suspicious of our assumptions about how the world appears to be. This means that the categories with which we as human beings apprehend the world do not necessarily refer to real divisions. For example, just because we think of some music as 'classical' and some as 'pop' does not mean we should assume that there is anything in the nature of the music itself that means it has to be divided up in that particular way. . . .

2 Historical and cultural specificity

The ways in which we commonly understand the world, the categories and concepts we use, are historically and culturally specific . . . This means that all ways of understanding are historically and culturally relative. Not only are they specific to particular cultures and periods of history, they are seen as products of that culture and history, and are dependent upon the particular social and economic arrangements prevailing in that culture at that time. The particular forms of knowledge that abound in any culture are therefore artefacts of it, and we should not assume that our ways of understanding are necessarily any better (in terms of being any nearer the truth) than other ways.

3 Knowledge is sustained by social processes

If our knowledge of the world, our common ways of understanding it, is not derived from the nature of the world as it really is, where does it come from? The social constructionist answer is that people construct it between them. It is through the daily interactions between people in the course of social life that our versions of knowledge become fabricated. Therefore social interaction of all kinds, and particularly language, is of great interest to social constructionists. The goings-on between people in the course of their everyday lives are seen as the practices during which our shared versions of knowledge are constructed. Therefore what we regard as 'truth' (which of course varies historically and cross-culturally), i.e. our current accepted ways of understanding the world, is a product not of objective observation of the world, but of the social processes and interactions in which people are constantly engaged with each other.

4 Knowledge and social action go together

These 'negotiated' understandings could take a wide variety of different forms, and we can therefore talk of numerous possible 'social constructions' of the world. But each different construction also brings with it, or invites, a different kind of action from human beings.' For example, before the Temperance movement, drunks were seen as entirely responsible for their behaviour, and therefore blameworthy. A typical response was therefore imprisonment. However, there has been a move away from seeing drunkenness as a crime and towards thinking of it as a sickness, a kind of addiction.

Task B3.4.1

Burr writes that 'just because we think of some music as "classical" and some as "pop" does not mean we should assume that there is anything in the nature of the music itself that means it has to be divided up in that particular way'.

➤ Think about the ways that art and literature are 'divided up'. Is there anything in the 'nature of' art and literature that mean they have to be divided into particular categories?

Task B3.4.2

We considered in Unit B3.2 how people are 'divided up' in particular ways, in particular according to nationality, race and gender.

➤ Think of other ways in which the world and the people of the world are divided up. How many of these divisions are 'social constructs'?

Sperber, D. (1996) *Explaining culture: a naturalistic approach*, Oxford: Blackwell pp. 24, 32–33, 81–82 (extracts)

What are cultural things made of?

Let us start as simply as possible. Cultural things are, in part, made of bodily movements of individuals and of environmental changes resulting from these movements. For instance, people are beating drums, or erecting a building, or slaughtering an animal. The material character of these phenomena is, so far, unproblematic. But we must go further. Is it a musical exercise, a drummed message, or a ritual? Is it a house, a shop, or a temple? Is it butchery, or sacrifice? In order to answer, one must, one way or another, take into account the representations involved in these behaviours. Whatever one's theoretical or methodological framework, representations play an essential role in defining cultural phenomena. But what are representations made of?

Let us note, to begin with, that two types of representations are involved: mental representations and public representations. Beliefs, intentions and preferences are mental representations. . . . Signals, utterances, texts and pictures are all public representations. Public representations have an obviously material aspect. However, describing this aspect – the sounds of speech, the shapes and colours of a picture – leaves out the most important fact, that these material traces can be interpreted: they represent something for someone.

Interpreting and explaining cultural representations

A representation sets up a relationship between at least three terms: that which represents, that which is represented, and the user of the representation. A fourth term may be added when there is a producer of the representation distinct from its user. A representation may exist inside its user: it is then a *mental representation*, such as a memory, a belief, or an intention. The producer and the user of a mental representation are one and the same person. A representation may also exist in the environment of its user, as is the case, for instance, of the text you are presently reading; it is then a *public representation*. Public representations are usually means of communication between a user and a producer distinct from one another. A mental representation has, of course, a single user. A public representation may have several . . .

Consider a social group: a tribe, the inhabitants of a town, or the members of an association. Such a group and its common environment are, so to speak, inhabited by a much larger population of representations, mental and public. Each member of the group has, in his or her head, millions of mental representations, some short-lived, others stored in long-term memory and constituting the individual's 'knowledge'. Of these mental representations, some – a very small proportion – get communicated repeatedly, and end up being distributed throughout the group, and thus have a mental version in most of its members. When we speak of *cultural representations*, we have in mind – or should have in mind – such widely distributed, lasting representations. Cultural representations so understood are a fuzzy subset of the set of mental and public representations inhabiting a given social group. . . .

Public representations are generally attributed similar meanings by their producers and by their users, or else they could never serve the purpose of communication. This similarity of attributed meaning is itself made possible by the fact that people have similar enough linguistic and encyclopaedic knowledge. Similarity across people makes it possible to abstract from individual differences and to describe 'the language' or 'the culture' of a community, 'the meaning' of a public representation, or to talk of, say, 'the belief' that witches ride on broomsticks as a single representation, independently of its public expressions or mental instantiations. What is then described is an abstraction. Such an abstraction may be useful in many ways: it may bring out the common properties of a family of related mental and public representations; it may serve to identify a topic of research.

Task B3.4.3

Burr gives the example of how views of drunks and drunkenness are socially constructed, and how these social constructs have changed over time. She also talks of how 'typical responses' that have been made to drunks and drunkenness have also changed over time.

➤ In a 'social group' you see yourself as a member of, how have the social constructions of the following people and issues changed over time?

■ Gays/lesbianism and homosexuality.
■ Divorcees/divorce.
■ People who suffer from 'mental illness'/'mental illness'.

■ Women who have abortions/abortion.

■ Criminals/crime.

➤ What have been 'typical responses' to these people and issues in your social group at different times?

➤ What particular 'cultural representations' (in Sperber's understanding of the term) of the people and issues are currently widely distributed in your social group, and what do 'typical responses' currently consist of?

Commentary

For Van Dijk there is a close relationship between social representations and ideologies. He defines ideologies as 'the basis of the social representations shared by members of a group' (1998:8). An important question concerning social representations is that of how far the individual is bound by networks of social representations. Oyserman and Markus (1998:117–18) assert that 'individuals may resist or fail to incorporate . . . public and mutually constructed ideas . . . into their meaning-making systems', but state that more research is needed into 'how many individuals in a given socio-cultural niche must share' social representations and 'with what level of incorporation and understanding, and of how much resistance or outright negation can be tolerated within a given cultural system'. Augoustinos (1998:165) claims, too, that 'people may not simply endorse or reject dominant views, but rather, develop complex configurations of thought in which some dominant ideological elements find expression in conjunction with individual and group-based understandings'.

CULTURAL CONSTRUCTS

UNIT B3.5

In Task B3.4.2 in Unit B3.4 you were asked to consider how the world and people in the world are commonly divided up. In the final unit in Section B we look at a very common division that has been made by social scientists and categorized 'cultures': the division between 'collectivism' and 'individualism'. This division has trickled down into numerous popular guides for those visiting, living in and working in 'foreign' cultural contexts, as well as academic texts in such diverse fields as education (and particularly language learning and teaching), psychology, health care, business and history. In Text B3.5.1, Extract 1, we include introductory sections from a book by a social scientist who has written widely on 'collectivism' and 'individualism', Triandis. We will consider, in the light of some of the perspectives in previous units in Section B, whether such a distinction is valuable in helping us to understand both ourselves and others.

Before we go on to consider what the terms 'collectivism' and 'individualism' mean, read the description of ten incidents that Triandis provides below.

TEXT B3.5.1,
EXTRACT 1
H. C. Triandis

Triandis, H. C. (1995) *Individualism and Collectivism*, Boulder: Westview Press
pp. 1–2 (extracts)

1. In Brazil, a waiter brings one menu for four people and gives it to the 'senior' member of the group, who orders the same food for all.
2. In France, each member of the group orders a different entrée at a restaurant.
3. In India, a senior engineer is asked to move to New York, at a salary that is twenty-five times his salary in New Delhi, but he declines the opportunity.
4. In California, a senior engineer is asked to move to New York, at a salary that is 50 percent higher than his salary in Los Angeles, and he accepts.
5. On a street in Moscow, an older woman scolds a mother she does not know because she thinks the mother has not wrapped her child warmly enough.
6. In New York, a woman asks for help from passers-by to escape from the beatings that her boyfriend is giving her; but no one helps.
7. In Japan, a supervisor knows a great deal about the personal life of each subordinate and arranges for one of his subordinates to meet a nice girl he can marry.
8. In England, a subordinate does not mention to his supervisor that his father has just died.
9. In Germany, a man walks on the grass in a public park and is reprimanded by several passers-by.
10. In Illinois, a man marries a woman his parents disapprove of.

 Task B3.5.1

In his book Triandis asks the question: 'What do the . . . incidents have in common?'

➤ Can you see anything that any of the incidents [listed in Text B3.5.1] have in common with another/other of the incidents?
➤ Can you provide explanations for what is said/done and what is not said/done by individuals in the ten incidents described?
➤ What do you think the writer's purpose is in asking what the incidents have in common?

Now read Extract 2 of Text B3.5.1.

TEXT B3.5.1,
EXTRACT 2
H. C. Triandis

Triandis, H. C. (1995) *Individualism and Collectivism* Boulder: Westview Press
pp. 2–3, 4–5

As we analyze episodes of this kind [listed in Text B3.5.1], we find that they can be explained by two constructs: collectivism and individualism. The odd-numbered episodes reflect an aspect of collectivism; the even-numbered ones an aspect of individualism. The fact that ten so diverse social behaviors can be explained by just two constructs indicates that the constructs are useful and powerful . . .

Collectivism may be initially defined as a social pattern consisting of closely linked individuals who see themselves as parts of one or more collectives (family, co-workers, tribe, nation); are primarily motivated by the norms of, and duties imposed by, those collectives; are willing to give priority to the goals of these collectives over their own

H. C. Triandis

personal goals; and emphasize their connectedness to members of these collectives. A preliminary definition of *individualism* is a social pattern that consists of loosely linked individuals who view themselves as independent of collectives; are primarily motivated by their own preferences, needs, rights, and the contracts they have established with others; give priority to their personal goals over the goals of others; and emphasize rational analyses of the advantages and disadvantages to associating with others.

The reader will want some explanation of why the ten behaviors mentioned above reflect these constructs. Brazil, India, Russia, and Japan are collectivist countries, though in different degrees. France, the United States, England, and Germany are individualistic countries, also in different degrees. Nevertheless, one can find both collectivist and individualistic elements in *all* these countries, in different combinations.

In Brazil, the waiter assumes that the senior member of the group will decide what to eat and that ultimately consuming the same food will intensify bonds among the members of the group, whereas in France the waiter infers that each person has personal preferences that must be respected.

In India, the engineer feels he must stay close to his parents and that New York is simply too far. If his father were dying, it would be the engineer's duty to be at his bedside and facilitate his passage to the other state. Under similar conditions in the United States, it is more likely that the parent would be placed in a nursing home. The parent and his son have their own lives and are independent entities.

In Russia it is assumed that the whole community is responsible for child rearing. If the parent is not doing an adequate job, an older person is responsible for upholding community standards. 'Putting one's nose in another person's business' is perfectly natural and expected.

One's supervisor in Japan is often like a father, one who is obliged to attend to the needs of his subordinates. Locating a suitable mate for a subordinate may be one of his duties. In England, where individualism is quite intense, the death of a parent may be private information not to be shared with a supervisor. . . . Germany, though overall individualistic, is also collectivist in certain respects. The German episode is illustrative of collectivist behavior. Walking on hard-to-grow grassy areas is a community concern, and witnesses to such 'deviant' behaviour may take action. In most cultures, people try to marry a spouse that their parents find acceptable. However, in very individualistic entities like the United States, it is assumed that people are independent entities and can marry someone regardless of parental disapproval. In individualist cultures marriage is an institution that only links two people and not their respective families. In collectivist cultures it links two families, in which case it is mandatory that the families find the mate acceptable. . . .

One of culture's most important aspects is 'unstated assumptions'. The assumption that we are bound together into tight groups of interdependent individuals is fundamental to collectivism. The assumption that we are independent entities, different and distant from our groups, is fundamental to individualism. If we look at the ten examples, we see that such assumptions hold. The Brazilian waiter saw a group of interconnected individuals, with a 'senior' member who would order the food. The French waiter saw individual preferences as unrelated to group influences. The Indian engineer saw himself linked to his parents; the American engineer saw his parents as having a life of their own. The elderly Russian woman saw herself linked to the mother passing by; the New Yorkers saw no ties to the woman asking for help. The Japanese supervisor saw himself linked to his subordinates and thus felt that it was his duty to take care of their personal problems. The English subordinate saw himself not linked at all to his supervisor, so the supervisor had no inherent right to obtain private information. The German citizens saw themselves linked to the community and felt a need to defend it from a person who broke the rules. The Illinois man saw himself as a discrete entity, only weakly linked to his parents.

Task B3.5.2

➤ Look again at the descriptions of incidents 1, 2, 3 and 4 in Text B3.5.1.

➤ Change 'Brazil' to France' in description 1, and 'France' to 'Brazil' in description 2. Also change 'India' and 'New Delhi' to 'California' and 'Los Angeles' in description 3, and 'California' and 'Los Angeles' to 'India' and 'New Delhi' in description 4.

➤ Now that you have changed the descriptions, do you think that these incidents could occur in the other places?

➤ If you think they could occur in the other places, what implications does this have in light of the points made in Text B3.5.1?

Task B3.5.3

➤ Evaluate what Triandis writes in this unit in relation to ideas we have previously considered in other texts throughout Section B. Below are quotations from some of these texts.

> We have an old habit of speaking about 'cultures', in the plural form, as if it were self-evident that such entities exist side by side as neat packages, each of us identified with only one of them . . . (Hannerz (1999), Unit B0.1, Text B0.1.1).

> . . . The dominant discourse relies on equating community, culture, and ethnic identity, and its protagonists can easily reduce anybody's behaviour to a symptom of this equation. So long as its human objects can be logged under some ethnic identity other than, say, British, German, or American, it can even claim to speak 'for' them, 'represent' them, explain them to others. (Baumann (1996), Unit B0.1, Text B0.1.2).

> Another important fact about cultures is that they are essentially open. Cultures are ideational entities; as such they are permeable, susceptible to influence from other cultures. (Fay (1996), Unit B0.2, Text B0.2.1).

> In the functionalist tradition, 'culture' is seen as background and resource, where the human subject is only seen in his/her role of executor of functions. 'Culture' thus comes to be viewed too simply as either behaviour (e.g. x people don't smile in public), or as fixed values and beliefs, separated from social interaction and socio-political realities (e.g. x culture values the elderly) (Roberts and Sarangi (1993), Unit B0.2, Text B0.2.2).

Cultural models . . . lead us to ask, when confronted with a piece of talk, writing, action, or interaction, questions like these:

- What cultural models are relevant here? What must I, as an analyst, assume people feel, value, and believe, consciously or not, in order to talk (write), act, and/or interact this way? . . .
- How consistent are the relevant cultural models here? Are there competing or conflicting cultural models at play? Whose interests are the cultural models representing? . . .
- How are the relevant cultural models here helping to reproduce, transform, or create social, cultural, institutional, and/or political relationships? What Discourses and Conversations are these cultural models helping to reproduce, transform or create? (Gee (1999), Unit B1.3, Text B1.3.1, Extract 2).

When I think of myself in cultural categories – which I do perhaps too often – I know that I'm a recognizable example of a species: a professional New York woman . . . (Hoffman (1989), in Pavlenko and Lantolf (2000), Unit B1.4, Text B1.4.1).

We are moving more towards belonging to multiple communities, symbolic communities, communities of choice, and further and further away from belonging to communities of traditional location (Hall, Unit B1.5, Text B1.5.2).

Stereotyping . . . has been defined as a particular extension of the fundamental cognitive processes of categorisation, whereby we impose structure and make sense of events, objects and experience. The process in itself requires the simplification and organisation of diverse and complex ranges of phenomena into general, labelled categories. In so doing attention is focused on certain similar identifying characteristics or distinctive features, as opposed to many other differences (O'Sullivan, Hartley, Saunders, Montgomery, and Fiske (1994), Unit B3.2, Text B3.2.1).

. . . after we have categorized a person as a member of a particular group, that classification affects how we characterize their behavior. The same behavior performed by a member of another group will be characterized in different ways on the basis of the structure of beliefs we have already developed about these groups (Gandy (1998), Unit B3.3, Task B3.3.4).

Social constructionism . . . invites us to be critical of the idea that our observations of the world unproblematically yield its nature to us, to challenge the view that conventional knowledge is based upon objective, unbiased observation of the world (Burr (1995), Unit B3.4, Text B3.4.1).

Commentary

It should be noted that the model developed by Triandis (1995) is more complex than is suggested in the short extract from his book included in this unit, and, indeed, he mentions the following: that the 'terms' 'individualism' and 'collectivism' are 'fuzzy and difficult to measure' (p. 2), that 'our assumptions are not universal' (p. 3), that 'there are people in each of the countries that were mentioned in the examples who would have acted very differently' (p. 3), and that 'what may be called "the situation" is very important' (p. 3).

Important questions arise, however, when such models are considered in light of what others have recently written about culture, cultural identity, and its representation, questions suggested in Task B3.5.3 in this unit. A significant problem when social scientists, such as Triandis, employ models along the individualism–collectivism dimension (in some cases, like Hofstede (1991), adding other dimensions, to investigate how cultures and communities are constructed), is that these 'constructs' are interpreted as 'facts' by writers of the numerous popular guides for those visiting, living in and working in, 'foreign' cultural contexts, which we mentioned in the introduction to this unit. Moreover, even in academic texts there is often a tendency to make statements of a generalized and questionable nature. Triandis himself (1995:74), for example, writes that 'personality is less evident in collectivist cultures than it is in individualist cultures because the situation is such a powerful determinant of social behaviour'.

At the end of Section B, we return to the writer featured in the first text extract in Section B, Ulf Hannerz (Unit B0.1, Text B0.1.1). In a recent publication, Hannerz writes that culture

> must not be a mystifying concept, but must point towards tools to think with. As a reflective stance, everyday cultural analysis would involve a sense of how we know what we know about other people: a sense of our sources of ignorance and misunderstandings as well as of knowledge. It may even suggest that differences between people are not absolute or eternal. Culture can be viewed in no small part as a matter of cumulative experience, and exchanges about that experience. It is a matter of doing as well as being, it is fluid rather than frozen. And such everyday cultural analysis might also tell us that culture may cut across social distinctions, so as to create at least some areas of sharing, and some possibility of mutual intelligibility (2001:69–70).

SECTION C
Exploration

Exploration

In Section C of the book the focus is upon relating what you have read and learned in Sections A and B to your own personal circumstances and experiences. The aim is to develop reflection and strategies for action which will increase your awareness about how you may approach intercultural communication. This is achieved through research tasks. These can be carried out either in groups or individually; but the value of researching in small groups, perhaps with others from different cultural backgrounds, is that you can compare notes and at the same time learn from each other's cultural perspectives.

As with the rest of the book, this section follows the broad themes of identity, otherization and representation. Explicit links will be made to Sections A and B, but there will also be links you will need to make by yourselves as an index of your own theory development. Ideas and themes raised in the units in the previous sections are therefore further developed in the units in this section.

The intention is to offer you research tasks that will develop both your 'noticing' skills and your strategies in undoing and dealing with essentialist cultural prejudices. They are designed to help you observe, gather data and reflect upon the deeper nature of cultural difference and hence to enhance your communication skills. There will thus be specific reference to the disciplines for interpersonal understanding which grow out of and are listed in Section A. This section of the book is based upon the premise that communication skills can be improved through analysis and reflection. Both to help you undertake the tasks, and also to underpin your communication skills, another aim of this section will be to develop a research methodology, which is in effect a methodology for raising awareness.

Another important premise is that you do not need to travel to 'other cultures' to collect data on intercultural communication and develop intercultural communication skills. Cultural difference is everywhere and we all actually engage with it in our everyday lives. This can be seen in the texts in Unit B0.1, and is illustrated in several of the examples in Section A. We will consider instances of cultural difference that occur within and between societies, communities and institutions; and especially within the process of globalization, *all* of these can be encountered within our own personal social settings. Section C therefore invites you to explore and develop your understanding of intercultural communication as an everyday activity.

 Task C0.1.1 Establishing approach

Consider these points.

➤ Why may the notion of travelling *to* a culture be an essentialist one? Does it comes from the thinking that reduces and otherizes the individual in the same way as sexism and racism? You may like to revisit Table 1 in Section A and recall what we say there.
➤ Consider the conceptual difference between cells i and ii in Table 1.1, and how the non-essentialist option leads to thinking differently about people and incidents around you and to helping us to escape from otherizing people.
➤ Within your own milieu, where could you use the phrase 'There is something culturally different about . . .'?

We suggest that you begin a research diary and note down these instances and your thoughts about them. You are advised to keep the diary as an ongoing record throughout all the research tasks in Section C.

An ethnographic approach

Task C0.1.1 is broadly ethnographic in approach. It is within an interpretive qualitative approach to research. This means that you begin researching everyday life by looking around you to see 'what is going on'. Your very basic research tools are observation and writing descriptions of what you see and hear in a research diary. These activities need, however, to be disciplined. Some of these disciplines are represented in the ones listed in Table 4 (Section A). They are also implied in the non-essentialist thinking outlined in Table 1. Here the researcher is asked to try very hard to put aside preconceptions and attempt to gain an understanding of things in their own terms. If you wish to read more about ethnography and the attendant disciplines of qualitative research and participant observation, there are many books available; accessible ones are Spradley (1980), Hammersley and Atkinson (1995) and Holliday (2002).

An important aspect of progressive forms of ethnography and qualitative research is the understanding that you as a researcher are, or become, part of the setting you are researching. You do not simply observe 'them' and 'their' behaviour, but, instead, how the participants in the setting interact with you. Understanding how you interact with other participants will also help you to understand what sort of people they are. An interesting book to read here is Coffey (1999). Adopting this approach is important if you are going to escape from an essentialist 'us'–'them' view of culture.

The disciplines listed in Section A therefore look in two directions. They consider both how we may look *outwards* at people who we perceive as culturally different to ourselves to gain an understanding of the complexities of their identities, and how we should look *inwards* at ourselves to understand how we may be imposing a view of what other people are on them. The outward and inward gazes are of the same order in that we are fundamentally the same as the *people* with which we wish to interact. We all have complex cultural formations which derive from complex societies. Thus, the inward and outward gazes will deeply interact and the distinctions between them will be over-simplistic. Tasks in this section are designed to develop an understanding of yourself which has a bearing on the development of the understanding of others.

Intercultural communication research task

At the end of most units there will be a research task specifically designed to investigate instances of intercultural communication within the framework of the disciplines outlined in Section A. This will connect the other issues and investigations within each unit to an intercultural communication event within your own milieu. The intercultural communication research task in each case will have the form expressed in Figure 12, though this form is of course designed to be adapted to individual needs.

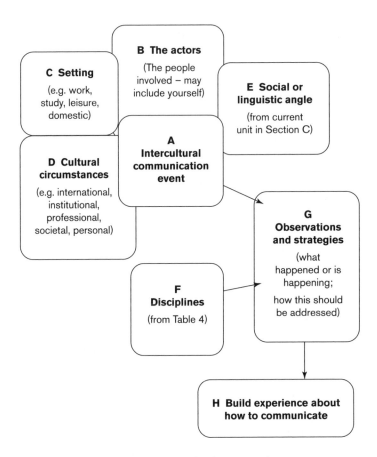

Figure 12 Format for intercultural communication research

The task will be focused upon an intercultural communication event of your choosing (as in Figure 12). You will begin the task by describing the overall scenario of the event in terms of **B** to **D** in the figure. You will be asked to address a particular angle **E**, which will arise from the discussion in the current unit, which may refer back to discussions in Section B of the book. You will be guided to apply particular disciplines and their attendant discussions from Section A. The overall approach to the task will be ethnographic in that, aided by the disciplines in **F**, the strategies in **G** will emerge by means of open-ended interpretation from observation.

The range of types of event covered by these tasks will depend on you, and will allow you to explore the intercultural domains in which you are interested. The examples in C and D show the possible width of choice, and are not exclusive. They are *working* categories, which only stand until better ones are found. They are *heuristic* in that they are there to help understanding, but do not represent real distinctions. It is as difficult and unsatisfactory to categorize settings and circumstances in this way as it is to categorize cultures. However, the following attempt to gloss them may be helpful. Work and study places could be companies, offices, building sites, schools or universities. Leisure settings could be football matches, clubs or cinemas. Domestic settings could be at home or in daily life which is not easily categorized. The event described in Unit A1.3, with girls on a bus, could be called domestic. International cultural circumstances would be where the 'difference' is connected with nationality; institutional, where it is connected with hierarchies, departments, territories, traditions or role and status differences, within work or study settings; professional, where difference is between groups of practitioners such as doctors and nurses, geographers and historians, painters and ceramicists, engineers and academics, all clearly overlapping with institutional circumstances. Societal circumstances, which clearly overlap with the others, are to do with the structure of society, perhaps with gender, age, class, race, ethnicity, family, education, social condition, power, wealth, participation and so on. Personal could be connected with interpersonal difference.

Task C0.1.2 Exploring breadth of setting and circumstances

➤ Look at a selection of examples in Section A or in the texts in Section B. Explore how far you can categorize them in terms of setting and cultural circumstances. Look particularly for overlaps in the categories offered in Figure 12.
➤ Where there are categories in Figure 12 for which you cannot find examples in Sections A and B, find examples from your own experience.
➤ See if you can replace the categories in Figure 12 with better ones of your own.

As you progress through the units in Section C, an overall task might be to *redesign* Figure 12.

The important *outcome* of the intercultural communication research model in Figure 12 is H, the experience you build about *how to communicate*. As has been stated elsewhere in this book, we are more interested in mastering the *process* of intercultural communication than with the content of how to do it with individual 'cultures'.

Ethical considerations

Because you will be invited to research real events with real people, it is important to consider the ethics of this practice. It is best if you are able to confide in the people who take part in your investigation and to ask their permission. You may need to be prepared to share with them what you are finding out. In all cases, when sharing your findings with colleagues, it is essential to have anonymized as much as you possibly can; and you must tell the people in your research that you are doing this. There will however be occasions where your research is very casual and impromptu, with a minimum of invasion of people's privacy, and too unplanned for you to ask permission. For advice on these issues, consult Punch (1994).

Theme 1
Identity

THE STORY OF THE SELF

Since childhood we have all been offered ways of understanding ourselves – from our family, education, friends and the society that surrounds us. In a sense we have been told who we are since our birth from a variety of sources. These messages may be contradictory, and so we may try to integrate these stories about what we are into a unified narrative of our own identity. This narrative is a key aspect of our sense of who we are – of our personal identity. As can be deduced from this perspective, the identity we assume is, at least in part, derived from the social context in which we live, the type of family we are born into, the education we receive and the friends that we are able to make as well as the society that surrounds us. This means that our identity is temporally and spatially framed or influenced. Who we feel ourselves to be is thus influenced by where and when we live our lives. To the extent that certain periods of history and certain geographical locations offer people living in them common features, our personal identity is, at least in part, shared with others from the same time period and location. Although the non-essentialist view promoted strongly in Section A encourages us to look at individuals, it cannot be denied that culture is nevertheless basically a group phenomenon which interacts with individual identity.

The following research task involves age groups. This will serve to demonstrate both that cultural difference can operate within as well as between societies and the way in which you, as a member of an age group, may be culturally constructed.

★ Task C1.1.1 Exploring age

➤ Interview people from different age groups.
➤ Select three adults of different ages: one in the 20–30-year-old age bracket, one in the 40–50-year-old bracket and one in the 60+ age bracket. Think of general topics to broach with these participants concerning the belief systems they feel they either subscribe to or feel people of their generation subscribe to.

Research questions and informants

Before beginning your investigation it is important to decide several things. You need to have an overall research question to which you are looking for an answer. This provides a sense of direction and purposefulness to your research. At the same time, the questions must be sufficiently open-ended to allow you to respond to people according to how you find them rather than according to what you have heard about them (Discipline 1, Table 4). This relates to an important principle in qualitative research – allowing the unexpected to emerge. In this task, two possible questions are:

1. In what ways are age groups culturally different?
2. Are age groups culturally different?

Consider which of these two questions best fulfils Discipline 1. Make more suitable questions if you need to.

Next you need to decide who exactly you are going to interview. This choice will depend on who you have access to and who would be good informants from each age group. These decisions will also depend on convenience and how much time you have. It is also important to realize the limits of your investigation. What you investigate will hopefully offer you insights and develop your understanding of the question you are researching, but you cannot say that what you interpret from the limited data you obtain is in any sense definitive and necessarily generalizable to other researchers and samples of populations. On the other hand, if others undertaking similar small-scale investigations derive insights similar to yours, then this acts to strengthen your findings. This is why researchers need to read one another's work.

Within an interpretive qualitative approach to research, we can learn from small instances of social life. The aim is not to prove how things are, but to make us think again and question our preconceptions.

Asking questions

Here are some interview questions that may be helpful.

■   When you were young, was it expected that young people should show respect to their elders?
■   Did you show this respect? How? Why? Why not?
■   What about now? Do you think there has been a change?
■   What do you think about this?

If you ask questions that distance the participant from their purely personal circumstances, i.e. by asking them questions about what others believed or did rather than questions such as 'Did *you* show respect to your father?', you are more likely to obtain a more general picture of the views held by certain generations.

You may like to choose other topics to ask questions on, e.g. sexual mores and behaviour, and attitudes to foreigners. The questions you choose are tools you use to try to 'unlock' underlying beliefs – which becomes your data. As they are tools (or instruments) you need to experiment until you find ones that work for you. You may elect to try to uncover such data using another strategy: you may ask the interviewee to tell you three things that were better in the past for young people than today and three things that are better now. You will then need to follow up the responses with probing questions to uncover why the interviewees hold the particular views they espouse. This allows you to attempt to try to uncover the values and beliefs each interviewee claims to hold. The methodology you choose is up to you, and is based upon your relationship with the interviewees and what you feel most comfortable with. The important thing is that you have thought through your approach before you undertake the interviews so that you know what you are aiming to achieve.

Organizing the research task

It is a good idea when undertaking a research project to draw up a timetable for the research. There are different ways to organize Task C1.1.1 depending on the number of people involved. Table 6 is an example timetable where the research task is done as a group project. Note the columns which refer to discussions. Looking for emerging patterns between each stage of interviews, which guide further interviews, assures that Discipline 1 is applied. If you are going to do follow-up interviews, this should be thought of before you start the research and the participants you choose need to be secured as available for the two interviews.

Table 6 Research timetable

	First week	*Beginning of second week*	*Second half of second week*	*Beginning of third week*
Interviewer 1	Interviews with: Participant 1 Participant 2 Participant 3	Discussion between interviewers and analysis of data.	Interviews with: Participant 1 Participant 2 Participant 3	Discussion between interviewers and analysis of data.
Interviewer 2	Interviews with: Participant 4 Participant 5 Participant 6	Looking for patterns in the data that can be probed further	Interviews with: Participant 4 Participant 5 Participant 6	Gathering together of findings from interviews
Interviewer 3	Interviews with: Participant 7 Participant 8 Participant 9		Interviews with: Participant 7 Participant 8 Participant 9	

Remember that initial questions only provide a surface response to most issues and these responses are often not sufficient in themselves for you to gain insights into the deeper thought processes and reasoning behind the responses. There can be no such thing as a scientific 'neutral' or purely 'objective' interview. Initial responses, therefore, need probing by follow-up questions. This can be done skilfully after the initial prompt questions at the time of the interview or you may prefer to first analyse the responses you have – especially if you have interviewed several people. You can then look for patterns in the responses that can then be followed up by further questioning in interviews with the same participants.

Another way to proceed, if doing this individually could be as follows.

1. Begin with one interview.
2. See what this tells you and where it leads you.
3. Investigate further with another interview with someone else, and so on.

This type of open-ended exploration could also involve use of other research tools such as looking at documents (e.g. things people write) or observing behaviour and appearance (e.g. how people stand around with each other, what people wear). You may also decide to turn the interview into a conversation, which may be less daunting and 'formal' for the participant. Seeing the interview as a conversation may also help you to learn something more about yourself, through your own role in the process.

Task C1.1.2 The interpersonal factor

➤ Reflect upon the interpersonal factor in researching people.
➤ Do you think that you, as the interviewer interviewing a set of people, uncover the same data as another interviewer interviewing another set of people? What factors, apart from a 'will to truth' may affect the answers your respondents make to your questions? How relevant are the following factors?

- Who you are and your relationship to the interviewee.
- The issue of whether people are able to distance themselves from their own cultural formation.
- The actual knowledge base of the respondents – the knowledge base upon which they claim to know what they state?
- The mood the person is in at the time of the interview.
- The degree to which the respondent may feel there is a boundary to what can be disclosed, i.e. talked about. This involves the socially learnt concept of taboo and the notion of what degree of intimacy is acceptable for disclosure to others.
- The issue of whether people want to appear likeable and 'nice' when talking to other people (maintain their positive face).

Hopefully you will agree that trying to uncover 'the truth' is a sensitive task. Would you agree that what one uncovers in interviews is rather 'versions of the truth' than 'the truth'? In this particular type of research – social research – you should not conclude, therefore, that such a feeling means what you are doing is flawed research. It is rather to understand a vital point about social reality. In the research project referred to on pages 152–155, it is perhaps not the quest to find out if the interviewees really are different from each other that is of interest, but rather to find out if the interviewees feel that they are different from other people from other generations. It is what people choose to assert that is interesting. It is the 'story of the self', i.e. one's identity, that is told by the self to the self and to others, that you are focusing on, and this story is important because it exerts a powerful influence on people's actions and behaviours.

Now we can conclude this unit with an intercultural communication research task. This follows logically from the previous task in that it should now be evident that interviewing people from age groups other than your own is in fact an example of intercultural communication. Hence, use Figure 12 to help complete Task C1.1.3.

Task C1.1.3   Interview as cultural interaction

➤ Event: retrospective.
➤ Actors: you and a person you have interviewed.
➤ Setting: as C1.1.1.
➤ Cultural circumstances: age difference.
➤ Angle: understanding self by finding out about others.
➤ Observation: reconstruct what happened. Your research diary (see Task C0.1.1) should be a useful resource here.
➤ Disciplines: 5, 7, 8.
➤ Outcome: draw conclusions about how the interviewee appeared to feel about her/his cultural identity from the way in which she/he behaved and told her/his story. Look into how your own behaviour might have contributed to what happened.

UNIT C1.2   **BECOMING THE SELF BY DEFINING THE OTHER**

As you may have found in Task C1.1.1, culture is pervasive – something that individuals absorb from their environment. The formation of one's own identity can, therefore, be seen, at least partly, to be shaped by external circumstances. It may also be apparent, from Task C1.1.3, that for the 'self' to be defined – to take shape – there is use made of 'contrastive others'. As is argued in the theory of deconstruction, things are what they are in terms of what they are not (see Text B2.5.3, Unit B2.5). In this sense cultural identity is inevitably exclusive (See Text B1.5.2, Unit B1.5). You are something because you are not something else. You are Canadian because you are not American, you are a conservative because you are not a socialist, you are a teenager because you are not an adult, and so forth. In Text B0.2.1, Unit B0.2, Fay attacks a view of culture – the 'standard view' – which sees culture as a force that penetrates its members mentally and that leads to socially and physically conditioned behaviour. He questions this 'standard' view which holds that members are seen to have absorbed the culture that surrounds them, thus becoming part of that culture themselves, with 'distinctive capacities and characteristics'.

■ **Stop and think:** What do you think Fay may have against this view of culture?

Fay's main criticism of this view of culture is that it is overly deterministic. It is for this reason that we state that identity is *partly* shaped by external circumstance, not that it is *completely*. Determinism is the view that we are completely formed by our environment and thus we are in a sense victims of circumstances. This view of culture, it is argued, may be criticized for viewing people as lacking agency, i.e. the ability to critically reflect upon and distance themselves from their environment and act upon it to change it.

This is an argument that runs throughout Cultural Studies and you will have to have taken a position on this when you read the various arguments presented in Section B. It is probably true to state here that although the various authors have differing views and positions on the nature and extent of influence of 'culture' upon individual actions – and no doubt you will also develop different insights from undertaking the tasks in this book and through reflection upon the results – they are, however, linked by the common theme that the more critical we can be about the process of how we construct ourselves and others in intercultural encounters, the better. In other words, we are aware of the danger inherent in the process of 'otherization' (as in the way the Smith family is demonized in Example A2.1.2, Unit A2.1) and the goal-directed and mediated nature of representation of others that we are exposed to and that the more we can develop our own critical understanding of this, the more we will be in control of our intercultural communication.

It is probably against the danger of this otherization and 'stagnant' view of others (i.e. cultural essentialism) that the concept of culture as shaping and an internally absorbed force that people then carry around with them is subject to certain attack in much of this book. On the other hand – as is often the case with reactions – we must be careful not to over-emphasize the voluntaristic, alternative view of culture as a purely choice-driven system. As much cognitive psychology suggests we do indeed learn to behave through interaction with our environment. Indeed, it is worth wondering where otherwise we are to learn about the world and how to behave in it.

In Task C1.2.1 you will investigate the degree to which people use contrasts (the contrastive Other) as a way of arriving at an understanding of who they are. It is important that you as researchers do not fall into this potential essentialist trap yourselves. Some of our research students have tended to present findings when researching British culture in contrastive terms: one group looking at personal interaction between strangers came to the conclusion from their research that 'the British are much politer than the Swedish. Because they always say "sorry" and "please"'. Another group concluded from observation of female dress codes in Britain that 'young British women are not as independent from men as young German women because they have to dress to sexually please men by showing a lot of bare flesh – even when it is very cold'.

It is easy to fall into the 'contrastive trap' of 'they are . . .' therefore 'we are . . .' But this is problematic because different cultural groups operate with different norms that only make sense *within* the groups, not necessarily *between* the groups. This is what is encompassed by the terms 'etic' and 'emic' levels of analysis. If we take a generally applicable human concept such as 'clothing' or 'interaction' we can take this as a generic 'etic' level concept; after all, all people, whatever cultural groups they belong to, 'interact'. In Culture X they do A; in Culture Y they do B. So far so good, but this is the limit of our understanding. As soon as you compare behaviour in Culture X with Culture Y because you are assuming that Behaviour A is in some way exclusively relatable to Behaviour B you fall into the danger of drawing false conclusions. The two behaviours are not comparable because they only have contrastive meaning within their own cultural and semiotic systems, i.e. when they are studied from within each culture. This study of cultural systems of meaning from within that system is referred to as the emic level of analysis. Because you, as a researcher, are also a cultural being, operating with certain cultural norms that are no doubt distinct from those you may be researching, you are in danger of interpreting them falsely if you use your own norms of reference. It may be that British people are not actually more polite than Swedish people but that 'sorry' and 'please' are simply used in different ways from their 'linguistic equivalents' in Swedish. They may be necessary systemic tags in one culture but not in another. To compare cultures as if they were operating from the same meaning template as one's own is to commit the 'emic fallacy'.

 ### Task C1.2.1 Contrasting yourself with others

➤ Decide on a particular cultural group that you see as distinct from yourselves. Try and define what it is about the group that signals it as different.
➤ You can approach this by doing the following:

> They are . . . whereas we are . . .
> They do . . . whereas we do . . .

Or

> We are . . . whereas they are . . .
> We do . . . whereas they do . . .

➤ Now work out what the effect of this otherizing impulse is when you contrast 'us' with 'them' when you assume that you are operating to the same system of norms and interpretative values.
➤ Devise a strategy for how you might be able to approach researching the other group at an emic level. What procedures, techniques and guidelines could you use?
➤ In the case of the group of Swedish students mentioned earlier, the following guidelines were drawn up. How do they compare to yours?

■ You have to get some 'insider' interpretation of data, not just rely on your own 'outsider' interpretation.
■ You need to develop trusting relationships with 'insiders'.
■ You need to look for examples of behaviour that don't fit with your first conclusions and thus resist closing your eyes and ears to new possible meanings.
■ You must be aware of how easy it is to draw on stereotypes rather than to learn to see what is actually there.

➤ Can you add any more to the list?
➤ Once you have done this go and research the group in question following the procedures, techniques and guidelines you have drawn up. Then look back at the list of differences you drew up previously. Are the differences still clear?

Note: criticality

At this point it is important to explain what is meant by the term 'critical'. It is a term that is used a lot in social science and has a precise meaning in that context. In many respects it is the key objective of this section of the book to develop critical thinking about culture and interaction. It does not mean that one holds a negative view of something – that is the more current, everyday meaning of the word. Being critical is seen as a good thing to be in that it shows a person has developed the ability to analyse something employing criteria they have developed for that purpose. It means a person is not simply accepting something as true because they have been told it is so. Being critical, therefore, takes independence of thought and a certain degree of intellectual courage as one may find that one is not in agreement with the way one is expected or supposed to think about something. This is a necessary ingredient of Discipline 2 (Table 4), in which one must often try very hard to resist what one's conditioning takes as 'obvious'. Being critical, however, needs to be based upon evidence and justification: in other words a vague feeling that something is not right needs to be refined into the ability to begin to understand the basis as to why it is felt that something is not right and be able to communicate this in a convincing fashion. Critical thinking can be seen to be a desirable achievement at the end of much reflection and analysis. Without reflection and analysis, thoughts are likely to remain vague and difficult to communicate in a convincing fashion to others.

Note: 'otherization'

Otherization is used to describe the process that we undertake in ascribing identity to the 'self' through the often negative attribution of characteristics to the 'other'. (See the definition and discussion in Unit A2.1. We may attribute these characteristics to other people so that the individual and their willingness or agreement to be subscribed to these characteristics is overlooked and indeed negated. In other words, otherization is a 'culture first view of individuals'. It is seen to be problematic in this book in that it does not allow for the agency of other people to be a factor in their identity construction. It does not permit the *negotiation* of identity between people, but imposes crude, often reductive identities on others.

   Having stated the case against over-hasty imposition of traits to others, this is not to say that the issue of cultural difference can be hypothesized away. People, as we all know, are different from each other and people do belong to distinct cultural groups which promote 'distinctive capacities and characteristics'. If this were not a reality then there would be no such thing as culture and there would be no need to study 'intercultural communication'. The point is that in intercultural communication it is wise not to impose categories to which you ascribe a person as belonging when you have minimal evidence for this, i.e. not to assume that a person can be understood firstly as a member of a certain cultural group. It is more felicitous to allow for negotiated identity in interaction.

   Indeed these categories or invoked templates may be mythical in nature – they may serve as 'mantras' to catch people within imposed webs of belonging. It is quite possible that any defined culture, as you experience it, does not seem to present the characteristics that its members profess it has or that other cultures profess that that culture has. In a sense this is not important as much as the fact that you are aware of the danger of these constructed images for your intercultural communication. It may perhaps be the case that genuinely successful communication relies upon trust developing between interactants from professedly distinct cultures and that this involves a process whereby the larger cultural templates (stereotypes) are gradually debunked in favour of a more dynamic and creative construction of identities between interactants. This does not occur in the examples in Units A2.2, A2.3 and A3.1, where the outcomes are unsuccessful.

Task C1.2.2   Your own 'distinctive characteristics'

➤ Determine the distinctive capacities and characteristics that you feel you can draw on for your cultural identity. To what aspects of your identity do they refer? How much do you draw on these and perhaps manipulate or negotiate them according to who you are communicating with and where you are communicating?

You may find Table 7 useful as a starting point for self-reflection. You will find that in this task you are dealing with the large-scale social understandings of how these particular aspects of identity are signalled and 'read'. These are what Gee refers to as Discourses with a capital 'D' Text B1.3.1, Extract 1, Unit B1.3. They are the socially sanctioned ways that a group of people orientate themselves towards representing and interpreting 'objects', i.e. the thing that is constructed. In this task the objects in each case are the identity components. While these constructed understandings may not necessarily be accurate, or you may not agree with them in essence, they can be argued to exist in the collective consciousness of a cultural group and the media that is read by that group and therefore inevitably exert an influence upon members of a cultural group. Because of this they need to be negotiated by individuals in that group, particularly by those who may not conform to them.

Here you are required to record your responses to a specific issue over a period of time. One way of doing this is to note your responses in your research diary. Research diaries provide a certain structure for your research and help to combat the vagaries of recall and memory. It is best to aim to record your responses to instances just after they occur. Once they are noted down you can revisit them later, preferably after a break, to be able to look at them afresh and to try to note any patterns that are in your responses. As well as keeping a narrative of your observations, you can also devise a framework within which you place your recordings or which you use to categorize 'raw data' – i.e. the responses you write for future analysis. Categories you may wish to consider are: your role, your relationship to any interactant, the time and place of each event, and your feelings (affective reaction). One way of organizing this is to devise a chart to fill in after each 'event'. You will probably find that the categories you finally use to analyse and collect the data develop as you undertake the research. You may wish to use the first few observations as test cases for helping to devise the categories you will use.

Table 7 Self-reflection chart

Identity component	Capacity/characteristic	Variety according to context of communication (give two examples of each)
Nationality		
Region		
Ethnicity		
Social class		
Gender		
Age		
Religion		
Role (e.g. 'mother')		

Task C1.2.3 How you manage your identity

➤ Keep a record of how you actually manage your identity according to the above identity components over the next 24 hours with people that you encounter.
➤ Once you have done this, consider the following questions.

■ Do you catch yourself representing different versions of yourself and struggling against other people's perceptions of you?
■ Are you aware of how you manipulate the possibilities available to you at the time?
■ Do you meet occasions where you are unable to do this because your interlocutor(s) have already decided who you are – i.e. otherized you?
■ How does this make you feel?
■ What do you do if this is the case?
■ What are your findings?

Identity is ideally a negotiated feature between interactants. However, you may discover that in many instances this is not possible because in interaction people may be assuming who the other person is without the willingness to enter into more fluid negotiation and time-consuming research of the other person. An interesting comment made by one student studying cultural identity is: 'It is much easier to hold and use undifferentiated categories about others than not to.'

We can complete this unit with a further intercultural communication research task. Use Figure 12 to help with this.

Task C1.2.4 Watching yourself

➤ Events: which take place normally within your own milieu.

➤ Actors: same each time.

➤ Setting: your choice.

➤ Cultural circumstances: same each time.

➤ Angle: how your image of yourself influences your interaction.

➤ Observation: monitor yourself, describe carefully and deconstruct.

➤ Discipline: 8.

➤ Outcome: as you become more aware of yourself, how do your perceptions of the Other people improve? In what ways are you more likely to avoid the traps into which Agnes, François and Jeremy fall in Units A2.2 and A2.3?

When to take notes

It is clearly impossible to describe what is happening *during* the process of communication events. Once you get into the habit of keeping your research diary regularly, you will also develop your ability to recall. You should then be able to make fairly detailed notes of what has happened at the earliest convenient private time after the event has happened, even if this is the following day. Also, there is no need to audio-record and transcribe events in order to collect useful data. Indeed, it is advisable not to with this type of informal research. Behavioural descriptions of what has happened, with the occasional note of what was said, can be very rich. Transcribing is very time-consuming and, unless your study is specifically a linguistic discourse analysis, may mean you are using up your limited time on this rather than developing your research.

UNIT C1.3   UNDOING CULTURAL FUNDAMENTALISM

If we believe or subscribe to a view that people have innate cultural traits – i.e. that they carry within them certain essential characteristics that belong to them and the larger group of which they are seen to form a part, rather as we carry genetic information within us (information that leads to different skin colour etc.) – then this may be argued to be the holding of a view that can be called 'cultural fundamentalism' or 'culturism' (see Unit A2.1).

While it is true that we are socialized into certain ways of depending on the context of our existence – i.e. we are 'trained in expectation', which means that we are 'programmed' to expect certain behaviours of others and to have certain behaviours expected of us by others – it is important to remember two factors that tend to override cultural uniformity:

■ For each individual each context is unique and these contexts may vary considerably between members of what may ostensibly be the same culture; this is true even within the same family. This means that it is, to a certain extent, illusory to hold a generalized notion that people are uniform within certain cultures.

■ Contexts are interactive in that people are not powerless to create new contexts. People can adapt to new influences and learn new ways of being. It is therefore questionable that the self is an unchanging, readily describable and definable entity. It is hard to define something that has the potential to change.

So while there may be certain commonalities between two people from the same cultural context (from the same temporal and geographical location) and a general notion of 'typicality' held between them (i.e. an understanding of expected behaviour or the norm for behaviour in various contexts), it is risky to assume that the contextual influences they have been exposed to result in two people with the same cultural outlook.

Note: introspection and subjectiviy

In Task C1.3.1, as indeed in Task C1.2.2, you are required to be introspective, i.e. to collect not only external data through observation, but also to become aware of your own subjectivity. Each person interprets the external world from their own experience and it is an awareness of this subjectivity that allows us to accept and recognize plurality and interpersonal difference. This awareness is very necessary for effective intercultural communication. It is the recognition of difference and then the negotiation of various subjectivities to achieve shared understanding that is central to skilled intercultural communication. Intercultural communication can be described, therefore, as a process of 'intersubjectivity'.

Task C1.3.1 Drawing a culture star

➤ Compare yourself with another person in your study group to see what influences there are upon both of you and how these:

1. may vary from each other, and
2. may be interpreted differently by you both.

➤ To do this you will draw a 'culture star'.

This idea of a culture star comes from Singer (1999) who considers the various 'cultures' in which individuals exist and from which they 'source' their identities. A person's culture is seen here to be the result of belonging to a myriad of 'small cultures' (Unit B0.2) each of which demands a certain normativeness. These small groupings are inherently unstable in that they come and go – as individuals enter and leave them – and they change according to the influence of their members. Some are more enduring than others.

Figure 13 is an example of one such culture star. Each band in the star is one in which the individual is potentially recognized by others, and recognized by themselves as a competent member of a group, i.e. one in which there are perceived norms of behaviour

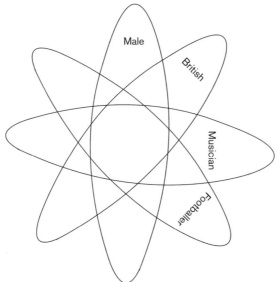

Figure 13 Culture star

and attested values and beliefs that the individual recognizes and either uses or navigates with and negotiates with as a member of the group. The choice over which groups you think are of influence, or of significance, is up to you.

➤ Once you have drawn a star you need to compare it with someone else's.
➤ When you have done this, consider how much variety there is between the two stars. You may then like to discuss what influences each cultural group has over you in terms of your personal identity and look at how this identity changes according to each cultural group to which you are affiliated (done by oneself to oneself) and ascribed (done by others to oneself).
➤ Considering these multiple belongings, can you actually choose one influence, or cultural group, e.g. 'nationality' or 'ethnicity', as one that successfully serves to describe both you and the person who has done the other star? Doing this must inevitably result from a process of 'cultural reductionism', i.e. a negation of the true complexity of each of you. Indeed, is there any way in which you can actually say that you and the other person are the same or is it that all you can perhaps say is that there are similarities in certain areas between you?

 Task C1.3.2 Belonging

➤ Look again at the bands of the stars you have drawn and identified. What are certain key expectations that you feel each band proposes as norms for members to subscribe to?
➤ In other words, consider how you know you belong, and how others in the particular group identified in the band know you belong to that small culture. What is it that holds members of each 'club' together as different from others?

This may be a very difficult task to accomplish – you may feel that while superficially there are key values and characteristic behaviours that you can identify, the more you think about it the more complex it becomes to be sure about these. This may be because the small cultures are in a constant state of shift and change. You may therefore like to think of what the standard image is that the group promotes or is seen to have by others, both within and without each group. From the fictional star this may be as follows. (This is a worked example; you do not have to agree with it.)

- Male: does not show emotions too openly.
- British: is proud of things British; appreciates humour – i.e. is able to 'take a joke'.
- Yorkshireman: is proud of things from Yorkshire and dislikes Lancashire; is not 'fancy' and 'Southern' but blunt and to the point – i.e. 'calls a spade a spade'.
- Musician: has things in common with other musicians such as knowledge of various pieces of music; is more expressive than a stockbroker.
- Football player: feels loyalty to others in the same football team; participates in 'male bonding' behaviour.
- Son in the Cole family: understands the rules of participation and the responsibilities of being a son in the family; works hard at being successful.
- Garage mechanic: has an understanding of car engines; is not scared of getting hands dirty.
- Motorcycle rider: has a knowledge and interest in motorcycles and things to do with motorcycles; has a special bond with other motorcyclists as opposed to car drivers.
- Regular pub goer: has an understanding of pub etiquette; is knowledgeable about the different kinds of beers available.
- London resident: has a knowledge of the city; subscribes to the rules of living in that city.

Of course, how you negotiate your membership in each membership group, or small culture, is up to you, but in order to 'negotiate' you obviously need to know certain basic features of each of these (see Gee's large 'Discourses' written with a big 'D' described in Text B1.3.1, Extract 1, Unit B1.3). Your individual negotiation within these Discourses can be seen to be your small 'discourses', written with a small 'd'. Another possible set of terminology for the same thing is to see the larger frameworks as discourse types (DTs) and your own negotiating with these as your discourse actions (DAs). The DTs can be seen to be large cognitive schemas (see Gandy, Task B3.3.4, Unit B3.3) and the DAs can be seen to be your personal relationship to the DTs. The Discourse Types are communally held, whereas Discourse Actions are personal instances of interaction. DTs exist because, for communication to occur, it is necessary for groups of people (within the same culture) to have norms by which they can communicate. From a discourse analysis point of view one could argue, therefore, that a culture is a set of DTs which members draw on to create their own DAs. Without the DTs there could be no DAs. It is also the DAs that constantly reconfirm the existence of the DTs.

From a look at your culture star you will notice that the small cultures that you belong to vary in the degree of autonomy they allow you through the degree of choice you have about being a member of each of them or not. This is not to say that you have to be an uncritical member of any of them, but that they vary in the degree of choice you have – to decide to be a member or not. You cannot, for example, choose the ethnicity you have or the place you are born or the family you are born into, but you can choose whether or not you will join a karate club or go to university or join a reading circle. To build on a concept presented in Unit A1.3 you may consider the experience of negotiating identity from the following cards metaphor: you can see yourself as having been dealt a set of cards by your life circumstances – 'culture cards'. Some of these cards you cannot change but others you can gain, get rid of, or change, and indeed play. Of course, some of the inherited cards you may choose to downplay or attempt to change: one thinks of people who actually attempt to change their gender through sex change operations; of the plastic surgery that Michael Jackson has had to change his features, or of a migrant who changes national cultures and languages (see Ribeyro, Text B1.1.1, Unit B1.1 and his description of someone attempting to change his cultural cards).

These changes are not, however, purely under the individual's control in that, as the large DTs that one may be opposing are not individually held but communally held, it may be that the community does not accept the new cards that an individual tries to play the culture game with. Remember that it is large and often stereotypically crude structures that may be used by others when interacting with you (see Unit A1.1 and Parisa's struggle in Example A1.1.1 to be understood for what she is). You may therefore find that identity is not just a negotiated entity between interactants; rather, it is like a game of cards with certain rules as to how you can play. Interacting may be seen as a game which you play with the cards at your disposal. Some of these cards may be powerful ones, whereas others may be less so. This depends on the power structure represented by the dominance of certain DTs in which you are using your DAs, i.e. playing the culture game. The word 'game' should not imply that the stakes are not high or that this activity is frivolous. It is also possible that what may be a weak card in one particular context may be a strong one in another. It may also seem obvious that the more cards you can play the wider the possibility of having useful cards in more situations. The more cards you have, the more membership possibilities you have. At certain times you may emphasize the cards you feel you have in common with the other people you're interacting with; at other times you may downplay or play up a culture card that you feel is opposed to or promotes your interests and goals in the communicative context in which you find yourself. Which cards you play thus depends upon a strategic consideration of which ones you can draw on and which ones you want to draw on in a particular context and on the goals you have. The same, of course, is true of the people you interact with. As mentioned before, the more cards you can draw on the more possibilities you have in playing the culture card game. A person who has an Indian mother, an English father, who was born in France and who was educated in the USA, evidently has many cards to potentially draw on. This does not necessarily make interaction with this person easier, however. People may like to play the culture card game with people who have a reduced set of cards and thus not risk being trumped by the other person, who may be playing the game with a set of powerful cards up their sleeve. It is perhaps uncomfortable for people to play the culture card game with a cultural chameleon. It's easier to play the game with a person who has their cards visibly on the table. For this reason it may be tactical for people to choose to deliberately hide their complexity in certain interactions. Again such a decision is strategic and up to the individual – it is a weighing-up of the benefits and losses that the playing of each card may bring within each context of interaction. What possible cards did the author Hope have in Text B2.5.1, Unit B2.5, considering the situation he was in? Perhaps he had no possible cards to play and therefore an ironical detachment to the situation was the only possible strategy for him?

Task C1.3.3

➤ Discuss your views on the cards metaphor as an explanation of intercultural interaction.

Task C1.3.4

➤ Prepare either a presentation or an assignment with the title 'An analysis of my own cultural formation'.

Task C1.3.5

➤ Look at the following anecdote, and try to explain it in terms of Discourse Types, Discourse Actions and the strategic use of 'culture cards':

> An Englishman who is the director of a private company in Spain addresses his workforce one day in Spanish, but with a slightly detectable non-Spanish accent. In his speech he uses the following term: '*Nosotros, los españoles, somos una gente muy orgullosa*' (translated: 'We Spanish are a very proud people'). A certain number of the Spanish workers exchange looks with each other upon hearing this that seem to express a mixture of discomfort and mirth.

Now it is time to convert the observations in this unit into observation of intercultural communication, with reference to Figure 12.

Task C1.3.6 Culture cards and stars

➤ Event: your choice, but it might take a series of events, with the same people, to find out what you need to know, especially if the other people come from small groups or societies which you know little about.
➤ Actors: you and two other people.
➤ Setting: within your milieu.
➤ Cultural circumstances: your choice.
➤ Angle: use of 'culture cards', the complexity of the culture star.
➤ Observation: use Table 8 and record as much detail as you can about the culture cards that are played by you and by each of the other two people. More rows can be added for other people.

> ➤ Disciplines: 2, 3. You are focusing here on the complexity; but you will need to try hard to put aside what you *imagine* about the other people and to base your investigation on what you *observe*.
> ➤ Outcome: analysis of the effectiveness of each interaction. Also, what you can learn about the complexity which the other person is bringing with them.

Table 8 Record of playing culture cards

Description of the context	Analysis of the cards you felt were at your disposal (a), that you played and their effectiveness (b), that you felt your interactants had at their disposal (c) and that they played and their effectiveness (d)
Person 1	(a)
	(b)
Setting 1	(c)
	(d)

UNIT C1.4   **INVESTIGATING DISCOURSE AND POWER**

As has been hinted at so far in Section C, communication does not take place in a power void. Power is manifest within all communication because the culture cards that one draws on are valued differently within different social structures. Certain images that are in circulation in a social group about other social groups may be drawn upon or countered by interactants. An interactant may insist on playing with these dominant discourses or images and thus not allow other interactants the individual freedom to create and present themselves as they wish. To thus attempt to curb someone's autonomy for intersubjectivity is to attempt to exercise power. As Bourdieu reminds us in Unit B1.2, because of the power structure of a society at a certain instance, some cards have greater social currency and value than others.

■ **Stop and think:** Look at the cards you potentially hold. How powerful are they in various different contexts?

In each interactive context you basically have two strategies for action. First you may choose to show 'solidarity' – i.e. play the cards that bind you to the person you are interacting with (e.g. draw upon a shared belongingness or identity). Second you may choose to use a distancing strategy, whereby you play cards that emphasize the difference in status between you. The decision about which strategy to use may vary according to context. The wrong use of the wrong strategy may have a detrimental effect in terms of an interactant's communicative goals. If you use distancing strategies when solidarity strategies may be felt by your interlocutor to be more appropriate, then you will appear to be cold and unfriendly – possibly snobbish. If, on the other hand, an interactant uses a bonding, solidarity strategy with someone who evidently feels of a different status, or from a distinct identity group, or is in an official role that would be compromised by solidarity, then the interactant may be rebuffed for using such a 'levelling' strategy. (Think of Jeremy's misuse of such a bonding strategy in his dealings with Jabu in Example A2.3.1, Unit A2.3). In many languages of the world, the actual degree of solidarity or distance is encoded in the personal pronouns chosen for use between two forms of 'you'. In French there is '*tu*' or '*vous*'. The use of these pronouns is by no means straightforward as '*vous*' can imply coldness and distance, but it can also be used to show respect, which is not the same as coldness. The way '*vous*' is interpreted depends very much on the context of its use. In English there is only one pronoun 'you' and so solidarity and social distance are encoded in other ways – through the forms of address people choose to use with each other and through politeness strategies, which includes the degree of directness or indirectness in language use.

Another example of the marking of solidarity or social distance in language use is the form of greeting employed in British English. The term 'mate', for example, is a marker of equality. However, if it is used with someone who feels of higher status and thus deserving of respect, the use of the term 'mate' may be interpreted as cheeky and an attempt to belittle that person's status. In this sense the term 'mate' can be a power strategy through its potential to 'level out' difference. It has a pragmatic force equal to saying: 'I do not consider you to be any better than me or in any position of authority over me in any way.'

Task C1.4.1   Trying to gain solidarity

➤ Analyse the following dialogue and decide whether a solidarity strategy or a distancing strategy is being employed, and which possible culture cards are being played. Also consider their effectiveness.

Those involved in the dialogue: Swedish woman and immigrant man (taken from an example given by a presenter at a conference in Gothenburg by a lecturer analysing intercultural discourse).

The situation: the 30-year-old Swedish lady approaches the 20-year-old immigrant man, who is sitting in a university café. She asks him for a cigarette by saying in Swedish:

'Can I buy a cigarette from you?'

The young man replies in Swedish:

> 'No, here, you can have one.'

He offers her one of his cigarettes. She then replies in English:

> 'No, really, let me buy it – I'm trying to give up.'

She offers him two crowns. The man waves his hand at the money and continues in Swedish:

> 'If you want a cigarette, take one – I won't take any money for it.'

The woman turns around and walks away without taking the cigarette.

This example may lead us to consider how we may be constrained in our interactive behaviour not only by contextual cultural factors but also by the self-view one has and the identity that that reinforces.

In many interactions we are perhaps constrained by notions of typicality and expectation fulfilment. Although it may be a rule that to stick to what is most expected, or in other words 'appropriate', is the safest way to communicate – especially with strangers – this is only so providing, of course, that the two interactants are plugged into similar notions of what is typical in those contexts.

■ How may the interaction described have been more successful? What is required of the interactants for this?

Task C1.4.2 Manipulating discourse

➤ Reread Example A1.3.1, Unit A1.3 ('Girls on the bus'). What have the school girls done to subvert the original power to wound of certain words traditionally used by men to negatively type women? Try to explain this in terms of Discourse Types, the use of culture cards and solidarity strategies. To what extent does your explanation coincide with the one below?

Possible explanation

The girls are appropriating a sexist and misogynistic Discourse Type, traditionally belonging to a male domain. They thus use terms of abuse from this DT: derogatory terms that equate females with animals and sexual licentiousness (the former suggesting inferiority to men, the second perhaps hinting at a fear that females whose libido cannot be controlled by social propriety are dangerous). The fact that it is girls using these terms to bond with each other rather than men – the girls would seem to demand of each other the use of insulting words from a particular type of 'male speak' as a form of greeting – would seem to subvert the words' original wounding power and intent. In a sense these words are disarmed by this female strategy. They lose their original meaning through being appropriated in this particular way. The girls are thus using a culture card from the male pack and playing with it themselves. The scene is shocking because it is normally only a DT within the male domain of possibilities to which this belongs. It is not a DT used by women – not women about women – and then not in such a public manner. Girls, traditionally, are not supposed to swear or use 'rough and rude' language in public either; this is not considered to be traditionally 'feminine'. The exchange in the bus, intended for the public at large, is thus part of a power strategy of the colonization and neutralization of a male space.

➤ Do some research on the various terms that the girls use and determine the significance of them.

Task C1.4.3 Analysing discourse

➤ Choose a section of interactive text to analyse.
➤ Collect the text (by recording it) either from the radio, the television or real life. Make sure that it is not too long – the example of the girls on the bus is sufficiently long. Choose the text carefully so that it involves people in social interaction, perhaps discussing or arguing points.
➤ Transcribe the text by writing it out. Avoid the use of punctuation or capital letters and leave gaps between words to reflect pauses in speech; also use double lines with parallel texts when two people are talking at the same time. Analyse the text by referring to DTs and DAs and to the use of various 'culture cards'.
➤ Prepare a presentation of the text explaining your analysis. It is useful to have the transcribed text on an overhead transparency.

Example of transcribed text

Interactant A: there's no point in trying to apologize now because
Interactant B: apologize for what
Interactant A: for not inviting us
Interactant B: but I thought you didn't want to come you know

➤ Now see if you can apply this type of analysis to other examples of intercultural communication in your own milieu, with reference to Figure 12.

Task C1.4.4 How close or far apart do we signal we may be?

➤ Events: of your choice, but where you can hear people talking, preferably on several occasions so that you can begin to see patterns of discourse emerging, and (see below) develop relations which allow you to interview.
➤ Actors: of your choice, but always the same small group.
➤ Setting: of your choice.
➤ Cultural circumstances: of your choice, but where the interaction is marked by some form of cultural difference.
➤ Angle: success and failure in using solidarity or distancing strategies. Look again at Jeremy's failure in trying to achieve solidarity with Jabu in Example A2.3.1. Notice

particularly that Jeremy does in fact have good intentions, but in a sense chooses the wrong content.

➤ Observation: use your research diary to note down as much detail as possible. If it is appropriate you might also interview the interactants to see how they feel about what is happening.

➤ Disciplines: 2, 13, 14. Although you are not one of the interactants, you need to employ these disciplines as though you were, so that you put aside your own preoccupations and presumptions about what might bring solidarity or distance, so that you can try and see things in the terms of the actors.

➤ Outcome: experience for your own interactions.

This is a complex and difficult research task. You will need to discuss this with others to explore the best way to proceed as delicately as possible.

UNIT C1.5 | ## LOCALITY AND TRANSCENDENCE OF LOCALITY: FACTORS IN IDENTITY FORMATION

When analyzing the way people read texts, Barthes sees the reader as potentially engaged in two acts: that of '*plaisir*' and that of '*jouissance*'. These psychological needs that the reader has are in fact contradictory tendencies. Barthes' terminology is sexual, suggesting that he approaches individual psychology from a Freudian perspective. '*Plaisir*' is the need the reader has to feel a sense of belonging. It is the reconfirmation of the world as one expects and feels it is. '*Jouissance*', on the other hand, is the opposite tendency: the urge to break the mould and to transcend the known (it means 'orgasm' in French). It is the excitement of transgressing the boundary of the accepted and the known.

If we relate this idea to that of individual identity generally, we may argue that these two tendencies are inherent in individual identity construction. To be part of the society one is in one needs to be familiar with the 'text' of that society – the rituals and the accepted modes of being and the values one is expected to uphold. This sense of belonging is a source of pleasure ('*plaisir*'). It is the sense of not being alone but of belonging to a group. This offers comfort and security. On the other hand there is potentially excitement and invention to be found through the breaking of this 'order'. Crossing the boundary of the accepted and experimenting with new forms can be invigorating and on an individual level may be felt to set oneself off against the crowd. The contradiction is that one can only achieve this transcendence if at one and the same time one is beholden to the values one is transcending – in other words, both aspects of cultural belonging and transcendence are forces (in many ways contradictory) that work together within individuals.

 Task C1.5.1 Sources of '*plaisir*' or '*jouissance*'

➤ Look at the following list and decide how each one may be a source of '*plaisir*' or '*jouissance*'.

- Feeling patriotic, e.g. supporting your national football team along with others from your nation.
- Going on an exotic holiday alone.
- Learning and speaking a foreign language.
- Breaking established taboos (e.g. cross-dressing, experimenting with banned drugs).
- Using language at variance with the expected and established norms of the society you are in (e.g. schoolgirls swearing on a bus).
- Using slang, or a local dialect, with your friends.
- Swapping jokes with friends and finding the same things funny.
- Smoking a cigarette with friends as a young teenager behind the bike shed at school.

Note: using dichotomous models

The dichotomy (the two possible options) used for analysis of '*plaisir*' and '*jouissance*' proves a useful heuristic device (a tool for analysis), but becomes more complicated to maintain as an either/or option the more one digs deeper into the examples. It would appear that the essence of '*plaisir*' is an indulgence in normativeness, i.e. in the psychological benefit of sharing. The essence of '*jouissance*', on the other hand, would appear to be the personal transcendence of the established cultural norms that surrounds the individual. However, transcendence may also become normative and hence a 'subculture' of people may together be transcending the more established norms of the wider culture; this may mean that the subgroup is enjoying '*jouissance*' together. If this is the case, then is this not in actual fact also '*plaisir*'? After all, it is shared and normative transcendence. It would appear that an initial act of '*jouissance*' can become a form of '*plaisir*' once it becomes shared and hence normative. Thus an act of rebellion – as, say, that of punk rock in the 1970s – soon becomes a form of '*plaisir*' for its adherents as it becomes an established mode of rebellion, including dress code, language and behaviour. In other words '*jouissance*' is not a cultural construct as '*plaisir*' is, but a psychological, personal one – it is about transcending the cultural formations that surround one.

This analysis starts with the use of a dichotomy – the use of two different extremes. These extremes thus serve to question and probe a phenomenon. It may be that these extremes in themselves are too crude to be useful as explanations in themselves. They may, however, prove a useful tool for analysis. This is what is meant by stating that they are 'heuristic devices'. You are free to use any such dichotomies as tools for your own analyses, always, of course, bearing in mind that they are tools for use that you have created and are not necessarily true reflections of an external reality in themselves.

It is worth noting that the pursuit of '*jouissance*' brings risks and sanctions from the cultural group being transcended (rejected) by the individual. Members of a culture work hard to protect their culture from being undermined, by re-establishing, on a daily basis, the norms by which the group in question operates (see Anderson 1983). This may mean attacking anything that is 'heretical' to those norms. Members have a duty to protect the norms the group lives by and the '*plaisir*' that this sources. Transgressors of these norms may be feared and suffer social ostracism (exclusion) and demonization (see Unit B3.5). Indeed, any cultural group would seem to need to have a serviceable Other – a thing against which the group finds its own identity. A punk in the 1970s was a punk because he/she was not symbolically a member of the 'dominant' society against which punks were rebelling. Unfortunately, the consequences of this process can lead to violence and cruelty. People are not seen as complex and variegated and changing but as serviceable objects for use in establishing a group's identity – even if this is at times a counter-identity. Think of the fate of 'witches' in medieval Europe, for example.

 ### Task C1.5.2 In- and out-groups

➤ Interview groups of young people about their musical tastes and the clothes they wear. Note how they thus create identities based on their professed musical tastes and the fashion they follow. Note if they associate with certain professed groups and how the borders between them as members of such a group and others are drawn.

➤ Also use observation to look at the activities that certain groups of youths engage in and their attire, thus noting to what extent activity type is also part of the overall image a group has and uses to define itself.

➤ When you have collected your data, see if you find any common themes. What can you apply from your findings to yourself as an individual and to your own identity formation?

➤ What is it that creates an in-group member and what is it that creates an out-group member?

Interviewing small groups instead of individuals should help the members of the group to show you how they help each other to create borders.

➤ Then think about yourself. In what ways do you balance '*plaisir*' with '*jouissance*'? Do you feel you belong to any oppositional counter-cultures that through group '*jouissance*' offer a different version of '*plaisir*' from the wider culture against which it is rebelling? Can you describe how this works?

Note: national identity

If we look at the world's cultural groups as now caught between tradition and modernity, between established and often agricultural communities tied to the land and city dwellers, freed from their link to the land through the use of technological invention, then we may see the world as divided between this fundamental tension of tradition and traditional values and modernity. In the search for a collective identity and the fear that modernity may be undermining this identity, people may psychologically return to or try to retain a sense of local cultural identity. Martin, the author of Section C, has experience of some Hungarians, living city lives, who also have nostalgia for traditional costumes, language and dialects, dances and songs. The discourse of national identity may manifest itself in a pride in local cuisine, in claims about the beauty and good nature of the women, in the bravery of the men, and there may be a mystical attachment to the countryside. In Hungary people may claim and feel a profound link with the Puszta – the Hungarian Plain. Argentinians may similarly refer to the Pampas. It is noticeable that romantic pictures of gauchos, the Pampas cowboys, adorn up-market restaurant walls in Buenos Aires. North Americans may conduct a similar romantic affair with the Wild West, which becomes emblematic not only of a geography but also of a way of life that projects the self-view of the pioneering spirit and toughness in the face of adversity, however mythical this may be.

Task C1.5.3 Artefacts and identity

➤ Interview members of your study group and use Table 9 to make a record.
➤ When doing this consider your nation's or region's use of these cultural artefacts and factors in the creation of a national/regional identity and a sense of traditional belonging.

Table 9 Cultural artefacts

Artefact/factor	Description	Function in terms of identity formation
Costumes/dress		
Dances		
Songs/music		
Language and dialect		
Cuisine		
Nature – landscape		
Fauna		
Flora		
Sports and sporting events		
Festivals and holidays		
Physical appearance of people		
Qualities of people		

Nationalism or regionalism is perhaps one of the most powerful sources of identity in modern society. More and more the world is divided into states with frontiers; the people within these states are encouraged to see themselves as belonging to these particular groupings and as being distinct from those in other states. In many cases these boundaries have been historically forged through war and political negotiation.

Having briefly looked at this powerful and emotive use of culture within and between nation states – a use of culture that is very politicized, and indeed a force which a lot of us are perhaps seduced by to some extent – it is also worth looking at another aspect of modernity that influences us in how we understand who we are. This is again represented as a dichotomy: the rural and the urban. Industrialization has led people away from the land and into metropolitan centres. The growth of cities is a key feature of life today, along with the increased use of technology within our lives, from fridges to cars to computers. We may also take pride in the way we see ourselves and the way we present ourselves to others through 'conspicuous consumption' – arguably a key characteristic of urban modernity. The man polishing his new car in the street on Sunday morning, the schoolgirl ostentatiously using her mobile phone on the way home from school, the newly married couple dedicating a year's wages and thought into getting the most up-to-date kitchen installed in their new home; these are people who help to define their existence and sense of who they are, at least in part, by these modern artefacts that act as indexes of success and status. The seeking of power through consumption is the bedrock of the capitalist system of existence and consumer objects become symbols of success. While this may be joked about – 'I have just indulged in some retail therapy', 'I shop therefore I am' – there is a poignancy that underlies these phrases.

We will briefly explore two aspects of this phenomenon in relation to culture and individual identity: first, the relative value of the rural and the urban in your context; and second, the commodification of cultural goods for consumption within the capitalist system and how this may impinge upon you. (See the discussion of globalization and identity in Unit B2.4 in relation to this.) The relationship between city and country is a complex one in many countries. The rural may be seen as the backyard of the city – a place for sports and relaxation by the city people, or a place to stay away from – a place of backwardness and poverty, or it may be mythologized and be romanticized as the location of the true soul of the nation. The urban may be seen as a place of wealth and possibility, invigorating and exciting, or may be seen as degenerate, dangerous and polluted, and a place to move away from.

 Task C1.5.4   Rural and urban images

➤ Look at the following terms from British and American English to describe people and homes. What do they suggest about the urban and the rural? What perspective is behind each word?

yokel	oik	hick	country retreat	yob
mugger		city slicker		man about town/city girl
peasant	yuppie		cottage	tenement
hillbilly	highrise	flat	suburbia	the hood

> How does each term fit into the general picture of the urban and the rural and the relationship between them? Do you have similar terms associated with the urban and the rural?
> Find out the relative conceptions of the rural and the urban in the society that surrounds you.
> You can collect data through interviewing people by asking them for key words (such as those above) and/or you can analyse the representation of the urban and the rural in advertising by deciding what key words you would use to describe the image of each.

Cultural objects may be made into saleable products: the country cottage may be sold as a second home to the urban rich and thus marketed as a form of Arcadia; clean air and flowers can become selling points or indeed commodities that can thus be bought and sold, and so cultural products from other places can be marketed in the 'global supermarket'; this may include holidays abroad, foods, drinks, martial arts, dances, music, sport – indeed anything and everything. A bottle of wine becomes the consumption of France and things French, to dance a tango is to imbibe a little 'Argentinianness', eating a Chinese meal is to have a mini-voyage into the exotic, walking through the Amazon rainforest on an eco-holiday is to buy into a small chunk of pristine purity, and so on.

■ **Stop and think**: How much are these cultural promises mediated by an image of the thing you are consuming? In other words, how much are you influenced by this when buying and consuming the commodity?

Task C1.5.5 Buying cultural promise

> What products do you buy that are packaged and are aimed at making you feel that you are transcending the confines of the local for you? Look at the things you have bought or the experiences you have paid money for recently.
> Use Table 10 to list the products you buy and explain the cultural promise that each one offers.

Table 10 Commodities as cultural promise

Commodity	Cultural promise of the commodity

For example, you may be influenced by the promise of science and the accomplishments of modernity when you decide to take some industrially produced medicine, or on the other hand you may be influenced by an image of natural healthiness and folk wisdom and decide to take a herbal remedy sold by an alternative health practitioner. Both forms of treatment are wrapped in cultural representation. Barthes goes as far as to state that when a person is drinking red wine, that person is not drinking red wine at all but the idea of red wine! It is easy to see how desire can thus be created and sold through the advertising of cultural products. Our urges for '*plaisir*' and '*jouissance*' can be taken advantage of. To what extent are we involved and perhaps manipulated in this cultural consumption?

Note: text

The word 'text' traditionally refers to a sample of writing. However, the word can be extended to mean anything that can be read – in this sense we can 'read' architectural styles, as well as visual images such as adverts and films. Indeed, there is an argument that can be made that we are thus 'readers' of the multitude of texts that surround us and it is the way we 'read' these texts that is how we make sense of the world. (See, for example, Text B2.4.1, Unit B2.4, for an analysis of how the idea of 'China' may be discoursally constructed and read by Westerners.)

 ### Task C1.5.6 The use of words

➤ Through an examination of texts within your everyday milieu, collect examples of the use of the following words and their derivations: 'modern', 'new', 'natural' and 'alternative'. Table 11 is an example of how to keep a record of each instance for each word. In the left column explain where the word comes from; in the right column tease out what you feel is the intended effect of the word and the connotations it carries in the context from which it is taken. You can then do the same for other words with other rows.

Table 11 Words and social images

Word: 'modern'	
Context 1 e.g. 'Spacious, *modern* apartment in city centre location' from estate agent blurb in shop window, UK.	Intended effect/reading of the word e.g. the apartment symbolizes what wealthy people aspire to – perhaps there is more than one bathroom and a fully-fitted kitchen

➤ Compare your findings and assessment of the effects of the use of the words with your study peers. You may like to do this task with other words that you feel are in some way significant today as indicators of the cultural clash produced by modernity and tradition.

Now refer to Figure 12 before completing Task C1.5.7.

Task C1.5.7 Diverse identities

➤ Event: of your choice.
➤ Actors: where there is evidence that different people who you presume come from the same cultural group tell different stories about their culture. There is an example of this in Unit B1.2, where Ming and Zhang give different impressions of 'Chinese culture'.
➤ Setting: of your choice.
➤ Cultural circumstances: of your choice.
➤ Angle: images of modernity, tradition and the alternative in people's accounts of who they are.
➤ Observation: listen to the way in which people characterize their cultural backgrounds. Find opportunities to talk to them about who they say they are and to find the deeper meanings behind their perceptions. Also try to find out how far the way in which the actors project themselves has to do with their reactions to new cultural circumstances, whether it is a new country or a new office. You may find Figure 12 useful.
➤ Disciplines: 4, 5, 6, 12. Figure 1 may be a useful guide to untangling what may seem conflicting perceptions as you try to build a thick description of what the actors are actually trying to project. By deconstructing the way in which you project onto them you can imagine what they may be reacting to. You must also be careful not to generalize what you hear beyond the person who tells you.
➤ Outcome: an understanding of the complexity that people bring with them, and an ability to see other people's thinking in the same way as you see your own.

Theme 2
Otherization

OTHERIZATION

Otherization has been presented to you already in this book (especially in Unit A2.1). However, it is helpful to analyse the term again. 'Otherization' is used to describe the process that we undertake in ascribing identity to the Self through the often negative attribution of characteristics to the Other. Otherization is a 'culture first' view of individuals. It is seen to be problematic by the authors of this book in that it does not allow for the agency of other persons to be a factor in their identity construction. It does not permit the *negotiation* of identity between people, but is often crudely reductive, and so it is typical of *unskilled* intercultural communication.

■ **Stop and think:** With reference to the previous units in this section think about the following questions.

■ Who controls the way you want to be understood or viewed?
■ Is it you or are you involved in a struggle to assert this?
■ Have you ever felt at times that you are being 'read' in ways contrary to the one you wish to be?
■ Why do you think this struggle arises?
■ What can you do about this?

Within all societies there are dominant ways of constructing the cultural Self and cultural Other, i.e. the accepted and promoted view from the culture(s) you are affiliated and ascribed to. In other words the cultures you belong to tell you who you are – or should be – as a member of those cultures. Examples of this can often be heard, e.g. 'Us Mexicans are . . .' or 'It's not British to . . .'. There are also, conversely, dominant ways of constructing the cultural Other: the cultures to which you belong tell you how those in different cultures (i.e. outsiders from your culture) are to be read and understood – e.g. 'The British are a cold people', 'Well what do you expect from the French?', 'How Italian of you!' If these modes of understanding the Self and the Other become part of the daily currency by which individuals make sense of the world around them, then these can be seen to represent the dominant constructions that have become internalized within the individuals of a particular society.

It would seem evident that to control these dominant ways of understanding the Self and the Other within a society is to exercise power. For this reason these representations are not immobile but are open to change: they change as members of the society in question struggle with each other over the power to control these representations. A society is thus a set of competing modes of construction of the Self and of Others. You may find, therefore, that your particular construction of your Self and of Others may run up against some of these competing constructions and this may be a reason why you have felt misread at times. Because these constructions of who you are and who others are are part of a power struggle there may be deliberate readings of you to the one you attempt to assert. In other words, you may be deliberately otherized by others for their own 'political' motives.

Task C2.1.1   Otherization and power

➤   Work on the following three examples. Discuss with your study peers how an otherizing impulse is perhaps being used as part of a power strategy.

Example C2.1.1

Sheena is a college secretary, in her early twenties and unqualified beyond school-leaving certification. She earns a salary of around £14,000 per year. Michael is a lecturer in the college; he has several post-graduate qualifications and earns about £25,000 per year. Collin, another lecturer, similar to Michael, decides to try and send a fax. He does not wish to disturb the secretary Sheena, who is on the computer, writing. Once at the fax machine he realizes he doesn't know the sequence in which he needs to press buttons to operate the fax machine, so he appeals to Sheena for help. Sheena then remarks loudly: 'Michael asked me the same question the other day. Honestly, you men!'

Example C2.1.2

Ian and Peter are two brothers, in their mid-thirties. Ian studied civil engineering at university and Peter studied fine art. Ian studied engineering mainly to do something different from his older brother Peter, but also because he felt it would lead to a more secure job. Peter developed his artistic inclinations mainly because of family praise about his early efforts at drawing and because he had often been told that his Uncle Reginald was a good painter and that there was a strong artistic streak in the family that he had inherited. Although he studied art, Peter is actually very practical with his hands and methodical. He likes working out how things work mechanically; he used to take his motorcycle engine apart and reassemble it just for fun as a teenager. Although Ian studied engineering he is not very good with his hands and as a student he played the bass guitar in a rock band.

When at home visiting their parents, their mother would make the following type of comments: 'Peter, as the artist in the family, what colour should we paint the kitchen?' and 'Ian, where should we best put our savings?' or 'How best should we design the living room extension?' Being typed as an artist was something Peter found very annoying and something he found it difficult to get away from. He remembered the joke a friend who studied maths at university made at his expense when he introduced him to a girl: 'This is Peter. He studies art with a capital "F".' Everyone laughed, including Peter, but it annoyed him deeply. From his point of view, the fact that people could label him an artist was a way of trivializing him and making him seem peripheral to 'important' things. Ian, as it happened, had the opposite problem: he felt people saw him as boring and not worth talking to as an engineer. At university he would pretend he was studying an arts subject when at parties for this reason.

Example C2.1.3

(Extracts from Barroso, M. and Reyes-Ortiz, I. (1996) 'Caribbean Chronicles' (Trans. by M. P. Hyde), *El País Aguilar*, pp. 65–70)

Extract 1

When in Europe a person talks about a 'multiethnic society', the term refers to Africans cleaning the Paris metro or picking apples in Lerida, Spain, or to Turks tightening bolts in Mercedes Factories. In Trinidad and Tobago, the term 'multiethnic society' means that there are various nations treading the same soil, who struggle over the same jobs and who eye each other warily in the street.

Extract 2

The further you descend the social hierarchy, the more the divisions of labour are evident. The sale of ice and everything to do with it has traditionally been the domain of the Negro, just as the sale of bread has been the domain of the Hindu. A Negro would have problems if he tried to open a bakery, and even more problems if he opened a cleaner's because Trinidadians believe that the hands that knead their bread and wash their clothes should be white or yellow. In the same way they believe that Negroes are not good at making money because they like to talk too much.

Extract 3

The law is ignored and there exist no clear models of conduct. 'You can't talk of Trinidad and Tobago as a society,' says Abu Bakr. 'The only dynamic is race. Our society has no shared goals. There exist separate groups and each group has its leaders. The whites control everything and are fearful of the Hindus; that's why they place the Negroes in positions of administrative power in the State because Negroes have no economic power and are not a threat to them.'

Analysis

■ Read the following analyses and then offer your interpretations. You may not agree with them. Indeed, if you do not, the reasons you may not do so could provide a useful starting point for your discussions.

In Example C2.1.1 there is an appeal to male and female stereotypes. The men, who are in higher positions in terms of status and salary in the work environment, are typed as being impractical and dependent on women – in this case by a woman who is on a lower salary and has a lower-status job. The implication is that as men they do not really deserve to have this higher status. Of course, the reason that the men may not be able to operate the fax machine is that in their work routine this is not normally something they do. Their being male may have very little to do with their inability to operate the fax machine. The underlying questioning of their status within the working context as being a consequence of their gender and not perhaps merit based on ability is, however, implicit in the secretary's 'joke'.

In Example C2.1.2 the pinning of qualities and abilities onto individuals and stereotyping them as either 'artistic and expressive' or 'practical and sensible' may run deep within certain societies. It would seem that a person needs to be one or the other – obviously not the case in this example of the two brothers. To be categorized as an artist would seem to disenfranchize one from being serious about 'more important' issues in life, whereas to be categorized as a scientist or 'non-artist' is to mean that one is perhaps not capable of being a colourful and interesting person.

In Example C2.1.3 we are given an account of Trinidad and Tobago, where it is suggested that race has a strong determining factor on who one can be in terms of the job one has and the economic position one has on the island. This division of labour, which fits with the power structure on the island, means that according to race people are thought of as capable of and deemed to rightly undertake certain functions. It would seem that a belief develops that race leads to occupation and that this becomes mythologized as a natural state of affairs. On a much larger scale than in the first two examples, people are reduced in their potential according to a crude label that is seen to explain them. In Example C2.1.1, technological incompetence is explained as a factor of maleness. In Example C2.1.2, the legitimization of opinions and outlooks is attributed to whether a person is artistic or not. In Example C2.1.3, race would seem to be a determinant of social function and potential. In all three examples, however, the reducing of the other to these characteristics and potentials is a form of power wielding. By reducing the other certain advantages can be accrued to the person or those within a system that encourages this. How may this be resisted?

Now we can connect this with our ongoing investigation of intercultural communication, with reference to Figure 12.

Task C2.1.2 Trap avoidance

➤ Events: of your choosing, ongoing.
➤ Actors: of your choosing.
➤ Setting: within your milieu.
➤ Cultural circumstances: personal.
➤ Angle: the way we reduce the foreign Other to sexist, racist or culturist stereotypes.
➤ Observation: deconstruct the thoughts you have when you interact with people who are culturally different. Begin by noting these thoughts in your research diary, until eventually you begin to analyse them at the point where you are actually interacting.

> ➤ Disciplines: 10.
> ➤ Outcome: culturist trap avoidance – being able to see the traps coming and changing the trajectory of your interaction.

UNIT C2.2 ## AS YOU SPEAK THEREFORE YOU ARE

Language is a bridge between people, but it is also a wall that divides people. Perhaps as noticeable as the colour of one's skin, the noises one makes to communicate with other human beings is an obvious indicator of 'difference'. Language, apart from allowing for the transmission of culture from one generation to the next, serves to identify its users as belonging to particular cultural groups. Indeed, to the extant that a language is only intelligible to those who use it, language is exclusive. In Text B1.5.2, Unit B1.5, Stuart Hall talks about community being exclusive and of language as the basis of community; this is equally true of language. Language is thus a great divider of people. As soon as people use language they are judged by the people who hear them as belonging to certain social groups, and the images and stereotypes that are attached to these groups may be conjured up and applied to them. Indeed a branch of linguistics called sociolinguistics is concerned less with the transactional content of language itself than with talk as being the assertion of belonging and identity.

There is, it may be argued, no such thing as neutral transaction in communication. All communication, apart from being about the 'what' that is said, is also about the negotiation of interpersonal relationships; of the signalling of the status of each interactant, of the power relationship between the interactants, of the social distance between them or the solidarity they may offer each other. This is deducible through the use of politeness strategies, of honorifics (terms of address) and other communicative devices. These devices obviously differ according to the language group and cultural background of the users, which in turn depends on the histories and evolution of the societies of the language users. Some societies may be more divided than others in terms of social class; some may be more homogenous than others. In a more divided society, politeness and the showing of deference may be very important for communicative success. Members of societies that are not perhaps so divided may have less need for politeness strategies and the demonstration of relative rank during their interactions with each other. There is a multiplicity of factors that lead to the particular way people orientate themselves to each other in various locations and these ways inevitably vary from location to location and from context to context within these locations. In Unit B2.6 Wierzbicka thus talks about culture specific ways of speaking, and in Unit B3.5 Triandis and Smith discuss ways of possibly linking this to differences in cultural value systems that, they hypothesize, exist in the world between different cultures.

Task C2.2.1 Language of address

➤ Think of all the different ways people may address each other in a language. Make a list of them with examples from the language group(s) you are familiar with. Table 12 may be of use. Continue the table for as many items you can think of.

➤ Discuss any similarities and differences with your study peers. To help you make comparisons you might like to think when, in English, the following terms may be used, i.e. between which people and in what contexts?.

First name   Family name   Mr/Mrs/Miss/Ms plus family name

Sir/Madam   Dr   Lord/Lady   The Right Honourable Gentleman/Lady

Hey, you!   Oi, you!   Father/Mother (and other family role titles)

Darling/sugar/honey (and other terms of endearment)

Familiar shortened version of name, e.g. Mick for Michael   Nickname

Duck/love

➤ Why do these terms vary and what factors do you take into account when using these forms of address?

Table 12 Cultural use of language

Language item	Interactants who use the item	Context of interaction

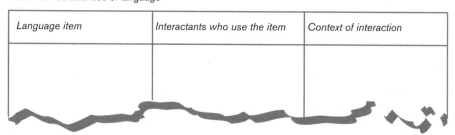

Note: etic and emic levels of analysis

We all use the communicative systems we have been socialized into. Because in one cultural group's language use there are a lot of politeness markers such as 'please' and 'thank you', it does not necessarily follow that the people who use these are more polite and respect each other more than those who do not use them habitually. It is just that in one group this is expected out of force of habit and in the other group it is not. It is very risky to judge other people by one's own cultural and linguistic habits and derive conclusions in this way. One has to understand other groups and the language use within other groups from a perspective from within those groups. When one moves from one linguistic and cultural group to another it is also risky to assume that the other group will use language in the same way. One needs to observe how language is used in the other group and not assume that one's primary group is the norm against which other groups' language use can be judged. We also need to be aware of the fact that when someone moves into our primary language use group that that person is probably not expert in the language use patterns of our group. In other words, we need to be wary of interpreting a person's personality or intentions through the linguistic behaviour of that person, as we would a person who has been socialized from birth into that pattern of language use. A person from a language group that uses fewer 'pleases' for requests may be seen as rude by a group that expects the more ubiquitous use of 'please'. However, rudeness may well not be intended at all.

'Languacism' could perhaps serve as a neologism to stand for the stereotyping of people according to their language use, as racism stands for stereotyping people according to race. The way language is used by groups of people may become connected with a judgement about the people of that group and certain values and characteristics may be ascribed to people in that group because of their language use. In British English people who drop the 'h' at the beginning of such words as 'home' and substitute 'f' for the 'th' sound in 'think' – i.e. 'fink' – may be considered uneducated or less intelligent than those who do not do this, merely because of the way they speak. It would seem that we otherize each other very readily from very minimal audial clues.

Discussion point

Think of how in your cultural context you may place people in boxes according to the way they speak. Think how you also respond to people speaking your language when it is not their first language and how you may also be tempted to judge them as having certain characteristics because of the way they use the language. Look at the following and try to explain them in terms of the above.

- A Swedish female states: 'The English are not honest because they are always saying "please" and "thank you" even when they don't mean it.'
- The word 'barbarian' derives from the Ancient Greeks who typed those who couldn't speak Greek as uttering meaningless noise like the sound 'babababa'.
- A Spanish man talking about the rise of Spanish in the USA states that Spanish will never rival English because it is the language of the poor.
- A Moroccan teenager enquires of a British tourist who is speaking Arabic to him why he is speaking Arabic if he is not a Muslim.
- Sarah, a working-class British girl from the county of Essex, who has a good job in the City of London, is paying for elocution lessons because she wants people to treat her as 'herself'.

You can now continue your ongoing investigation of intercultural communication in your own milieu, with reference to Figure 12.

 Task C2.2.2 Exploring language

➤ Events: conversations between people, conversations *with* people *about* culture.
➤ Actors: of your choice.

➤ Setting: of your choice.

➤ Cultural circumstances: of your choice.

➤ Angle: cultural use of language.

➤ Observation: note down the different ways people from different cultural groups, whether national or other, greet each other. Also, have conversations with people about how they feel about the way they are addressed by their culturally different interactants.

➤ Disciplines: 4. You will need to create a thick description by piecing together different fragments of evidence, both about how to collect the data and about how to communicate with your informants.

➤ Outcome: awareness of how to tune your language to the languages of others.

Conversations

Having conversations with informants is an alternative to the more formal interview. It enables you to search out meanings and ideas in dialogue with your informant. The development of your own thoughts also helps to build the thick description.

THE 'LOCATED' SELF

UNIT C2.3

This unit looks at the issue of the degree to which we are shaped in our outlook by our environment. It raises issues about the extent to which we can be truly considered individuals and also the range of possible selves we can be according to circumstances. It therefore suggests that we need to be very careful about making judgements about others if we are not aware of the context in which others live or have lived and not aware that we too could equally well hold different values and have different outlooks were we in different circumstances.

Discussion point

In groups consider the following questions.

1a If you live in a place in the world or in a time where there is a high level of infant mortality, how may this be reflected in parent–child emotional attachment?

1b If you live in a place in the world or in a time where there is a low level of infant mortality, how may this be reflected in parent–child emotional attachment?

2a If you live in a place in the world or in a time where there is a high level of sexually transmitted disease, some of it fatal and with no known cure, how may this affect the sexual mores of the society experiencing this situation?

2b If you live in a place in the world or in a time where there is effective and readily available contraception and treatment of sexually transmitted disease, how may this affect the sexual mores of the society experiencing this situation?

3a If you live in a period of history in a society where there are food shortages, or recent experience of food shortage, how may this influence the view that that society has of eating and desirable body shape?

3b If you live in a period of history in a society where there is an overabundance of food, how may this influence the view that that society has of eating and desirable body shape?

■ What possible social mores, values and beliefs may emerge as normal, do you think, in each of the circumstances described in questions 1 to 3? Figure 14 may help you.

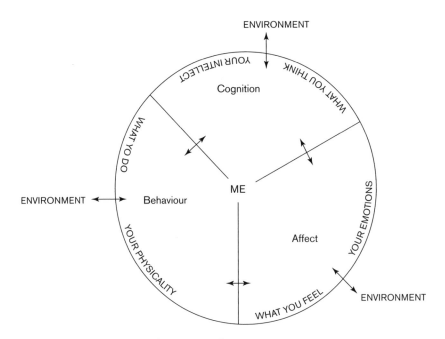

Figure 14 Three spheres of human experience

■ After looking at Figure 14 decide in what way the circumstances described may be reflected in the cognitive, affective and behavioural domains of individuals.

Task C2.3.1 Exploring language

Refer to Figure 12.

➤ Events: conversations *between* people, conversations *with* people, observations of people's behaviour.
➤ Actors: of your choice.
➤ Setting: of your choice.
➤ Cultural circumstances: of your choice.

➤ Angle: observation of how people behave and what values they state they have concerning selected issues.

➤ Observation: think of some social phenomena that you have noticed and that you feel give rise to certain cognitive, affective and behavioural expression. Decide how you may organize the collection of data to test this.

➤ Disciplines: 3, 11.

➤ Outcome: awareness of how circumstance influences all of us in the affective, cognitive and behavioural domains.

INTEGRATING THE OTHER

UNIT C2.4

Often when we consider other cultures we compare them to our own. Because we know and understand our own culture better than the 'foreign' one we tend to feel that the foreign one is strange. We have been taught since birth to interpret and understand one another in certain ways, and when we meet a different system of interpretation we may feel that it is therefore not the 'right' way to do things. If we have become accustomed to sleeping from 11pm to 7am, we might think that people who have a siesta are odd. Similarly, we may feel that people who eat other foods to us are strange, or family structures that are different to ours are unnatural. In other words, we tend to defend our cultural inheritance as the norm and see other modes of existence as mistaken. This perhaps natural reaction to difference, is something we need to be wary of and try to overcome, for, in effect, there is no blueprint or copyright to existence and there are always interesting things to be found and learnt in the ways other communities manage their existence. Different communities have come up with different solutions to the challenges of communal existence within the environments in which they exist. Your cultural milieu – the one that you feel you belong to – is but one attempted solution. The problem is that there are many within various communities who profess that their vision of how life is to be lived is the only true and correct way and that other ways are aberrations. This leads to intolerance and of course to conflict. Rather than reject the way other communities live and the values they have learnt to subscribe to, another way forward is to try to understand and learn what one can from these different cultural outlooks.

It is of course imperative to maintain a moral sense of what one believes is right and wrong – in other words, openness to other cultures does not imply an abstention from judgement but rather an abstention from *prejudgement* based on ignorance. Openness implies the willingness to learn through researching other cultures and this aids in the development of one's own moral sense.

In the next task you will be asked to find a positive aspect to behaviour that may initially appear negative. It is perhaps a natural reaction to find different behaviour threatening or disconcerting, and we may indeed judge such behaviour as rude or negative. However, if we train ourselves not to jump to such hasty conclusions, we may be able to reassess difference in less negative terms.

Task C2.4.1 Turning thinking around

➤ Look at the following example. It is based on a true event. Try to transfer it from a negative experience to a positive one – in other words, do not prejudge it but work with it to see if there are any positive lessons to be learnt from it.

Example C2.4.1

When Peter, an Englishman, had been working for about a month in a town in the north of Morocco as a teacher he decided to try and further a friendship he was developing with several local Moroccan teachers in his school. He decided to invite them for supper to his apartment. This they readily accepted and agreed to turn up at 8pm that evening. He prepared a meal. By 9pm he began to realize that his guests were not coming and cleared away the food. The next day he went into school wondering what excuse they would have. He entered the staff room and met his two friends. They smiled and offered him mint tea. Instead of showing any embarrassment they seemed to regard their relationship as not soured in any way. He enquired what had happened the night before and why they had not turned up. One of them then explained that they had been on their way to his flat but on passing a café they noticed that there was an interesting football match on, so they sat down and watched it. As far as he could glean, that was the extent of the excuse. In fact, it was not an excuse at all but a statement of what happened, pure and simple. He went off to his class feeling confused.

As he lived in this new environment he began to adapt to it. He would at times be invited for mint tea to the homes of people who, frankly, he had little interest in. This could use up a whole evening as one was expected to remain chatting for hours, not just drink the tea and be off as is the custom in England ('to pop in for a quick cuppa'). He therefore developed the tactic of accepting an invitation to avoid the discomfort and rudeness of refusing it to someone's face, and thus keep his options open for the evening: if nothing better presented itself, he would go; if something more interesting turned up, he wouldn't. The next day he would just smilingly explain that something else cropped up.

➤ Peter was brought up in a system in which the demands of politeness and 'face' require either that one goes against one's real wishes and accepts invitations that one would really prefer not to accept, or that one finds elaborate excuses (an ill child is a very useful one) to avoid commitment. What may be the possible benefits of this alternative system?

Note: face

This is a concept that refers to a person's self-image and to how a person's self-esteem and sense of identity are related to the degree to which that person's self-image is supported in encounters with others. A threat to a person's face is therefore a threat to a person's self-concept – to how that person prefers to see himself or herself and to be seen, or at least regarded, by others.

To try and combat the tendency to see difference in negative terms, we need to look at how we can see the positive aspects that other perspectives and modes of existence can offer us and how we can appreciate these and even work them into our own way of being.

Task C2.4.2 Liberation into the Other

➤ Make a list of experiences you had when you entered another cultural milieu by concentrating on the things you have found liberating in this experience. By filling in Table 13 try to assess what it is in your own cultural milieu that you find repressive. Use the table to record your experience. One example is given. Add more rows if you need to.

Table 13 Cultural preferences

Description of different cultural experience and aspect that you found liberating	Analysis of own cultural milieu and aspects of it that this suggests you find repressive in it
Example	
Working with agricultural workers from my village as a student – picking apples. The ease with which everyone made jokes about each other – the enjoyment of this.	The fact that in more professional circles people tend to take themselves rather seriously and forget that they have foibles and that these can be a healthy source of amusement.

Otherization is based on the assumption that the cultural Other is not as complex or as sophisticated as the cultural Self, and that the Other can therefore be reduced to essential and often negative characteristics. This rendering of the Other as inferior or bad may be a psychological prop to make the Self seem superior. In Mark Twain's *Huckleberry Finn* there is an obvious example of this with Huck's drunken and dangerous father – who has obviously got few redeeming characteristics – holding a view of 'Negroes' as inferior, when in fact we are presented with the noble and compassionate figure of the runaway slave Jim. His otherization is thus shown by Twain to be a baseless psychological prop based on self-delusion. It is a device designed to preserve his own face.

Task C2.4.3 Stages for appreciation

➤ Consider this list of stages that could be used as a guide to overcoming otherization when confronted with difference. Put these stages in the order you feel they should be in. Then think about whether there are any stages missing and to what extent you agree with it or not as a model.

1. Reappraisal of own norms of behaviour.
2. Integration of new norms into one's own cultural system.
3. Making sense of new norms.
4. Investigation of new phenomena – information-seeking stage.
5. Shock and possible anger at difference.
6. Adaptation and adoption of new norms through practice into own cultural system.
7. Assumption that difference doesn't really exist.

(The intended stages are as follows: 7, 5, 4, 3, 1, 6, 2.)

Now continue your investigation of your own milieu, with reference to Figure 12.

Task C2.4.4 Being positive about the Other

➤ Events: of your choice, ongoing.
➤ Actors: you and others of your choice.
➤ Setting: of your choice.
➤ Cultural circumstances: of your choice.
➤ Angle: trying to be positive about the Other.
➤ Observation: continue your observation of your own thinking while taking part in intercultural communication. Reassess the list in Task C2.4.3 against your own lived experience of working out how to communicate. Integrate notes about this into your research diary. Observe and note the ways in which your interactants do the same.
➤ Disciplines: 4, 9.
➤ Outcome: developing experience of how to communicate.

UNIT C2.5 'ARE YOU WHAT YOU ARE SUPPOSED TO BE?'

Task C2.5.1 Are you saying what you are supposed to?

➤ Look at the following quote that the author of Section C collected one evening.

> When I was at school in the Republic of Ireland I had to learn Gaelic. I was forced to spend 30 per cent of my time, not learning something useful like

maths or science, that would serve me in life. I was a victim of a nostalgic, misguided and retrograde Irish nationalism that the politicians of the day decided to inflict upon us school kids to make themselves feel better.

In order to do this task you need to have a rudimentary knowledge of the historical and political context of the Republic of Ireland. Ireland was colonized for hundreds of years by the English (and British) with the English language displacing the native language. The Celtic Irish have also remained predominantly Catholic, while the English and British have been predominantly Protestant. The Republic of Ireland achieved independence this century after a long and bitter struggle. Eire (the Republic of Ireland) is now about 95 per cent Catholic and 5 per cent Protestant.

➤ When we receive statements from people we need to know who the person is that makes the statement in order to be able to process the statement and make a judgement about it. Who do you think the person is who made this statement? What identity tags would you find useful for further placing and understanding this statement?

The following are tags that we may tend to use for interpreting what is said:

- nationality
- gender
- age
- ethnicity
- religious affiliation
- social background
- current life context (married or single or divorced, father or mother, job etc.)
- sexual identity

➤ Re-read the above quote. Then look at the possible authors of the quote and make notes on your reaction in each case.

Person: with minimal descriptors (basic typology)	Your reaction: explain why
A middle-aged, Protestant Irish woman	
A middle-aged, Catholic Irish man	
An English person who attended school in Ireland due to the fact that their parents worked there for a period of time	
An immigrant Ugandan Asian who arrived in Ireland as a child in the 1970s	

➤ Who of the above do you think it was most likely to be and why?

➤ Are you surprised to learn that it was the second person in the list? Why?

Due to 'tags' and our interpretation of them we bring expectations about what we think people must believe and may tend to interpret the Other accordingly. This is dangerous, as it may override individual difference and we need to be on our guard against it. Sometimes the context of a person's discourse can become so oppressive that it is not possible for the person to speak freely.

The following task is designed to illustrate the fact that it is not just what is said that is important but who says what is said and the social and political context in which that person says what is said that is also important for our interpretation and understanding of what is said. Are people limited in what they can therefore say by the fact of who they are and the context of their speaking? Is it perhaps the case that certain people can say certain things and certain people cannot because of who they are supposed to be? Do you feel this pressure? Are there certain things that you refrain from stating because of who you are deemed to be?

Task C2.5.2   What we can say

➤ Can you give examples and explain why it is difficult to perhaps say certain things?

Thing that should not be said	Social and 'political' reason

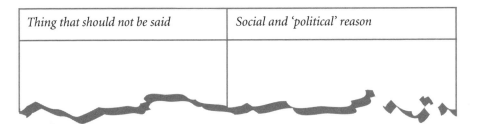

Tasks C2.5.1 and C2.5.2 are designed to raise awareness as to how we may otherize people through what we expect them to say. We may do this by imposing stereotypical notions onto people based on vague notions we carry as to 'who' they are. Thus an Irish Catholic may be expected to be nationalistic and pro the cultural 'Irishification' of Ireland. We may think that such a person should naturally be in favour of this and be disconcerted if he or she is not. We must also be careful of assuming that what people say is in any case what they actually think and believe, as the context of utterances may be a factor in allowing what can be said by certain people according to their 'typography'. Unit B2.1 is relevant to this point with texts by Sugimoto on the fabrication of national identity in Japan (B2.1.3) and Boye Lafayette de Mente on the public face (*tatamae*) versus private thought (*honne*) that is argued to exist in Japanese society (B2.1.2).

As well as otherizing the people we communicate with we may also otherize ourselves through our own self-conceptions. We may do this through using the following mechanism: to say that one is something is to thus say that one is not something else. To be Canadian or to be Turkish Cypriot is not to be American or not to be mainland Turkish.

'Are you what you are supposed to be?' SECTION

We perhaps use our neighbours more for this process of self-definition as they are the ones we encounter more frequently. As discussed earlier, we tend to represent these others in more negative terms than the self (see Unit B2.1). Said (1978) argues that the historical imperialism of Europe in the rest of the world has meant that Europeans constructed the colonized Other based on the repressions that the colonizers held themselves. Thus the colonized have been depicted as emotional and non-rational, as potentially immoral and degenerate and thus in need of firm guidance. This argument is also one found in feminist literature, which argues that women have been otherized in this manner and typed with having these same characteristics – ones that a repressed male psyche has projected onto them. In this way colonized subjects and women are argued to have become 'serviceable others' used for the construction of the identity and self-view of the dominant.

In the next task you are asked to look at your own potential use of this potential 'serviceable Other' in the construction of your 'Self'. The question you are asked to investigate here is that of what boundary lines you draw in the process of self-definition.

Task C2.5.3   Using the Other to define the Self

➤ Events: of your choice.
➤ Actors: yourself and others of your choice.
➤ Setting: of your choice.
➤ Cultural circumstances: of your choice.
➤ Angle: analysing how we use a contrastive Other to define the identity of the Self.
➤ Observation: Collect either introspective data about how you psychologically contrast yourself with others (use your journal), or interview people to see what they say about others and the implications this has for their self-view.
➤ Disciplines: 10, 12, 13, 14.
➤ Outcome: developing an understanding and a sensitivity of how stereotypes may be used in everyday discourse and thought to establish the Self. Learning to be on guard against this.

If we become aware of this function – this basic binary division and dichotomization process that we employ and that sets up a Self versus an Other – we can at least be on our guard against this tendency. There is a need to take people met as they are and not to impose a stereotype used for one's own purpose of self-definition. This is difficult because, as we will see in Theme 3, our images and stereotypes of Others are mediated by the societies we are in and by the media itself, which tend to reinforce stereotypical images of Others.

Theme 3
Representation

'YOU ARE, THEREFORE I AM'

There can be no doubt that we absorb the messages around us about 'the Other' that the media and the culture we are in project. There is also no doubt that today the media is a very powerful tool for those who want both to control society and to sell ideas and products to its members. For this reason we have included a section in this book on 'representation', which is the way the world is presented to us. Representation and otherization are similar processes. One could argue that otherization is a form of representation that projects the Other but in a negative 'inferior' manner. However, a subtle difference that we feel exists is that whereas otherization is a natural consequence of dichotomization and the affirmation of the Self – and is therefore something we have to be wary of as individuals – representation is more political in that it is controlled by external bodies that offer images and understandings of 'the Other' for us to consume. Theme 3 of Section C concentrates on looking at how our understanding of the world and the people in it may be mediated.

■ **Stop and think:** Think of the inherited stereotypes and images of others that you have been exposed to in your cultural milieu. Use the table below to list them. With your study peers, discuss where you think these images have come from and the purposes you think they serve. Who gains and who loses by them?

Stereotype and example of phrases used to convey this stereotype in the media/everyday discourse	Examples of contexts in which you have come across this stereotype

A further problem with being programmed to associate certain peoples with certain characteristics is that certain characteristic become looked for in certain groups, and even though other groups of people may exhibit the same characteristic in equal measure, this can be overlooked. One may well approach other people looking for confirmation of the characteristics they are supposed to exhibit and may thus also overlook other characteristics that may disconfirm the stereotype. It would seem that once cognitive schemas (mental frames of reference) are in place they become the lenses through which the world is observed and it is difficult to change them. In a sense, experience of the world can become contaminated by the glasses that you have been handed to look at it through (this is what we mean by 'mediated' experience).

Task C3.1.1 Familiarity breeds illusion

➤ Investigate how an object is represented through either the media or in discourse (the way people talk about something) in the cultural context you are currently in.

➤ First, you need to decide what the object is that you are to investigate and collect data on. Will it be a material object such as a car or an item of food, or will it be a less consumable object such as a group of people, e.g. travellers, asylum seekers, Americans, or indeed the British countryside or the Hungarian Plain? You need to consider both the visual and the non-visual in this project. Both are semiotic systems that work to represent objects.

➤ Once you have decided on the object, you need to devise a work plan for data collection. Will you be collecting images and text together? What sites will you go to to collect data? How much data will you collect and how will you record and later analyse the data? You also, therefore, need to devise a timescale for data collection and analysis.

➤ In the analysis phase it is important to move beyond description of the data you have collected to suggest how the object the data refer to is represented and how this is achieved. This means analysing the data and linking it to a theoretical system of interpretation. As an example of this, one group of students in a class decided to analyse the use of nature as a backdrop to products being sold in TV advertisements. The theoretical approach was a psychological one that suggested there is an urge in industrial society for escapism from the urban and congested. This desire to escape to a pure, natural Arcadia is manipulated to promote products through association with this urge. Thus a soap is advertised in association with a pristine, tropical waterfall. This theory about the psychological desire for escapism from modern society for something pure and elementary was the basis upon which the ads were analysed and gave the data analysis a theoretical coherence it would have otherwise lacked.

➤ Once you have collected your data and analysed it, prepare a presentation of your findings.

It is useful to combine images in your presentation of your findings. These can either be taken with a digital camera, and used in a PowerPoint presentation, or you may prefer to circulate the images to the audience in handouts. In the latter case it is wise to label each image and direct the audience's attention to each image at the apposite moment in the presentation. While it is important to develop a theory as to how the data works, it is also important to remain open to new interpretations offered by others which may further develop your understanding of the data. For this reason allowing time for responses from an audience to your presentation is a vital part of the process. The presentation is not the end point.

UNIT C3.2   'SCHEMAS': FIXED OR FLEXIBLE?

It may, at this point, be useful to look at what the difference is between a stereotype and a type. It is inevitable that we carry around with us mental structures which we impose on the world in an attempt to make sense of it. These cognitive structures, or schemas, are essential for us to navigate our way through life and are the building blocks of learning. The first time we encounter something new we form a mental schema of that event and then the next time we encounter a similar event we use the schema from the first encounter to help us navigate and understand the event the next time. It is, however, unwise to let a mental schema become hardened, so that it no longer takes account of new data. Schemas, while psychologically inevitable, need to be constantly updated and seen as imperfectly constructed models, not absolute replacements for reality.

Task C3.2.1   Navigating the world

➤ Write down the schema you have for a typical event – e.g. a wedding, or going out for a meal. Break it down into expected stages. The ideal model – i.e. the most expected template – is sometimes called the 'prototype', and even if this is not followed to the letter, it is the model we have by which we can then judge 'deviancy', and thus know if something is unusual or significant.

Knowing the cultural schema of events such as dancing a salsa or ordering a meal in McDonald's, is derived from empirical experience of that 'event'. It is reinforced each time that it serves as a useful guide for behaviour in that particular context or 'genre'. Of course the schemas of these different genres can be very different in different countries. When we are faced with a new genre, even within our own culture, we may be nervous and find the event tiring because we have to watch others and learn how to do it. For example, the author of Section C recently attended a funeral – the burial of a friend's husband – and as he had never been to a burial before he found himself anxious not to do the wrong thing. He was quiet and followed the others. He noticed he was one of the few without a black tie; he felt self-conscious about this, hoping it wouldn't be seen as disrespectful by the family of the deceased. He now has a schema for burials, which hopefully he won't have to employ too often! Schemas are therefore used to reduce anxiety and to reduce the amount of thought we need to employ in different cultural events. This is natural. I would suggest that when we experience an event such as 'visiting a friend's house' or 'going to a wedding', or 'eating a meal in a restaurant', or 'meeting the parents of a girl/boyfriend for the first time' or 'visiting the doctor' in a different culture from the one you are generally acclimatized to, it is best to learn the event as if it were the first time and to tentatively feel one's way. It is very useful to have a cultural informer – someone on the inside who can help guide you. 'Don't forget to wear a black tie' would have been useful information in the author's case. The problem is that if we have a schema for an event already established in our national, regional or ethnic cultural milieu, we are likely to make the error of thinking that the event in the other culture should be the same – or similar. When expectations are upset one may experience a certain degree of shock that can perhaps translate into resentment, anger and perhaps negative judgement of the other culture. This is because expectations have not been fulfilled and one may therefore feel vulnerable and 'adrift'. To further illustrate problems that may occur when one imports a schema from one cultural context into another let's look at the author's 'drinking in the pub in Britain' schema compared to his learnt schema for the same ostensible event in Spain.

In Spain the schema may be: enter the bar and greet the people there with a general '*Buenos dias*', go to the bar; see if there are any friends around; offer to get them drinks; order the drinks at the bar; drink and accept any offers of other drinks from others; when you want to go ask how much you owe, often clarifying with the barman/woman which drinks you are responsible for; make sure you say goodbye to everyone you know and to those you don't with a general '*Hasta luego.*'

A Spanish man greeting strangers in a bar in England would probably be disappointed in the lack of reciprocity of his greeting. The locals would be suspicious or amused; the Spaniard would feel the locals are perhaps unfriendly. He may be seen as dishonest or evasive if he doesn't offer to pay for the first drink he asks for upon being served that drink. An Englishman entering a Spanish bar may be seen as a little odd or ingenuine if he uses 'please' and 'thank you' all the time. These terms tend to be reserved for asking favours and for having rendered a favour, and are thus not used so 'lightly'. The Englishman would also be seen to be a little over-zealous or ill at ease if he attempts to pay for his drink immediately. In both instances the transgressor of norms would seem to reinforce larger suspicions and negative traits that may be attributed to non-locals of various origins. This example is designed simply to show how we need to rebuild our schemas when in different cultures and not feel that we can 'get by' with our previous ones. There is a schema for 'visiting a Spanish bar' which is distinct from the schema 'visiting an English pub'. This is a schema that needs to be learnt in order to navigate one's way successfully through the new cultural situation.

Task C3.2.2   Sketching a map

➤   Research a cultural schema. This is different from Task C3.2.1 in which you were asked to note down the components of a schema you felt you were familiar with. To do this task you need either to attend an event that you are not familiar with or to attend an event you are familiar with but look at it through 'ethnographic eyes'.

Note: ethnographic observation

The term 'ethnographic eyes' means that you should strive to make the familiar 'strange'. You need to act against the taken-for-grantedness that familiarity brings and try to see the event from the perspective of a cultural debutant – an outsider. One way to do this is to imagine you are watching the event and then going to explain it to a child who has not experienced that event before. To do this mini-ethnography it is useful to develop 'ways of seeing'. You need to start from the point that nothing that you see is normal or self-explanatory – everything you see is meaningful and tells you something about the society you are in. Look for the details and note them down. You may like to look at the spatial distribution of participants and objects in the event you have chosen to analyse – where are objects and where are people in relation to each other? What kind of people are where? You may ask whether females position themselves differently to males – i.e. is there a difference in distribution of people according to gender? What may this suggest about the relations of the sexes in that society and about the relative power of each group? Is age a factor? How are people dressed and what are the semiotics of this? Do people show their belonging to different cultural groups within the event you have selected? You may like to look at speech – who talks to who and when? Who holds the floor (i.e. speaks) most? Do people touch at all, and again what are seen to be the conditions governing this – the unwritten rules by which the people in the event seem to be guiding themselves? The questions you can ask are many and they are for you, the ethnographer, to decide. It is useful to have questions that you want to find answers to but you may want to enter the event initially without any precise questions to answer and wait and see if anything suggests itself as worthy of further investigation.

This stage of ethnography is very descriptive – you observe what is occurring, note it down and try to see patterns of behaviour. This means revisiting the event (does the time of day change the pattern of behaviour?). However, the exciting part of the project is the next stage, which is, having noted the patterns you have seen – i.e. gathered 'empirical' evidence – trying to understand the 'why'. What are the possible reasons for the patterns of behaviour you have observed? There are two paths to follow at this juncture: that of interviewing participants, or indeed analysing your own motives if you are a participant observer (i.e. an acculturated participant in the event under study). One tactic you may use for further development of understanding is to present people from the group under study with the 'evidence' you have collected and then ask them why they think such patterns seem to operate. Again, you will then need to find patterns in the responses you collect. Another path is to read literature on cultural analysis and on other ethnographic studies of a similar nature to develop theoretical perspectives with which to interpret your data. Does a feminist account of the events make sense? Does it partly or completely explain what you have observed? Does a Marxist account shed light on it, or does transactional analysis help? Is a Freudian or Jungian interpretation useful? Of course it takes many years to build up a knowledge of such theories! Remember, however, that it is the ability to coherently argue an interpretation that is important and that all theories are, after all, coherent arguments.

Once you have undertaken this study in your groups, present it to colleagues and be ready to defend your interpretation from their questions and to listen to new insights they may offer after having listened to your presentation.

Note: the mediated nature of schemas

The fact that we have mental schemas about what we expect in certain events raises the question about how we develop these schemas, i.e. where they come from. While many of them come from our own experience, it is also probably true that many of them are mediated, i.e. that we are offered the schemas for interpretation before we experience situations and that we thus enter these situations, not finding our own way, but imitating and copying a blueprint that has been offered to us. This mediation may be through what other people tell us, through TV and film or via the printed word. At times this may be like following a script that someone else has written and that we are actors in trying to get it right. This may be particularly true of events that one does not do very often, such as getting married. Again the cultural power invested in the control of schema formation is obvious and the media can be seen to have a pivotal role in this.

Note: the need for flexibility in schemas

A type is therefore a schema; it is a pattern of typicality that helps us to organize the world around us so that events can have meaning. It can also, however, become something of a straitjacket and may degenerate from something potentially helpful into something less helpful. If a schema does not become modified each time a person experiences a certain event then it can be argued to have become hardened and can help less and less with describing and offering a path through the reality of the changing world around us. The hardening of schemas could be argued to suggest a sloppiness of thought when this happens; a schema thus may become a stereotype when this occurs (see Gandy's quote in Task B3.3.4, Unit B3.3). A stereotype is thus the point at which a schema becomes rigid and no longer capable of, or indeed a genuine attempt at, describing or understanding the object it is focused on in a full and non-reductive manner. In a sense it is the giving up of investigation and becomes simply the promotion of a certain characteristic of the object it is focused on beyond its real occurrence in nature. Again the media can encourage us in this sloppiness of thought by repeatedly portraying objects in reduced and inaccurate ways. This may of course serve certain political purposes.

Task C3.2.3 Exploring media representations of the Other

➤ Events: of your choice.
➤ Actors: of your choice.
➤ Setting: of your choice.
➤ Cultural circumstances: the media operating in a setting of your choice.
➤ Angle: discourse analysis.
➤ Observation and strategy: collect instances of representations of a chosen object/ group of people. Analyse how this is undertaken and achieved. Look at how messages about this object are communicated to the 'reader'. Think about who this advantages and disadvantages.

Exploration

➤ Disciplines: 15, 16, 19.
➤ Outcome: awareness of how we as individuals may be susceptible to the manipulations of the media or popular discourse in our interpretation of objects or other people.

UNIT C3.3   **'WHAT'S UNDERNEATH?'**

In this unit we will look at how stereotypes and the reinforcement of what are seen to be 'intrinsic' values and ways of being, exist in much popular humour. As O'Donnell points out in Text B3.2.2 (Unit B3.2) from an analysis of sport, and in particular football commentaries on national teams, the Germans are represented as being 'mechanical' and the Swedes are seen as 'emotionless'. Think of the traits that are attached to various others from your cultural context. One way of doing this is to analyse the source of the 'humour' of jokes about others. If stereotyping is about not allowing the 'object' the freedom to be what it may be or what it may want to be, but is rather the imposition upon that object of a certain way of interpreting that object, then certain jokes can be seen to be part of this reinforcement process – which is inevitably a power strategy in that it restricts the freedom of the object it 'describes'. It is a power strategy because stereotyping is about shutting down the possibilities and potentialities of the Other and is thus used to disempower and consequently disadvantage certain people. Jokes are a common cultural phenomenon that involve representation on a grand scale, and for this reason it is felt they form an improtant part of the analysis of popular discourse and representation and are looked at here.

 Task C3.3.1   What's so funny about it?

➤ Read the following joke and 'unpack' it in terms of the stereotyping that it may reveal.

Mexican joke about Galicians
A Galician pilot brings his plane to land in Mexico. Upon touching down on the runway he has to slam the brakes on so that the plane screeches to a halt and even then it is right at the end of the runway when it stops. The pilot remarks to the co-pilot, 'These stupid Mexicans. Look at how short they build their runways.' The co-pilot replies, 'Yes but look at how wide they build them too!'

The joke may be considered to be amusing in that it is the Galician who is deemed to be 'stupid', not the Mexican: he lands his plane across the runway, not using it as he should, yet he insists it is his view that is right. We may laugh at the stupidity of this Galician pilot and his inability to see his own 'stupidity' and 'obstinacy'. Of course the pilot is designed to represent all Galicians – this is the nature of jokes – it is not just a joke about one foolish person who happens to be Galician. The joke is a 'jibe' at Galicians.

Galicians are people of Celtic origin from the north-west corner of the Iberian peninsula – they are part of Spain. Spain was the colonizing power in Mexico and so the joke has a strong political edge to it. What is more, Galicia has traditionally been a poor and backward part of Spain, and so many immigrants to the Americas (Spanish America) have been Galicians ('Gallegos' in Spanish). Being poor and 'uneducated' yet at the same time being 'colonizers' from Spain, they form the butt of this Mexican joke. This is the political context in which the joke operates.

Task C3.3.2   Stereotypes in jokes

➤   Events: group joke-telling.
➤   Actors: of your choice.
➤   Setting: of your choice.
➤   Cultural circumstances: people bonding by joke-telling.
➤   Angle: cultural use of stereotypes in jokes.
➤   Observation: note down examples of different jokes you encounter. Describe the cultural setting very carefully. Interview people about what it is in the 'joke' that they see as the main point of the joke and their attitudes towards this point.
➤   Disciplines: 17, 18.
➤   Outcome: awareness of how jokes may operate to perpetuate stereotypes against groups of people, operate politically against certain people, and reinforce prejudices against and promote disadvantage for those people in society.

Note: politics with a small 'p'

Politics with a small 'p' refers to the daily jockeying for position and advantage that individuals may indulge in as part of the everyday struggle of existence and the search for advantage. It is thus political to present oneself in a certain way to certain people so that one may achieve one's aims. This is not the same as whole-scale ideological subscription that politics of the left-wing or right-wing variety refers to.

'MANUFACTURING THE SELF'

UNIT C3.4

In Unit C3.3 we looked at how jokes may be used to stereotype others and to gain a certain advantage over those others which may psychologically satisfy the teller. Jokes are thus, to a certain extent, exercises in the domination of others. Of course not all humour is negative. In a play entitled *Comedians*, the writer Trevor Griffiths talks of humour that is based on fear and increases negative feeling towards others and humour that is liberating in that it teaches us something about ourselves and how we may be using stereotypes. An example of this may be the tongue-in-cheek comment the author of this section heard a black British comedian make when in front of an all-white audience in a working men's club in northern England. Upon being heckled he enquired: 'Could the person who made the comment please stand up. I'm sorry, but you all look the same to me!' The joke provoked laughter as it inverted the usual 'racist' comment by certain white people that 'they [black people] all look the same to me' – a comment which de-individualizes and hence dehumanizes the people at whom it is aimed.

In this unit we will look at how we may indeed stereotype ourselves as well as others – how we may be encouraged to see ourselves in certain ways, perhaps in ways that others have maybe told us we 'are'. This may be to make us feel 'good' and 'important' or it may result in us having a negative image of ourselves.

The cultural context we exist in offers us models as to how we should see ourselves and the values and beliefs we should ascribe to. The media also promotes images of what it is to be a member of the nation state one is in. Of course this is not uniform and there are often competing images available to us.

Discussion point

What are the values and beliefs that you feel are promoted in your cultural milieu and where is this promotion undertaken?

I recall, from my childhood, at breakfast, looking at the image on the back of the cornflakes box. It depicted an 'ideal family' – white, one boy, one girl, blond-haired, healthy-looking, a domesticated mother and a strong-jawed father, both in their early thirties, middle-class, all enjoying being together as a unit, flying a kite in a meadow. Of course this image may not sell well in the more multicultural population that Britain has become over the last thirty years, not to mention the fact that the number of single-parent families has increased substantially. This image was promoting the ideal of the nuclear family – the family as an independent, compact economic and emotional unit – and presumably the basis as to the way society should be structured. The family should be aspiring to middle-classdom and this is to be achieved through attachment to the Protestant work ethic and conscious self-control, part of the ideology of which, through family planning, is to have a small number of children (the ideal being one boy and one girl). The strong jaw of the father suggests unswerving devotion to work, the aim of which is to provide for one's family. The wife behind him enjoys (signalled by the smile) being a 'homemaker' – her reward being clean, healthy children and a happy husband. Nature is also seen as 'man's' backyard – a place in which to enjoy leisure time – a conquered and tamed space. The white skin colour of this ideal family acts as an unmarked default norm – see Text B2.3.1 in Unit B2.3.

There is thus often a gap between the promoted ideal and what you feel you are. This can be a pressure not only from the media, but also from your peers who have imbibed certain ideals from certain sources and thus attempt to reproduce these ideals. This pressure is particularly acute among teenagers and can be a source of much unhappiness for those who do not fit in. It can also be used by marketing companies as a pressure that helps sell certain products aimed at the teenage market. An advertisement in Britain in the early 1990s featured a cream that was supposed to clear up facial spots. A teenage girl who had such a spot was seen wearing a bucket over her head at a party. Once she used the cream she could take the bucket off. The message is clear: if you are a girl and have spots on your face you are so ugly it's better to wear a bucket over your head than to openly accept the 'blemish'. You should be so worried of what people think of you physically that wearing a bucket is a solution. The message also suggested that continuing to have a spot is antisocial and a sign of slovenliness as the solution is within reach – it just requires you to go out and buy the cream. Remaining spotty is thus an active choice and becomes your fault.

Task C3.4.1   Creating the need

➤   From an analysis of the advertisements that you are subjected to in your particular cultural context, complete the table on page 206.

Task C3.4.1 may illustrate how much we are influenced in our conceptions of ourselves through the media and how this may lead to certain outcomes in our behaviour and help to shape our beliefs. Of course, consumerism and the advertising industry that promotes it may not be the only force that shapes our behaviour; it may be religious doctrine or political ideology, or indeed it may be a collection of beliefs that we have amassed that make us into what we feel we are. The fact that many of these beliefs are contradictory is something that we have noted before in this section. Trying to overcome these inherent contradictions may lead to certain insecurities – it may be hard to reconcile certain religious doctrines and beliefs with materialism and consumerism, and this may lead to certain retreats away from the one or the other in an attempt to maintain a unified 'Self'. This may partly explain the move by certain people towards more fundamentalist notions of explaining our existence and our purpose on earth. It is one way of trying to reconcile the abundance of contradictory choice that exists in an increasingly interconnected world. Burkhalter's article (Text B1.5.1, Unit B1.5) looks at how on the Web we can actually now play at being different people – a white person can claim to be black, a woman can become a man and so forth. It is as if the Self can be 'invented'.

The retreat from such a potentially bewildering world where the traditional tags we have employed to 'locate' people and ourselves as 'beings' that we can thus 'read' and 'understand' may also be a consequence of a globalization that may be seen to be imposing a uniform 'cultureless' pattern on the world. International tourism, more and more, seems to offer a similar formula wherever it occurs, with local culture only intruding to the extent that it is colourful and an entertaining sideshow. A dervish may twirl for tourists in Turkey, a demonstration paella may be prepared for tourists in southern Spain, Brazilian dancers may do a samba for you and Cypriots may offer a rendition of 'Zorba the Greek' on a bouzouki, all within a uniform 'international' space of the resort hotel. Culture is thus commodified and reduced in its impact to entertainment, amusement and pleasure. The same may be said of food. International chains offering a standard fast food meal, such as MacDonald's, can be found all over the globe; Coca-Cola has penetrated the earth and crossed boundaries that religious and political ideals have not been able to. Perhaps there is also thus a retreat away from this perceived 'deculturing' by certain groups of people and this may also explain the move towards

**Task C3.4.1
Creating the
need
(continued)**

Advert 1 Brief description of advert:		
Promoted values	Antithesis of the values promoted and from which you may be 'suffering'	Plugging the gap – what action you are expected to undertake and the ideal result of that action
Advert 2		
Advert 3		
Advert 4		

cultural and religious fundamentalism as an alternative. It may be the psychological reaction to what may be seen as an assault on one's identity. It is perhaps not too risky to assert that people thus seek the familiar wherever they are and that familiarity is a useful psychological prop that keeps more worrying issues as to who one may be – the other possible modalities of existence that are potentially available to one – at bay. This may explain the way expatriates root each other out in overseas settings, or why immigrants prefer to congregate in certain areas of their new countries of abode. They are thus able to return to the familiar (see Abdul Razak Gurnah's quote in Task B3.1.1, Unit B3.1.)

Task C3.4.2   How do I come out of this?

➤ Revisit the jokes collected in Task C3.3.2. However, this time you are required to look not at the image of the Other that is promoted by the jokes, but at the image of the Self that is promoted. The following table is designed to help you in this.

Joke number and image of the Self promoted	Analysis as to how this is achieved

Task C3.4.3 What's this really saying?

➤ Read the following newspaper article, which is from the *Houston Chronicle* dated Friday, 5 July 2002. Once you have read it, analyse the potential messages that the article contains in terms of the assumed roles and values that one may take from it about what it means to be male or female in the society the article is aimed at.

Male teachers are odd men out in female dominated profession

By Greg Toppo

Associated Press

Zach Galvin teaches English, drama and public speaking in Natick, Mass. But high living costs make it hard to make ends meet in the Boston suburb.

'I'm earning a salary in a town that I'll never be able to afford to live in,' he said.

Galvin, 32, said he makes more than $50,000 a year, but can't afford to buy a down payment on a house. Other guys his age often make $70,000 to $80,000.

'They say, "You're doing great work, but you're a fool to be doing that job",' Galvin said. 'It's tongue-in-cheek, but there's some truth in it.'

Gathered at their annual meeting this week in Dallas, members of the National Education Association talked about why so few men go into teaching – statistics show that only one in four public school teachers is male.

'It's not macho – it's not cool,' said Ned Good, a middle school teacher in Burr Oak, Mich.

Good, the only male out of 12 teachers in his tiny school district, echoed the comments of many who said teaching still carried little prestige for men.

'Your job as a male is to provide for your family – it's not to be a nice guy and do what you can to help others,' he said.

'MINIMAL CLUES LEAD TO BIG CONCLUSIONS'

This final unit will look at how we may attribute personality and hence a theoretical notion as to 'who' other people are, their entire value system and beliefs, from often 'minimal clues'. We may in this way tend to 'idealize' and 'demonize' others accordingly. This unit begins with the questioning of the notion that people, anyway, hold stable personalities and coherent sets of beliefs, but that we are in fact perhaps more contextual and consist of a range of selves. We may think we are consistent in different situations, but how far is this empirically the case? While it is the case that not to hold any central value system and notion of who one is would lead to having no clear sense of identity and would also be a problem for ourselves and those around us – in that we would be untrustworthy or at best seen as hypocritical – it is worth looking at how we may present different aspects of our Self according to the situations we are in, or how different aspects of our Self may come to the fore in different circumstances.

Task C3.5.1 Am I really like that?

➤ Note down how you see yourself, i.e. the qualities that you feel you hold to and present – e.g. 'calm', 'open', 'outgoing', 'shy', 'sensitive'. Enquire of people you know how they see themselves – this can be done by presenting them with a tick list and asking them to tick the five qualities that best sum themselves up. Leave a blank for them to fill in and answer to the question 'How easy was this for you to do and why?' Look at the self-descriptions – how close are they to the descriptions you would have assigned to these people? How close do you think the view you have of yourself is that which others have of you? Do different people who know you in different contexts see you in different ways? How can you gauge this?

When we meet people we tend to make judgements as to their personalities; we may be led to do this by generalized stereotypes that we have inherited previously. In other words our judgement can be a result of mediation. We may carry a prejudice against certain people in this way. We may assign qualities to people according to certain 'minimal clues'. One that comes to mind is when someone says they are vegetarian and British; this may also mean that the following is attributed to that person: they are an animal lover and have 'alternative' and certainly not 'conservative' political views. If the person is female, she is feminist; if male, he is likely to be highly strung etc. We tend to ignore or not look for further contextualization before casting judgement on someone. Someone may be a vegetarian for a number of reasons, including health-motivated and religious reasons, or simply from not liking the taste of meat.

Task C3.5.2 So that's why I treat you as I do!

➤ Collect, throughout a day, information on how you respond to other people and how you attribute qualities to them. (Use the table on the following page to help you.) Do this with people who are relatively new to you, or strangers. In each case you need to think about the minimal clues (signs) that you use in each case to do this.

Person and context	Minimal signs that lead to attribution	Attribution

Obviously if we feel that people are attributing large-scale theories about who we are and the value and belief systems that we have according to minimal clues, then this may become a frustrating barrier for us in our communication with people. Look at the problem Parisa has with this in Example A1.1.1, Unit A1.1. When we enter different cultural contexts this procedure may be even less useful than it may be in what one feels is a context in which you feel these signs can be more 'justifiably' read and interpreted. In the following part of this unit we will look at the way 'hair' may be interpreted. Hair – be it facial, the stuff we have on the top of our head (or lack of it) and other body hair – is a good example of the facility we have for building up large assumptions about people based on minimal clues. In England blond girls may be the subject of such typing – of being stupid and promiscuous. The expressions 'dumb blonde' and 'bimbo' attribute these qualities to blond-haired girls, particularly if they are working-class and secretaries.

As for men and hair, I will limit an example in the form of an anecdote about having a beard. Recently I attended a conference for examiners of English and met up with several other examiners who I recognized from the previous year's conference. I let it slip in the conversation that I was awaiting my viva voce, to which one of the female examiners remarked, 'Oh, if you get a PhD it'll go nicely with the grey streak in your hair and beard.' Another of the female examiners then added, 'Oh yes, it'll make a perfect set!' I then decided to enquire further and asked how the beard I have may fit into the whole. The first woman stated that the problem with beards is that the men who have them are 'anoraks' (lonely obsessives), but that this was for men with longer beards; a shorter, grey beard was OK for an academic with the title 'Doctor'. I felt relieved that I had trimmed my beard the day before!

Task C3.5.3   Why do they behave like that to me?

➤ What about you? What signs do you think your hair is giving off about you in the cultural contexts in which you exist? What about others and the way they are read according to their hair? The following table may be of use for analysing this.

Person and context	Description of hair	Interpretation given (you believe)

We need to recall that this use of minimal clues is reductive and that it is also a mediated interpretation in that the image of blonds, say, or men with beards, is brought to us through the discourse of others. In a sense we are told how to interpret these signs. We may forget that there are a number of ways of interpreting signs and that to look for other interpretations rather than to opt for one interpretation is a useful way to try to counter this reductive practice.

Task C3.5.4   It depends how you look at it

➤ Look at the following examples and decide how there may be different interpretations of each event according to which perspective – i.e. through which eyes – you view the events. What may these interpretations be?

Example C3.5.1

I was dressed up in a graduation gown and waiting in a queue with others to receive my master's award from my university. In front of me was a student from Mauritania called Djack. As one's name was read out one went forward to the podium, shook the proffered hands of various deans and dignitaries, and then returned to the aisle. As the student's name was read out and the award given, the audience would clap. When Djack's name was read, he muttered to me, 'Just you wait and see the claps I get – "He got a master's and he's black!"' Indeed, I noted that the claps he received were louder and more effusive than they had been previously.

Example C3.5.1 boils down to different interpretations and intentions. What do you suppose the intentions of the audience were? Why did the black student see this as an example of racism?

Example C3.5.2

Mike and Jane, an English teaching couple, had moved to the Dominican Republic to work in a private English medium school there that belonged to a big sugar company. They were housed in a company apartment, like many other company employees. Soon they were asked by a local woman if they wanted to employ a maid. Everyone seemed to have a maid and Mike thus felt that it would be mean not to have one – it gave a job to someone, after all. The maid – Josefina – also worked for some of the local Dominican families. When Mike discovered what a small amount the maids were paid he and Jane decided to double Josefina's wage when she worked for them.

➤ How may this action be viewed in different ways by the different participants? Try to get inside the minds of the following participants and see how the same act may be interpreted in distinct ways – not always favourably: from Mike's perspective, from Josefina's perspective, from the perspective of Señora Piña, one of the local company employees who hires Josefina as a maid.

When a person's intentions are read in a way other than they are intended to be read, then we may talk about this as being an instance of 'mis-communication' (MC). It is much easier for this to occur if one is ignorant of how the other person or people you are with is/are likely to read events. The more sensitive one can become to this multiple reading of events, the better. Literature is of course one of the key ways of gaining insights from other perspectives. In this sense the more we read the accounts of others the less trapped in our own solipsism we may be. Conversely the less we read about or have the opportunity to think about and investigate others, the more likely we are to misunderstand them.

 ### Task C3.5.5 Exploring miscommunication

➤ Events: of your choice, from your own experience.
➤ Actors: yourself in interaction with others.
➤ Setting: of your choice.
➤ Cultural circumstances: of your choice.

➤ Angle: how your intentions from the language you use to the semiotics of your clothes or hairstyle etc. have been misread.

➤ Observation: note down the different ways people from different cultural groups, whether national or other, have, in your view, misread you. You need to note the clues that you read that may indicate this too. Try to analyse how it is that this has happened – what are the cognitive steps these people may have taken to do this misreading?

➤ Disciplines: 17, 19.

➤ Outcome: awareness of how you may be misread through a dominant reading of you and of how you in turn may be doing the same thing to another person.

References

SECTION A

Keesing, R. M. (1994) 'Theories of culture revisited' in Borofsky, R. (ed.) *Assessing Cultural Anthropology*. New York: McGraw-Hill pp. 301–312

Unit A1.2

Kubota, R. (2002) 'The impact of globalization on language teaching in Japan' in Cameron, D. and Block, D. (eds) *Globalization and English Language Teaching*. London: Routledge pp. 13–28

Moeran, B. (1996) 'The Orient strikes back: advertising and imagining in Japan' in *Theory, Culture and Society* 13/3 pp. 77–112

Unit A2.2

Holliday, A. R. (2002) *Doing and Writing Qualitative Research*. London: Sage

Unit A2.3

Fairclough, N. (1995) *Critical Discourse Analysis: The critical study of language*. London: Addison Wesley Longman

Holliday, A. R. (2000) 'Exploring other worlds: escaping linguistic parochialism' in Davison, J. and Moss, J. (eds) *Issues in English*. London: Routledge

Nzimiro, I. (1979) 'Anthropologists and their terminologies: a critical review' in Huizer, G. and Mannheim, B. (eds), *The Politics of Anthropology: From Colonialism and Sexism Towards a View from Below*. The Hague: Mouton pp. 67–83

Wagner, R. (1981) *The Inventions of Culture*. University of Chicago Press

Unit A3.2

Fairclough, N. (1995) *Critical Discourse Analysis: The critical study of language*. London: Addison Wesley Longman

Kabbani, R. (1986) *Europe's Myths of Orient: Devise and Rule*. London: Macmillan

SECTION B

Unit B0.1

Anderson, B. (1983) *Imagined Communities*. London: Verso

Barthes, R. (1973) *Mythologies*. London: Granada

Cohen, A. P. (1985) *The Symbolic Construction of Community*. London: Routledge

Potter, J. and Wetherell, M. (1987) *Discourse and Social Psychology: Beyond Attitudes and Behaviour*. London: Sage

Watson, C. W. (2000) *Multiculturalism*. Buckingham: Open University Press

Ylanne-McEwen, V. and Coupland, N. (2000) 'Accommodation Theory: A Conceptual Resource for Intercultural Sociolinguistics' in Spencer-Oatey, H. (ed.) *Culturally Speaking: Managing Rapport through Talk across Cultures*. London: Continuum pp. 191–214

Unit B0.2

Alasuutari, P. (1995) *Researching Culture: Qualitative Method and Cultural Studies*. London: Sage

Bauman, Z. (1990) *Thinking Sociologically*. Oxford: Blackwell

Geertz, C. (1973) *The Interpretation of Cultures*. New York: Basic Books

Street, B. (1991) 'Culture is a verb'. Plenary Lecture at the BAAL Conference Sussex University, 1991

Tylor, E. (1871) *Primitive Culture*. London: John Murray

Ylanne-McEwen, V. and Coupland, N. (2000) 'Accommodation Theory: A Conceptual Resource for Intercultural Sociolinguistics' in Spencer-Oatey, H. (ed.) *Culturally Speaking: Managing Rapport through Talk across Cultures*. London: Continuum pp. 191–214

Unit B1.1

Strinati, D. (1997) 'Postmodernism and Modern Culture' in O'Sullivan, T. and Jewkes, Y. (eds) *The Media Studies Reader*. London: Arnold pp. 421–433

Wetherell, M. and Maybin, J. (1996) 'The Distributed Self: A Social Constructionist Perspective' in Stevens, R. (ed.) *Understanding the Self*. London: Sage/Open University pp. 219–279

Unit B1.2

Gabriel, Y. and Lang, T. (1995) *The Unmanageable Consumer: Contemporary Consumption and Its Fragmentations*. London: Sage

Unit B1.3

Fairclough, N. (1992) *Discourse and Social Change*. Cambridge: Polity Press

Foucault, M. (1980) *Power/Knowledge: Selected Interviews and Other Writings 1972–77*. Brighton: Harvester Press

Gee, J. P. (1990) *Social Linguistics and Literacies: Ideology in Discourses*. London: Falmer Press

Gumperz, J. J. (1996) 'The Linguistic and Cultural Relativity of Conversational Inference' in Gumperz, J. J. and Levinson, S. C. (eds) *Rethinking Linguistic Relativity*. Cambridge: Cambridge University Press pp. 374–406

Jaworski, A. and Coupland, N. (1999) 'Introduction' in Jaworski, A. and Coupland, N. (eds) *The Discourse Reader*. London: Routledge pp. 1–44

Sapir, E. (1947) *Selected Writings in Language, Culture and Personality*. Los Angeles: University of California Press

Whorf, B. L. (1956) *Language, Thought and Reality*. New York: Wiley

Unit B1.4

Bakhtin, M. M. (1984) *Problems of Dostoevsky's Poetics* (Trans. by C. Emerson). Austin, Texas: University of Texas Press

Geok-Lin Lim, S. (1996) *Among the White Moonfaces*. Singapore: Time Books International

Hoffman, E. (1989) *Lost in Translation*. London: Verso

Schumann, J. H. (l976) 'Second Language Acquisition; The Pidginization Hypothesis' in *Language Learning* 26: pp. 391–408, reproduced in Brown, H. D. (ed.) (1995) *Readings on Second Language Acquisition*. Englewood Cliffs, New Jersey: Prentice Hall Regents

Wierzbicka, A. (1994) 'Emotion, Language and Cultural Scripts' in Kitayama, S. and Markus, S. R. (eds) *Emotion and Culture: Empirical studies of mutual influence*. Washington, DC: American Psychological Association pp. 133–196

Vygotsky, L. S. (1986) *Thought and Language* (Trans. by A. Kozulin) Cambridge, Mass: MIT Press

Unit B1.5

Chiawei O'Hearn, C. (ed.) (1998) *Half and Half: Writers on Growing Up Biracial and Bicultural*. New York: Pantheon Books

Gergen, K. J. (1996) 'Technology and the self: from the essential to the sublime' in Grodin, D. and Lindlof, T. R. (eds) *Constructing the Self in a Mediated World*. London: Sage pp. 127–140

Jones, S. and Kucker, S. (2001) 'Computers, the Internet, and Virtual Cultures' in Lull, J. (ed.) *Culture in the Communication Age*. London: Routledge pp. 212–225

Unit B2.1

Billig, M., Condor, S., Edwards, D., Gane, M., Middleton, D. and Radley, A. (1988) *Ideological Dilemmas*. London: Sage

Said, E. (1978) *Orientalism*. London: Routledge and Kegan Paul

Said, E. (1993) *Culture and Imperialism*. London: Chatto and Windus

Unit B2.2

Baudrillard, J. (1993) 'The Evil Demon of Images and the Procession of Simulcra' in Docherty, T. (ed.) *Postmodernism: A Reader*. Hemel Hempstead: Harvester Wheatsheaf pp. 194–199

Berger, A. A. (1995) *Cultural Criticism: A Primer of Key Concepts*. London: Sage

Bignell, J. (1997) *Media Semiotics*. Manchester: University of Manchester Press

Unit B2.3

Denzin, N. K. (1994) 'Postmodernism and Deconstruction' in Dickens, D. R. and Fontana, A. (eds) *Postmodernism and Social Inquiry*. London: University College London Press pp. 182–202

Derrida, J. (1982) *Margins of Philosophy* (Trans. by A. Bass). Chicago: University of Chicago Press

Fairclough, N. (1995) *Critical Discourse Analysis: The Critical Study of Language*. Harlow: Longman

Fay, B. (1996) *Contemporary Philosophy of Social Science: A Multicultural Approach*. Oxford: Blackwell

Gergen, K. J. (1999) *An Invitation to Social Construction*. London: Sage

Hall, S. (1997) 'The Spectacle of the Other' in Hall, S. (ed.) *Representation: Cultural Representations and Signifying Practices*. London: Sage/Open University

Pennycook, A. (1998) *English and the Discourse of Colonialism*. London: Routledge

Unit B2.4

Kellner, D. (1995) *Media Culture: Cultural Studies, Identity and Politics between the Modern and Postmodern*. London: Routledge

Sarup, M. (1996) *Identity, Culture and the Postmodern World*. Edinburgh: Edinburgh University Press

Strinati, D. (1997) 'Postmodernism and Modern Culture' in O'Sullivan, T. and Jewkes, Y. (eds) *The Media Studies Reader*. London: Arnold pp. 421–433

Thompson, J. B. (1995) *The Media and Modernity: A Social History of The Media*. Cambridge: Polity Press

Watson, R. (1997) 'Ethnomethodology and Textual Analysis' in Silverman, D. (ed.) *Qualitative Research: Theory Method and Practice*. London: Sage pp. 80–98

Unit B2.5

Bakhtin, M. M. and Medvedev, P. N. (1978) *The Formal Method in Literary Scholarship: a critical introduction to sociological poetics* (Trans. by A. J. Wehrle). Baltimore: Hopkins University Press

Berg, D. N. and Smith, K. K. (1985) *The Self in Social Inquiry: Researching Methods*. Newbury Park, California: Sage

Denzin, N. K. (1994) 'Postmodernism and Deconstruction' in Dickens, D. R. and Fontana, A. (eds) *Postmodernism and Social Inquiry*. London: University College London Press pp. 182–202

Denzin, N. K. (1997) *Interpretive Ethnography: Ethnographic Practices for the 21st Century*. Thousand Oaks, California: Sage

Edgar, A. and Sedgwick, P. (1999) *Key Concepts in Cultural Theory*. London: Routledge

Geertz, C. (1973) *The Interpretation of Cultures*. New York: Basic Books

Unit B3.1

Chomsky, N. (1992) *Chronicles of Dissent*. Stirling: AK Press

Hall, S. (1996) 'The Social Production of News' in Marris, P. and S. Thornham (eds) *The Media Studies Reader*. Edinburgh: University of Edinburgh Press pp. 424–429

Razak Gurnah, A. (2001) *By the Sea*. London: Bloomsbury

Unit B3.2

Anderson, B. (1983) *Imagined Communities*. London: Verso

Barthes, R. (1973) *Mythologies*. London: Granada

Hall, S. (1996) 'The Question of Cultural Identity' in Hall, S., Held, D., Hubert, D. and Thompson, K. (eds) *Modernity: An Introduction to Modern Society*. Oxford: Oxford University Press

Hall, S. (1997) 'The Spectacle of the 'Other'' in Hall, S. (ed.) *Representation: Cultural Representations and Signifying Practices*. London: Sage/Open University pp. 223–290

Smith, A. D. (1990) 'Towards a Global Culture?' in Featherstone, M. (ed.) *Global Culture: Nationalism, Globalization and Modernity*. London: Sage

Wodak, R., De Cillia, R., Reisigl, M. and Liebhart, K. (1999) *The Discursive Construction of National Identity*. Edinburgh: University of Edinburgh Press

Unit B3.3

Gandy, O. H. (1998) *Communication and Race: A Structural Perspective*. London: Arnold

Strongman, K. T. (1996: 4th edition) *The Psychology of Emotion*. Chichester: Wiley

Unit B3.4

Augoustinos, M. (1998) 'Social Representations and Ideology: Towards the Study of Ideological Representations' in Flick, U. (ed.) *The Psychology of the Social*. Cambridge: Cambridge University Press pp. 156–169

Hewstone, M. and Augoustinos, M. (1998) 'Social Attributions and Social Representations' in Flick, U. (ed.) *The Psychology of the Social*. Cambridge: Cambridge University Press pp. 60–76

Moscovici, S. (1976) *Social Influence and Social Change* (Trans. C. Sherrard and G. Heinz). London: Academic Press

Moscovici, S. (1998) 'The History and Actuality of Social Representations' in Flick, U. (ed.) *The Psychology of the Social*. Cambridge: Cambridge University Press pp. 209–247

Oyserman, D. and Markus, H. R. (1998) 'Self as Social Representation' in Flick, U. (ed.) *The Psychology of the Social*. Cambridge: Cambridge University Press pp. 107–125

Van Dijk, T. A. (1998) *Ideology*. London: Sage

Unit B3.5

Hannerz, U. (2001) 'Thinking About Culture in a Global Ecumene' in Lull, J. (ed.) *Culture in the Communication Age*. London: Routledge

Hofstede, G. (1991) *Culture and Organizations: Software of the Mind*. London: McGraw-Hill

SECTION C

Anderson, B. (1983) *Imagined Communities*. London: Verso

Coffey, A. (1999) *Ethnographic Self*. London: Sage

Hammersley, M. and Atkinson, P. (1995) *Ethnography: Principles in Practice*. London: Routledge.

Holliday, A. R. (2002) *Doing and Writing Qualitative Research*. London: Sage

Punch, M. (1994) 'Politics and ethics in qualitative research.' In Denzin, N. K. and Lincoln, Y. S. (eds) *The Handbook of Qualitative Research*. London: Sage pp. 83–97

Singer, M. R. (1998) *Perception and Identity in Intercultural Communication*. Yarmouth, Maine: International Press, Inc.

Spradley, J. P. (1980) *Participant Observation*. New York: Holt Rinehart and Winston

Further reading

Suggestions are included below for further reading on issues raised in the book. Where appropriate, suggestions are made for accessible introduction to the issue(s) for the reader, for more in-depth and specialised reading, and for books which collect together key papers and book extracts previously published elsewhere.

Culture and cultural studies

Accessible introductions to key issues in cultural studies are as follows.

Baldwin, E., Longhurst, B., McCracken, S., Ogborn, Smith, M. and G. (1999) *Introducing Cultural Studies.* Hemel Hempstead: Prentice Hall Europe

Barker, C. (2000) *Cultural studies: Theory and Practice.* London: Sage

Barker, C. (2002) *Making Sense of Cultural Studies: Central Problems and Critical Debates.* London: Sage

Chaney, D. (2002) *Cultural Change and Everyday Life.* Basingstoke: Palgrave

Giles, J. and Middleton, T. (1999) *Studying Culture: A Practical Introduction.* Oxford: Blackwell

Thwaites, T., Davis, L. and Mules, W. (1994) *Tools for Cultural Studies: An Introduction.* Melbourne: Macmillan Education Australia

For a useful dictionary on terms and key figures in culture and cultural studies, the following is recommended.

Edgar, A. and Sedgwick, P. (1999) *Key Concepts in Cultural Theory.* London: Routledge

If you are interested in doing further reading on the concept of 'culture' in anthropology and the social sciences, the following titles are recommended.

Clifford, J. and Marcus, G. E. (1986) *Writing Culture: The Poetics and Politics of Ethnography.* Berkeley, California: University of California Press

Fay, B. (1996) *A Contemporary Philosophy of Social Science.* Oxford: Blackwell

Geertz, C. (1973) *The Interpretation of Cultures.* New York: Basic Books

Smith, M. J. (1998) *Culture: Reinventing the Social Sciences.* London: Sage/Open University

If you are interested in doing further reading on postmodernism, the following titles are recommended.

Dickens, D. R. and Fontana, A. (eds) (1994) *Postmodernism and Social Inquiry*. London: University College London Press

Lyotard, J-F. (1984) *The Postmodern Condition*. Manchester: Manchester University Press

Sarup, M. (1998: 2nd edition) *An Introductory Guide to Poststructuralism and Postmodernism*. London: Harvester Wheatsheaf

Collections of previously published papers and book extracts on aspects of culture include the following.

Anderson, W. T. (ed.) (1996) *The Fontana Postmodernism Reader*. London: Fontana

Docherty, T. (ed.) (1993) *Postmodernism: A Reader*. Hemel Hempstead: Harvester Wheatsheaf

If you are interested in doing further reading on approaches to researching culture, the following titles are recommended.

Alasuutari, P. (1995) *Researching Culture: Qualitative Method and Cultural Studies*. London: Sage

Atkinson, P., Coffey, A., Delamont, S., Lofland, J. and Lofland, L. (eds) (2001) *Handbook of Ethnography*. London: Sage

Brewer, J. D. (2000) *Ethnography* Buckingham: Open University

Coffey, A. (1999) *The Ethnographic Self: Fieldwork and the Representation of Identity*. London: Sage

Denzin, N. K. and Lincoln, Y. S. (1998) *Strategies of Qualitative Enquiry*. Thousand Oaks, Calif.: Sage

Holliday, A. R. (2002) *Doing and Writing Qualitative Research*. London: Sage

McGuigan, J. (1997) *Cultural Methodologies*. London: Sage

Silverman, D. (ed.) (1997) *Qualitative Research: Theory Method and Practice*. London: Sage

Taylor, S. (ed.) (2002) *Ethnographic Research: A Reader*. London: Sage/Open University

Collections of previously published papers and book extracts on aspects of culture include the following.

Alexander, J. C. and Seidman, S. (eds) (1990) *Culture and Society: Contemporary Debates*. Cambridge: Cambridge University Press

Mumms, J. and Rajan, G. (eds) (1995) *A Cultural Studies Reader: History, Theory and Practice*. London: Routledge

Storey, J. (ed.) (1998: 2nd edition) *Cultural theory and Popular Culture: A Reader*. London: Prentice Hall

Identity

Accessible introductions to identity are as follows.

Billington, R., Hockey, J. and Strawbridge, S. (1998) *Exploring Self and Society*. London: Macmillan

Gergen, K. J. (2000: 2nd edition) *The Saturated Self: Dilemmas of Identity in Contemporary Life*. New York: Basic Books

Stevens, R. (ed.) (1996) *Understanding the Self*. London: Sage/Open University

Woodward, K. (1997) *Identity and Difference*. London: Sage/Open University

If you are interested in doing further reading on approaches to identity, the following titles are recommended.

Burkitt, I. (1991) *Social Selves*. London: Sage

Giddens, A. (1991) *Modernity and Self-Identity: Self and Society in the Late Modern Age*. Cambridge: Polity

Goffman, E. (1959) *The Presentation of Self in Everyday Life*. New York: Anchor Books

Hall, S. and du Gay, P. (eds) (1996) *Questions of Cultural Identity*. London: Sage

Jenkins, R (1996) *Social Identity*. London: Routledge

Sarup, M. (1996) *Identity, Culture and the Postmodern World*. Edinburgh: Edinburgh University Press

Wetherell, M. (ed.) (1996) *Identities, Groups and Social Issues*. London: Sage/Open University

A collection of previously published papers and book extracts on identity is:

du Gay, P., Evans, J. and Redman, P. (eds) (2000) *Identity: A Reader*. London: Sage/Open University

If you are interested in doing further reading on globalization, culture, and identity, the following titles are recommended.

Beck, U. (2000) *What is Globalization?* Cambridge: Polity Press

Featherstone, M. (1995) *Undoing Culture: Globalization, Postmodernism, and Identity*. London: Sage

Friedman, J. (1994) *Culture, Identity and Global Process*. London: Sage

Held, D. (ed.) (2000) *A Globalizing World?* London: Routledge

Tomlinson, J. (1999) *Globalization and Culture*. Cambridge: Polity Press

If you are interested in doing further reading on consumption and identity, the following titles are recommended.

Bourdieu, P. (1984) *Distinction: A Social Critique of the Judgement of Taste*. London: Routledge and Kegan Paul

Chaney, D. (1996) *Lifestyles*. London: Routledge

Gabriel, Y. and T. Lang (1995) *The Unmanageable Consumer: Contemporary Consumption and Its Fragmentations*. London: Sage

Miller, D., Jackson, P., Thrift, N., Holbrook, B. and Rowlands, M. (1998) *Shopping, Place and Identity*. London: Routledge

If you are interested in doing further reading on the impact of information technology on notions of 'identity', 'community' and 'culture', the following titles are recommended.

Lull, J. (ed.) (2001) *Culture in the Communication Age*. London: Routledge
Smith, M. A. and Kollock, P. (eds) (1999) *Communities in Cyberspace*. London: Routledge

If you are interested in doing further reading on the impact of information technology on language, the following title is recommended.

Crystal, D. (2001) *The Language of the Internet* Cambridge: Cambridge University Press

Culture, identity and communication

If you are interested in doing further reading on culture, identity and communication, the following titles are recommended.

Bremer, K., Roberts, C., Vasseur, M-T., Simonot, M. and Broeder, P. (1996) *Achieving Understanding: Discourse in Intercultural Communication*. Harlow: Longman
FitzGerald, H. (2003) *How Different Are We? Spoken Discourse in Intercultural Communication*. Clevedon: Multilingual Matters
Gumperz, J. J. and Levinson, S. C. (eds) (1996) *Rethinking Linguistic Relativity*. Cambridge: Cambridge University Press
Pan, Y., Wong Scollon, S. and Scollon, R. (2002) *Professional Communication in International Settings*. Oxford: Blackwell
Schieffelin, B. B. and Ochs, E. (eds) (1987) *Language Socialization Across Cultures*. Cambridge: Cambridge University Press
Scollon, R. and Wong Scollon, S. (1995) *Intercultural Communication*. Oxford: Blackwell
Spencer-Oatey, H. (ed.) (2000) *Culturally Speaking: Managing Rapport through Talk across Cultures*. London: Continuum
Wierzbicka, A. (1991) *Cross-Cultural Pragmatics: The Semantics of Human Interaction*. New York: Mouton de Gruyter

Culture, identity, and language learning and teaching

If you are interested doing further reading on issues of culture and identity in language teaching and learning, and applied linguistics, the following titles are recommended.

Block, D. and Cameron, D. (eds) (2002) *Globalization and Language Teaching*. London: Routledge
Byram, M., Morgan, C. et al. (1994) *Teaching-and-Learning-Language-and-Culture*. Clevedon: Multilingual Matters

Byram, M. (1997) *Teaching and Assessing Intercultural Communicative Competence.* Clevedon: Multilingual Matters

Canagarajah, A. S. (1999) *Resisting Linguistic Imperialism in English Language Teaching.* Oxford: Oxford University Press

Hinkel, E. (ed.) (1999) *Culture in Second Language Teaching and Learning.* Cambridge: Cambridge University Press

Holliday, A. R. (1994) *Appropriate Methodology and Social Context.* Cambridge: Cambridge University Press

Holliday, A. R. (in press) *The Struggle to Teach English as an International Language.* Oxford: Oxford University Press

Kramsch, C. (1993) *Context and Culture in Language Teaching.* Oxford: Oxford University Press

Lantolf, J. P. (ed.) (2000) *Sociocultural Theory and Second Language Learning.* Oxford: Oxford University Press

McKay, S. L. and Wong, S-L. C. (eds) (2000) *New Immigrants in the United States: Readings for Second Language Educators.* Cambridge: Cambridge University Press

Norton, B. (2000) *Identity and Language Learning: Gender, Ethnicity, and Educational Change.* Harlow: Pearson Education

Pennycook, A. (1994) *The Cultural Politics of English as an International Language.* Harlow: Longman

Pennycook, A. (2001) *Critical Applied Linguistics: A Critical Introduction.* Mahwah, New Jersey: Lawrence Erlbaum

A collection of previously published papers and book extracts on culture, identity, and language learning and teaching is as follows.

Candlin, C. N. and Mercer, N. (eds) (2001) *English Language Teaching in its Social Context.* London: Routledge

Discourse and discourse analysis

In addition to Gee (1999), accessible introductions to discourse and discourse analysis are as follows.

Fairclough, N. (2003) *Analysing Discourse: Textual Analysis for Social Research.* London: Routledge

Wetherell, M., Taylor, S. and Yates, S. J. (eds) (2001) *Discourse as Data: A Guide for Analysis.* London: Sage/Open University

If you are interested in doing further reading on approaches to discourse and discourse analysis, the following titles are recommended.

Fairclough, N. (1992) *Discourse and Social Change.* Cambridge: Polity Press

Fairclough, N. (1995) *Critical Discourse Analysis: The Critical Study of Language.* Harlow: Longman

Gunnarson, B-L., Linnell, P. and Nordberg, B. (eds) (1997) *The Construction of Professional Discourse*. Harlow: Longman

Johnstone, B. (2002) *Discourse Analysis*. Oxford: Blackwell

Potter, J. and Wetherell, M. (1987) *Discourse and Social Psychology: Beyond Attitudes and Behaviour*. London: Sage

Sarangi, S. and Coulthard, M. (eds) (2000) *Discourse and Social Life*. Oxford: Oxford University Press

Van Dijk, T. A. (ed.) (1997) *Discourse as Social Interaction*. London: Sage

Van Dijk, T. A. (ed.) (1997) *Discourse as Structure and Process*. London: Sage

Willig, C. (ed.) (1999) *Applied Discourse Analysis: Social and Psychological Interventions*. Buckingham: Open University

Wodak, R. (1996) *Disorders of Discourse*. Harlow: Longman

Wodak, R. and Meyer, M. (eds) (2001) *Methods of Critical Discourse Analysis*. London: Sage

Wodak, R. and Reisigl, M. (2001) *Discourse and Discrimination*. Harlow: Longman

If you are interested in doing further reading on the role of discourse in the construction of national identity, the following titles are recommended.

Barker, C. and Galasinski, D. (2001) *Cultural Studies and Discourse Analysis*. London: Sage

Wodak, R., De Cillia, R., Reisigl, M. and Liebhart, K. (1999) *The Discursive Construction of National Identity*. Edinburgh: University of Edinburgh Press

Collections of previously published published papers and book extracts on discourse and discourse analysis include the following.

Jaworski, A. and Coupland, N. (eds) (1999) *The Discourse Reader*. London: Routledge

Schiffrin, D., Tannen, D. and Hamilton, H. E. (eds) (2001) *The Handbook of Discourse Analysis*. Oxford: Blackwell

If you are interested in doing further reading on the ideas of Vygotsky and Bakhtin, the following are recommended.

Sampson, E. (1993) *Celebrating the Other: A Dialogic Account of Human Nature*. London: Harvester Wheatsheaf

Shotter, J. (1993) *Cultural Politics of Everyday Life*. Buckingham: Open University

If you are interested in doing further reading on the ideas of Foucault, the following are recommended.

Danaher, G., Schirato, T. and Webb, J. (2000) *Understanding Foucault*. London: Sage

Rabinow, P. (ed.) (1985) *The Foucault Reader*. New York: Pantheon

Otherization

An accessible introduction to otherization can be found in:

Pickering, M. (2001) *Stereotyping: The Politics of Representation*. Basingstoke: Palgrave

Key texts on notions of 'the Other' and otherization are as follows.

Bhabha, H. K. (1994) *The Location of Culture*. London: Routledge
Fanon, F. (1967) *Black Skin, White Mask*. London: Pluto Press
Said, E. (1978) *Orientalism*. New York: Random House
Said, E. (1993) *Culture and imperialism*. London: Vintage

Notions of 'the Other' and otherization are also central in literature on postcolonialism. Accessible introductions to postcolonialism include:

Loomba, A. (1997) *Colonialism/Postcolonialism*. London: Routledge
Young, R. C. (2002) *Postcolonialism: A Very Short Introduction*. Oxford: Oxford University Press

Other recommended books on postcolonialism include the following.

hooks, b. (1992) *Black Looks: Race and Representation*. Boston, Mass.: South End Press
Moore-Gilbert, B. (1997) *Postcolonial Theory: Contexts, Practices, Politics*. London: Verso
Pennycook, A. (1998) *English and the Discourse of Colonialism*. London: Routledge
Person, K. A. Parry, B. and Squires, J. (eds) (1997) *Edward Said and the Cultural Readings of Imperialism and the Gravity of History*. London: Lawrence and Wishart

A collection of previously published papers and book extracts on postcolonialism is:

Williams, P. and Chrisman, L. (eds) (1993) *Colonial Discourse and Post-Colonial Theory*. London: Routledge

Discussions of otherization are also to be found in texts on race and racism. Collections of previously published papers and book extracts on race and racism include the following.

Back, L. and Solomos, J. (eds) (2000) *Theories of Race and Racism*. London: Routledge
Cashmore, E. and Jennings, J. (eds) (2001) *Racism: Essential Readings*. London: Sage
Fine, M. et al. (1997) *Off White: Readings on Race, Power and Society*. London: Routledge

A book that focuses specifically on this role of discourse in otherization is:

Wetherell, M. and Potter, J. (1992) *Discourse and the Legitimation of Exploitation*. New York: Columbia University Press

Processes of otherization in the mass media are discussed in the following.

Cottle, S. (ed.) (2000) *Ethnic Minorities and the Media*. Buckingham: Open University Press

Van Dijk, T. A. (1991) *Racism and the Press*. London: Routledge

Representation

An accessible introduction to representation is:

Hall, S. (ed.) (1997) *Representation: Cultural Representations and Signifying Practices*. London: Sage/Open University

If you are interested in doing further reading on representation in the mass media, the following are recommended.

Allan, S. (1999) *News Culture*. Milton Keynes: Open University

Ang, I. (1996) *Living Room Wars: Rethinking Media Audiences for a Postmodern World*. London: Routledge

Bell, A. (1991) *The Language of the News Media*. Oxford: Blackwell

Bell, A. and Garrett, P. (eds) (1998) – *Approaches to Media Discourse*. Oxford: Blackwell

Berkowitz, D. (ed.) (1997) *Social Meaning of News*. London: Sage

Bignell, M. (1997) *Media Semiotics*. Manchester: University of Manchester Press

Dines, G. and Humez, J. M. (eds) (1995) *Gender, Race, and Class in Media: A Text Reader*. London: Sage

Fairclough, N. (1995) *Media Discourse*. London: Edward Arnold

Van Dijk, T. A. (1998) *Ideology*. London: Sage

Van Ginneken, J. (1998) *Understanding Global News*. London: Sage

If you are interested in doing further reading on sport and representation in the mass media, the following are recommended.

Boyle, R. and Haynes, P. (2000) *Power Play, Sport, the Media and Popular Culture*. Harlow: Pearson

Rowe, D. (1999) *Sport, Culture and the Media*. Buckingham: Open University

Collections of previously published papers and book extracts on representation in the mass media include the following.

Boyd-Barrett, O. and Newbold, C. (eds) (1995) *Approaches to Media: A Reader*. London: Arnold

Marris, P. and Thornham, S. (eds) (1996) *Media Studies: A Reader*. Edinburgh: University of Edinburgh Press

O'Sullivan, T. and Jewkes, Y. (eds) (1997) *The Media Studies Reader*. London: Arnold

If you are interested in reading more about visual representation, the following are recommended.

Kress, G. and Van Leeuwen, T. (1996) *Reading Images: The Grammar of Visual Design.* London: Routledge

Kress, G. and Van Leeuwen, T. (2001) *Multimodal Discourse: The Modes and Media of Contemporary Communication.* London: Arnold

Mirzoeff, N. (ed.) (1998) *The Visual Culture Reader.* London: Routledge

Pink, S. (2000) *Doing Visual Ethnography: images, media, and representation in research.* London: Sage

Rose, G. (2001) *Visual Methodologies: an introduction to the interpretation of visual materials.* London: Sage

If you are interested in representation in advertising, the following are recommended.

Goffman, E. (1979) *Gender Advertisements.* Basingstoke: Macmillan

Messaris, P. (1997) *Visual Persuasion: The Role of Images in Advertising.* London: Sage

Williamson, J. (1978) *Decoding Advertisements: Ideology and Meaning in Advertising.* London: Marion Boyars

If you are interested in issues of culture, representation and otherization in travel and tourism, the following are recommended.

Selwyn, T. (1996) *The Tourist Image.* Chichester: John Wiley

Urry, J. (1990) *The Tourist Gaze.* London: Sage

Social constructionism

In addition to Burr (1996), an accessible introduction to social constructionism is:

Gergen, K. J. (1999) *An Invitation to Social Construction.* London: Sage

If you are interested in doing further reading on social constructionism, the following are recommended.

Berger, P. L. and Luckmann, T. (1966) *The Social Construction of Knowledge: A Treatise in the Sociology of Knowledge.* Harmondsworth: Penguin

Gergen, K. J. (2001) *Social Constructionism in Context.* London: Sage

Potter, J. (1996) *Representing Reality: Discourse, Rhetoric and Social Construction.* London: Sage

For further reading on the social construction of personality and emotions, the following are recommended.

Harre, R. and Gerrod Parrott, W. (eds) (1996) *The Emotions: Social, Cultural and Biological Dimensions.* London: Sage

Parkinson, B. (1995) *Ideas and Realities of Emotion.* London: Routledge

Greenwood, J. D. (1994) *Realism, Identity and Emotion.* London: Sage

Matthews, G. and Deary, I. J. (1998) *Personality Traits.* Cambridge: Cambridge University Press

If you are interested in reading further on social representations, the following are recommended.

Flick, U. (ed.) (1998) *The Psychology of the Social.* Cambridge: Cambridge University Press

Moscovici, S. (2000) *Social Representations: Explorations in Social Psychology.* London: Sage

There is also a useful online journal, *Papers on Social Representation.* The website address is http://www.swp.uni-linz.ac.at/content/psr/psrindex.htm

Index